# APRIL FOOLS' DAY EVERY DAY IN THE COURTS

*Leslie M. Carwell*

Hardcover Book (English)
ISBN 978-1-7750712-1-1

Paperback Book (English)
ISBN 978-1-7750712-2-8

Electronic Book (English)
ISBN 978-1-7750712-0-4

First Edition, 2019

Published by ***Merillion Press***

https://merillionpress.com/

# APRIL FOOLS' DAY EVERY DAY IN THE COURTS

KEROUACKING THE LEGAL LANDSCAPE

A COMPILATION OF COURT CASES

ROOTED IN JURASSIC ANTIQUITY
PROCESSED IN KREMLINESQUE SECRECY
ENDING WITH CHAPLINESQUE RESULTS

Compiled and Edited by Leslie M. Carwell

***Then came the churches***

***Then came the schools***

***Then came the lawyers***

***Then came the rules***

# CONTENTS

# PREFACE

# HOW TO READ THIS BOOK

Chapter titles are not organized under judicial terminology, for few cases come before the courts with a single complaint. Most frequently there would be 5-6 different – somehow interconnected areas of the law – with the hope, that some of them will stick. Thus, generic chapter titles better describe the common thread, the search for redress of grievances. Most of the time it's a money extraction attempt disguised in judicial terms, such as Product Liability, Discrimination, etc...

Settlement amounts that happened generations ago have been converted to approximate current values, and other currencies have been converted to US dollars.

Throughout the book, the term lawyer is used mostly even though Counsel, Barrister, Solicitor, Attorney, and Judge also feature prominently. For the purposes, of this collection they are all members of the legal profession regardless of their specific title or role in it.

Each story presented is a synopsis of the written court decision, the actual writings of the judges. No originality is claimed. A short and plain – which is to say, non-legalistic – version of events in a format understandable to a wider audience.

References and citations are taken from the original documents, as filed and stored by government agencies. In addition, each story in the book is linked to the original source document. If the reader wants to know more and read it all, the link provided will bring up the corresponding document in PDF format.

These documents range from 1- 55 pages, depending on the complexity of the case and the verboseness of its author. In total, about 1,300 pages are available to rifle through or approximately 4 additional books of this size. And for the absolutely devoted, these documents have dozens of citations (precedents) by the courts, which lead to further digging.

Readers of eBooks can simply tap on the link(s) on their screens and readers of print versions can type in their browsers' window the URL (Uniform Resource Locator) provided and the associated document comes up.

# INTRODUCTION

Look at your calendar. It's April again. Your taxes are due in 2 weeks.

See what some of your hard earned money is earmarked for at the Department of Justice:

Boomerang unexpectedly returned and smacked you in the face?

This is America, not Australia. We got you covered!

Train whistled at you and caused your tinnitus?

It's a disability, file a claim!

Spilled coffee on your laps? Or better, someone else spilled coffee on you?

There is money coming your way, precedent is plenty!

Horse emptying his bowels on your lap?

That's an "impact" and if the horse can't pay, its owner surely can!

Bought a pair of binoculars? Looked into the sun and hurt your eyes?

Mislabelled, it's as clear as daylight!

Stepped into a hole? Your grandfather's grave?

No, you are not a klutz. There is a legal remedy for this!

Stole a gun and shot yourself?

Worry not; you're technically unsophisticated and underage too!

Are you too short to fly a Boeing 747?

It's a handicap. Also discrimination and let's see if we can shrink that bird!

Are you being sued for paternity?

Turn around and countersue for a stud fee!

Got a permanent erection?

It must be your motorcycle, or the seat, or both!

Dead fly in bottled water?

Head to court, even if you didn't drink the water!

Forced to eat spicy food on a hijacked plane?

It's the airline's fault and those terrorists!

Refused school admission seven times in a row?

That's academic malpractice, we can help!

Just robbed somebody and got shot by police?

How can you be blamed for that? It's police brutality!

What are you? Litigation sissy? Or a tourist?

We are here to help you.

We are Bicker, Crook & Leach the law firm known for billing for a better future. Sue Conner is ready to take your call. Dial now!

You may think this is all made-up. Poor schmuck. Apart from the "law firm" it's all true. They are drawn exclusively from a trade renowned in legend for its immunity to both conscience and altruism.

Judging by the title the reader might prematurely conclude: here we go again, another lawyer bashing book. Far from it. It's an admirable feat what the industry has managed to pull off in full daylight, in every country, at every level and for so long. And without consequences.

Except maybe Saddam Hussein. He started out in law school, but didn't finish it. Possible cause of his demise?

What this means in practice is what ended up in this collection.

A comparable profession – say a team of engineers – got together and built an oil refinery. At start-up, the plant produced yogurt, instead of gasoline. Unlike in lawyerdom, word would get out quickly and heads would roll. Options, like reliance on talismanic phrases, running for the dense cover of ambiguity would not be available.

As the late English humorist A. P. Herbert noted: "In other trades to be wrong is regarded as a matter of regret; in the law alone is it regarded as a matter of course."

Lawyers and litigation have been lampooned by the likes of Shakespeare, Dickens, Napoleon, Twain, Mencken and a long list of other, lesser-known critics.

Not least the many books written by lawyers themselves, many of which can be found in the Bibliography section on the back pages. They are the insiders; they must know something others don't.

Titles like "The Trouble with Lawyers" by two distinguished academics of the legal profession – written 40 years apart – might indicate that something isn't right. Other titles of the genre are more specific. "Lawyers and Other Reptiles" or "Whores of the Court" or "The Terrible Truth about Lawyers" come to mind.

Some of these books offer a wide range of criticism. From mild to milder.

Others put it more sharply:

"The first thing we do, let's kill all the lawyers" says Shakespeare's character Dick the Butcher in Henry VI, a play written more than 400 years ago.

Napoleon, (whose father Carlo was a lawyer) ruler of France once said: "The practice of the law is too severe an ordeal for poor human nature. The man who habituates himself to the distortion of the truth and to exultation at the success of injustice will, at last, hardly know right from wrong." That was more than 200 years ago.

In the multiple awards winning movie "Mighty Aphrodite" Cassandra delivering the following line: "I see disaster. I see catastrophe. Worse, I see lawyers!"

In the year 2000, the late Common Pleas Judge Fred Cartolano in Cincinnati complained from the bench: "There are too many lawyers, too many law schools and too many opportunities for dishonest behavior. There are only so many fleas that can feed on a dog," the judge said. "We have lawyers coming out of the woodwork. There's not enough business for all the lawyers out there."

Oklahoma Judge Wayne E. Alley didn't mince words either. He said: "This case makes me lament the demise of dueling. Pistols at 10 paces would guarantee a salubrious reduction in the number of counsel to put up with."

Strong suggestions to be sure. As if, there is a persistent reputational deficiency hanging over the trade and lily-white is not the word to describe it. But you don't need to be a connoisseur of judicial vibrancy in order to appreciate the full majesty of the law. You need only forget any notion of justice.

How else – and despite the glut of lawyers – can the United States rank 67th (tied with Uganda) of 97 countries in access to justice and affordability of legal services? (Deborah Rhode)

That's easy. Having developed this shoot-yourself-in-the-foot model, America has built a judicial hellhole and moved in. Reality-evasion is in top gear and has become surreal enough; it's pointless to satirize it. Reality became ridiculous enough on its own.

And destroying society this way needs no analysis.

Cases like:

How a 21-year old aspiring opera singer was nearly laughed out of court in 1959 and how a 20-year old aspiring opera singer in 2002 laughed all the way to the bank with an $11 million judgment for her injuries. But that wasn't enough, she had this lingering anger and had another go at the compensation apple and sued for higher interest rates on the award, hoping to further soothe her anxieties. (See Chapter VII)

Ten years ago former administrative judge Roy L. Pearson in Washington D.C. sued a family owned dry-cleaner for $65 million. Their crime; a misplaced pair of trousers. (See Chapter VII) Subsequently, he lost the case, but .....What does someone as unhinged as Pearson get in return? The District of Columbia, Court of Appeals Board on Professional Responsibility suspended him on May 23, 2018.

For 90 days.

It only took 11 years and 13 judges to get here. And that should do it. An appropriate response to society's interest in protecting and safeguarding its legal and judicial systems... The logic of allowing this type of excess is pants-on-head retarded (pun intended) and fascinating in its perversity. Do some entirely symbolic embroidery around the edges and nothing changes.

As the case so often is, however, the longer the analysis the more diluted the point.

This book is solely focused on the industry's highlights – or lowlights. Come along for the ride. The intent is not to add a foot to Mount Everest, delivering still another cautionary tale about the unhinged times now upon us, but to entertain. Enjoy the heat of litigious zeal, gravitas-laden theatrics, everyone virtue-signalling their tails off to look sympathetic. Blue-ribbon excuses and at times, awards, off the Richter scale. Above all, although can't tell from reading.......it appears money is changing hands. The legal services industry is projected to rake in $290 billion this year. You've been warned.

# CHAPTER I

# ACCIDENTS

*"After being bombarded endlessly by road-safety propaganda it was almost a relief to find myself in an actual accident." James G. Ballard (1930 – 2009) was an English novelist*

This category is a gathering of mishaps, mostly bizarre chains of events. Unfortunate results - such as injury - are often entitled to compensation, mostly under an insurance policy, or workman's compensation scheme. The common thread running through these filings, unsurprisingly, is not sedate travel in the bus lane with no overtaking or risky manoeuvres. These are very different from the ones broadcast every morning on radio traffic reports. This is not to say, that a minor fender-bender cannot trigger legal carnage. Suffering any kind of damage is not always necessary and not all accidents involve vehicles.

## 1-AN IMPACT

**Court:** Court of Appeals of Georgia

**Date:** 1928

**Report:** None in original

**Case number:** 38 Ga. App. 581; 144 S.E. 680

**Link:** https://merillionpress.com/cases/I-001.pdf

**Plaintiff (Appellant):** Christy Brothers Circus

**Defendant (Appellee):** Velna TURNAGE

**Opinion By:** Alexander W. STEPHENS, Judge

**Prior History:** Velna Turnage was an unmarried white lady, and one afternoon she decided to go to an entertainment show of Christy Brothers Circus. She was seated in the front row to enjoy the performance up close and also in clear view of everybody else in the tent. One act featured several horses and horsemen and while in attendance a horse, which was going through a dancing performance immediately in front of where she was sitting and – obviously insufficiently trained – caused to back towards her, and while in this situation the horse evacuated the contents of his bowels into her lap.

That this occurred in full view of many people, some of whom were circus employees, and all of whom laughed at the occurrence. As a result Ms. Turnage was caused much embarrassment, mortification, and mental pain and suffering.

She sued for damages in a certain amount, that the damage alleged was due entirely to Christy Brothers' negligence and without any fault of her own. The lower court agreed with her and awarded damages. Christy Brothers claims the plaintiff has insufficient evidence to justify a suit and timely appeals.

**Before this Court:** There may be a recovery of damages for mental suffering, humiliation or embarrassment resulting from a physical injury of which they are inseparable components. . . . Any unlawful touching of a person's body, although no actual physical hurt may ensue, yet, since it violates a personal right, constitutes a physical injury to that person. . . . The unlawful touching need not be direct, but may be indirect, as by the precipitation upon the body of a person of any material substance. ...

The lower court, fairly to the defendant, submitted all the issues presented. The evidence authorized the inference that the plaintiff was damaged, by reason of humiliation and embarrassment.

**Verdict:** in the sum of $500 ($7,500 today), and the verdict found for her in that amount is AFFIRMED.

## 2-Bullu Antagonized

**Court:** Queen's Bench Division of the High Court of Justice, City of Westminster, London, England

**Date:** 1957

**Report:** None in original

**Case number:** [1957] 2 QB 1

**Link:** https://merillionpress.com/cases/I-002.pdf

**Plaintiffs (Appellants):** Johannes H. W. BEHRENS and his wife Emmie BEHRENS

**Defendant (Appellee):** BERTRAM MILLS CIRCUS Ltd.

**Opinion By:** Patrick A. DEVLIN, Judge

**Prior History**: Johannes H. W. Behrens and his wife Emmie were midgets. He was 30 inches high and claimed to be the smallest man in the world; he was uncommon among midgets in that he was perfectly proportioned. His wife was 36 inches high and was not perfectly proportioned; she was trained to play a number of musical instruments, such as an accordion and a saxophone of a special size, well enough to enable her to contribute to the entertainment with some form of musical act when she was on the stage.

Bertram Mills Circus Ltd., well-known circus proprietors, held a circus at Olympia in London every Christmas season, and for that purpose rented the Grand Hall at Olympia and the annex behind it. Beyond the funfair they had a menagerie where they kept animals for show, some of the animals being those which performed in the circus, among them six Burmese elephants. Every time there was a circus performance the elephants were twice taken from the elephant house to the circus ring and back, once for the parade at the beginning of the circus and once for their act.

In August, 1953, Whitehead, the Behrens' manager, obtained from Bertram's a license for a booth in the funfair and on Saturday, January 2, 1954, it was arranged that Whitehead's two children should go to Olympia in the afternoon. The children arrived in the main entrance about 2 o'clock and Whitehead was there to meet them. His daughter, Santa had brought with her the dog Simba. He then sent the two children to look around the funfair while he resumed his place in the booth at the pay box. He kept the dog; it had a lead which he attached to one of the legs of his chair.

The circus performance had begun at 1.45. The elephants had already been out for the opening parade and back again to their house. In due course they came out again in order to do their act. As the third elephant in the procession, Bullu, was [6] passing opposite Whitehead, the dog, Simba, ran out snapping and barking.

Bullu trumpeted with fright, Simba turned back and made to go into the booth and Bullu went after her. Behrens was got out of the booth and then Mrs. Behrens. The dog was killed. None of the elephants touched either of the couple, but the front of the booth and other parts of it were knocked down and some part fell on Mrs. Behrens, causing her serious injuries. The trainer got the elephants back into line again very quickly – the whole thing was over in a few seconds – and the procession went on and they performed their act.

Mrs. Behrens was seriously injured and was incapacitated until the middle of June, 1954, when she was fit to do light work. After her recovery she was unable to play her musical instruments as well as she had done before the accident. They did not take work again until two and a quarter years after the accident, when they resumed exhibition or fairground work.

They justified that long period of inactivity on the ground that their occupation consisted of a joint act of entertainment and that Mrs. Behrens was rendered unfit to play her musical instruments. In fact the act was not a joint act, for the part played by Mrs. Behrens was only subsidiary, the main attraction being the advertisement of Mr. Behrens as the smallest man on earth, and he could have obtained work without her and her injuries did not put an end to his professional livelihood. No diminution in joint earning power after a period of eight months from the accident was proved.

**Before this Court:** The Behrens allege, that the Circus wrongfully kept the elephants, which were wild animals and of a dangerous, mischievous and/or vicious nature, and that the injuries and loss which they had suffered were the result of the failure of Bertram, claiming damages.

Bertram denied liability; they denied that the elephants were wild or of a dangerous, vicious or mischievous nature, or that they were wrongfully kept on the premises at Olympia. They further contended that the matters complained of were caused by the wrongful act of a third party in causing or permitting the dog to be on the premises.

Liability for damage done by a wild animal while out of control cannot be limited, as suggested by Bertram, to the damage flowing from its vicious or wicked propensities. Wild animals are not in the same category as domestic animals; the owner of a wild animal keeps it at his peril and is liable for all the damage which it does if it escapes from control. In any event, the danger from escaping elephants comes not only from their mouths or teeth but from their momentum and natural quality of bulk. A frightened stampeding elephant does not stop to reason but bulldozes its way through whatever lies in its path.

Mrs. Behrens received half the benefit of the joint earnings and may therefore be taken to have been paid half. Her injuries were considerable and they have left some permanent side effects of pain and discomfort. The medical history in relation to Mr. Behrens is almost negligible. He went to the hospital with his wife after the accident, but was not admitted; and in fact the first time he was seen by a doctor was nearly three years later for the purposes of this action. He preferred to stay at home and accept the loss of earnings; and in the very peculiar circumstances of this case I have held that his choice was a reasonable one. Can he then recover his loss of earnings as damages? I think that he is entitled to recover.

**Verdict:** The result is that there will be JUDGMENT for the male plaintiff for sums totaling £480 and for the female plaintiff for £2,930. (US $35,000 and $208,000 respectively today.)

## 3-Loosening of Teeth

**Court:** Supreme Court of Pennsylvania

**Date:** 1963 JUL 02

**Report:** None in original

**Case number:** 411 Pa. 346

**Link:** https://merillionpress.com/cases/I-003.pdf

**Plaintiff (Respondent):** Harry B. FREER

**Defendant (Appellant):** Leroy PARKER

**Opinion By:** Michael A. MUSMANNO, Justice

**Prior History:** Freer, averred in his complaint that, as a result of the automobile collision, for which Parker was responsible, he sustained various hurts, injuries and disablements, one of them being "loosening of teeth." At the trial his dentist testified that prior to the accident Freer suffered from some loosening of teeth but that the violence of the collision had further loosened his teeth. They were "mobile," that "you could shake them with your fingers," and that he "splinted the teeth together to try to allow the bone to regenerate and tighten the teeth."

Parker argues that at the lower court, there was a demonstrated variance between allegata and probata, (It's a general rule of evidence that the allegata and probata must correspond; that is, the proof must at least be sufficiently extensive to cover all the allegations of the party). Parker claims, that this variance is so great, it entitles him to a new trial.

**Before this Court:** It would be great, if for instance a plaintiff avers that his left arm was severed as a result of the litigated event and then stamps into court on a wooden leg, his arms intact. The defendant can well object, because he has been caught by surprise. But if Freer – as is the fact in this case – states in his complaint that, as a result of the legal bone of contention his teeth were loosened and the lay – as well as medical evidence – addresses itself to teeth loosening, it is difficult to see how Parker can reasonably argue that he was left in the dark as to what to expect at the trial of the case.

Even if Freer already chewed on loose teeth prior to the accident, but the teeth were made looser by the accident, what still happened was that his teeth were loosened. A loose tooth can always become looser. In fact, that is more or less the melancholy story of teeth.

A tooth first manifests the slightest variation from perpendicularity; then it leans a little more, but like the Leaning Tower of Pisa, it is still firmly imbedded in the terra firma of the jaw bone. One day, however, the tooth bearer will note, as he masticates a tough steak or bites into a bit of gravel in his oyster sandwich, that the tooth under surveillance wobbles a little more, but it is still useful and still resolute for further masticatory assaults on foods of a stronger constituency than mush.

A person may have a number of teeth in that state; they may even resemble a slightly pushed over picket fence but they are still good teeth, still serviceable tusks. If, because of violence applied to the mandibles, the whole dental battery is jostled and the individual molars, bicuspids, grinders and incisors are shaken in their sockets, it is certainly proper to say that there has been a loosening of teeth. A further loosening, it is true, but still a loosening.

In whatever stage of looseness a man's dental pearls may be, he is entitled to keep them in that state, and if they are tortuously subjected to jostling, jarring and jouncing, the tortfeasor may not be excused from responsibility for the further chewing dilapidation of his victim on the basis that he had bad teeth anyway.

Here, the defendant could not possibly plead ignorance to knowledge of the plaintiff's "loosening of teeth." If a man's teeth are 10 per cent loose before an accident and 60 per cent loose after an accident, "loosening of teeth" accurately describes the deplorable dental deterioration, and adequately acquaints the defendant with what he must face at the trial in the way of claimed damages.

**Verdict:** Judgment AFFIRMED.

## 4-Tumultuous Journey

**Court:** Supreme Court of Pennsylvania

**Date:** 1961 DEC 05

**Report:** Non in original

**Case number:** 405 Pa. 312 (Pa. 1961)

**Link:** https://merillionpress.com/cases/I-004.pdf

**Plaintiff (Respondent):** Eugene GASH

**Defendant (Appellant):** William A. LAUTSENHEZER

**Opinion By:** Michael A. MUSMANNO, Justice

**Prior History:** On February 7, 1955, Eugene Gash, the plaintiff in this case, was driving his car, a 1953 Chevrolet, northwardly on Mosside Boulevard between Wilkinsburg and Monroeville. Mosside Boulevard at the point of the untoward occurrence is about 18 feet wide and made up of "blacktop composition." The weather on the day of the unusual happening was cold but clear, the road not perceptibly icy except perhaps in some rare spots.

Suddenly Gash, beheld a car coming toward him on his own side of the road. To avoid the obviously impending collision he cut abruptly to the right. He hit the berm which, because of deep frozen ruts, became an unpassable barrier. The continuing momentum of the car, finding no outlet forward, swung the rear end toward the left, sweeping in a clockwise direction. The car skidded across the road and then, hitting the left berm, tilted, toppled and fell 15 feet into a gully at the bottom of the embankment. Through the gully ran a creek, the water carrying on its surface particles of ice.

At the end of his tumultuous journey Gash found himself lying on what he at first thought was the floor of the car but which turned out to be the inside of the roof, the car having completely capsized in its precipitous descent. Taking inventory of his situation, amid the broken glass and wreckage of his car, Gash concluded that despite the calamity he might have suffered, he had sustained only an injury to his right leg. However, another possible calamity now obtruded. The car was wedged in the gully in such a fashion that neither door (it was a two-door car) could be opened and the creek was flowing through it, with its particles of ice.

Gash could hear automobiles passing on the highway above, but despite his continued blowing of the horn of his car, he could attract no one to heed his plight. As his perilous state continued and augmented in gravity, something quite extraordinary happened. He felt a sudden jolt and his car spun around in the creek, releasing him from the imprisoning wreck and icy jailor. He looked to see what had occurred and found that another car had come to join him in the creek. It was because of this almost miraculous and certainly fortuitous visitation that possibly his life was saved, even though in the succoring process he sustained another injury, this time to his back.

As a result of this second injury he sued William A. Lautsenhezer, the man who, willingly or unwillingly, had provided the means for extricating Gash from the watery trap which might eventually have cost him his life. But we are here not concerned with the morals or ethics of the situation. We are passing only on the legal aspects of the strange event.

Moreover, it is by no means fatefully written that the arrival of Lautsenhezer in his own way constituted a wholly Samaritan interposition. What turned out to be a providential rescue of the plaintiff could also have been his coup de grace because had Lautsenhezer's car struck Gash in some manner other than the way in which they met in the aqueous arena, Lautsenhezer's car could have done what so far the creek had not accomplished, that is to say, killed Gash.

It is certainly within the realm of possibility that Gash could have extricated himself from his dilemma without the intercession of Lautsenhezer, or he could have been rescued by others through less unorthodox methods.

Be that as it may, at the trial, after the plaintiff had related what we have condensed above, the trial judge entered a compulsory non-suit on the basis that the plaintiff's narrative did not offer a suitable premise upon which to base a charge of negligence against the defendant. The trial judge summed up the situation in the following pseudo syllogism: "The plaintiff says: I was in the creek, I got there without any fault of my own. The defendant came into the same creek and hit me. I don't know how he got there or why but I want you to say that it was because of his fault. This amounts to a sort of Gertrude Stein, I was, I was not, I was, I was not. He was, He was, He was. Equals $10,000, please."

**Before this Court:** The literary allusion is interesting but the argument presented is erratic. The imagined soliloquy does not conform to the proved facts. The plaintiff not only said he was not at fault, he proved he was not at fault. He had been traveling on his own right side of the road, a car aiming at his destruction loomed without warning ahead of him, and he swerved to avoid the potential destroyer. From that point on, the law of gravitation, the nature of the terrain, and the geography of the locale all combined to take Gash into the bed of the creek which, as uncomfortable as it was, did provide him sanctuary from the aggressor on the road and under the circumstances, he had the right to occupy it undisturbed by the second aggressor.

The defendant here, however, offered no explanation of the grotesque condition of affairs which took him into an area where certainly normally, he had no right to be. Since his violent arrival in the creek inflicted injury on the plaintiff, the defendant incurred the obligation to explain why he departed from the roadway, and it would then be a question for the jury to determine if he also was without fault for his headlong leap into the glacial watercourse.

It will be recalled that the trial judge conjured up an equation in which he said that "I was" and "I was not" equalled $10,000, but the Judge had no right, under the circumstances revealed, to dispose of the case on a fanciful equation.

**Verdict:** Judgment REVERSED to a lower court with an order to proceed to judgment.

## 5-Escape from Hospital

**Court:** Appeals Court of Massachusetts, Essex

**Date:** 1993-JUN-14

**Report:** 92-P-45

**Case number:** None in original

**Link:** https://merillionpress.com/cases/I-005.pdf

**Plaintiffs (Respondents):** Tracy A. ROHDE and another

**Defendants (Appellants):** LAWRENCE General Hospital and others

**Opinion By:** Gerald GILLERMAN, Judge

**Prior History:** On November 12, 1987, shortly after 1:00 A.M., the Andover MA, police brought Rohde to Lawrence General Hospital, after finding him at the scene of a minor car accident expressing strange and irrational thoughts. Rohde was not physically injured, but the police thought he might have "some kind of mental problem." While being interviewed at the hospital, Rohde jumped from the carrier on which he had been placed, and assaulted a clinician. The police promptly handcuffed him to the carrier.

After examining Rohde, Dr. John Lucas, a defendant, recorded the diagnosis "acute psychotic episode" on the hospital's emergency admitting form. At the bottom of the form Lucas entered the order "leather restraints." Lucas also completed a written application to the hospital, on a form provided by the Department of Mental Health, for the temporary hospitalization of Rohde.

Lucas stated in this application that in his opinion Rohde "requires hospitalization so as to avoid the likelihood of serious harm by reason of mental illness," that Rohde was delusional, not oriented as to day, month or year, and that he was "dangerous to others: assaulted EPS worker – patient has bizarre behaviour: he cut up money and credit cards." The transfer of Rohde to a licensed mental health facility could not take place until certain test results were obtained, and he remained in the hospital's care for the night.

The nurse's notes of the defendant Cheryl Edwards, the "primary nurse" on duty until 7:00 A.M., record that at 6:00 A.M. Rohde's handcuffs were removed and he was secured in four-point (each arm and each leg) leather restraints.

Sometime after 6:00 A.M. Rohde woke up to find himself alone in his room, experiencing strange and bizarre thoughts. "I was paranoid ... I thought they were out to get me and my family. I thought to myself that I had to try to get out of the hospital and that it was a good time to try since nobody was in the room or in sight."

Rohde managed to free himself from the restraints, which he says were not securely fastened, and fled from the hospital. At 7:15 A.M. he was seen running down the hallway, out of the hospital and into an unlocked automobile (its engine was running) in the hospital parking lot. He drove off in the automobile, and soon crashed into a fence and suffered serious injuries. Rohde's suit alleges that the defendants were negligent in failing to secure the restraints on him, and in failing to supervise him while he was under restraint.

The hospital and the three individual defendants join in the main argument that the decision of the medical panel was correct, because the plaintiffs failed to offer expert testimony his injuries resulted from the defendants' failure of performance.

**Before this Court:** A medical malpractice tribunal, appropriately convened, found that the plaintiffs did not present sufficient evidence of negligence by any of the defendants to raise a legitimate question of liability for judicial inquiry. The plaintiffs declined to file the required bonds, and judgments were entered in the Superior Court dismissing the complaint against the four defendants.

**Verdict:** This is a "garden-variety case where ... attendance was needed but lacking at the time of need.... Such cases do not call for the paraphernalia of experts ...."We conclude that the plaintiffs should have been allowed to proceed against Lawrence General Hospital without posting a bond, but we AFFIRM the judgment in favor of the individual defendants Dr. John W. Lucas, Cheryl Edwards and Marguerite Reeves.

## 6-Help Thy Neighbor

**Court:** Supreme Court of Pennsylvania

**Date:** 1986 MAY 29

**Report:** None in original

**Case number:** (1986) 353 Pa Super 505; 510 A2d 776

**Link:** https://merillionpress.com/cases/I-006.pdf

**Plaintiffs (Appellants):** Ruth J. PACHESKY and Robert PACHESKY, her husband

**Defendant (Appellee):** Frank D. GETZ

**Opinion By:** Frank J. MONTEMURO, Judge

**Prior History:** In the early morning hours of December 6, 1978, Ruth Pachesky was returning from work. Her home was at the crest of a hill and as she approached her home, she observed a stationary car in the middle of the street just below the crest of the hill. In passing she noticed that the car's lights were on, the engine was running, the windows were up, and that a man, who proved to be Frank D. Getz, was slumped motionless over the steering wheel. Believing he was being overcome by carbon monoxide, she parked her car, ran into her house and told her husband what she just saw.

The two of them returned to the scene, pounded on the windshield and shouted in an attempt to arouse Getz. When he failed to respond, they tried to open the passenger side door and found that it was locked. Ruth then ran around to the driver's side, opened the door, rolled down the window and turned off the ignition. As soon as the ignition was turned off, the car began to drift backwards down the hill. The open door struck Ruth, knocking her to the ground and inflicting certain personal injuries. Evidence at trial indicated that Getz was intoxicated.

In September of 1981, this case was tried before the Court of Common Pleas of Allegheny County and a jury. The jury found that: (1) both Pachesky and Getz were negligent; (2) their respective negligent acts or omissions were substantial factors in bringing about Ruth's injuries; and (3) of the total causal negligence, 20% was attributable to Getz and 80% was attributable to Pachesky.

On October 9, 1981, the Pacheskys filed a motion for new trial, which was briefed and argued by the parties, and subsequently denied, by that court on July 13, 1983. Judgment was entered on the verdict and this timely appeal followed.

**Before this Court:** The Pacheskys' specific contention is that the jury's attribution to Pachesky of a greater percentage of the causal negligence was contrary to the weight of the evidence. Her own testimony was to the effect that she turned off the ignition without checking if the parking brake was engaged or if Getz had his foot on the brake; nor did she determine whether the transmission was in 'park,' 'neutral' or 'drive.'

She, of course, was an experienced driver and knew or should have known that the vehicle would roll back down the hill, unless the brake was set or the transmission was in 'park,' after the ignition was turned off. The jury had evidence before it from which it could determine that a reasonably prudent person, under like circumstances, would have taken the precaution of determining those matters before placing herself in such a dangerous position. Nor can a new trial be awarded on the basis that the verdict was against the weight of the evidence merely because the trial judge would have reached a different conclusion on the evidence presented.

**Verdict:** While Getz's causal negligence was patently not insignificant, our sense of justice is nevertheless unoffended by the jury's apportionment. Not only are we unable to find any "palpable abuse of discretion" we are of the opinion that the court's evidential analysis and subsequent disposition were quite proper.

Judgment AFFIRMED with one judge dissenting.

## 7-Fort-Erie Exotic Dancer

**Court:** Ontario Supreme Court - Court of Appeal

**Date:** 1990 JUN 19

**Report:** [1990] O.J. No. 1063

**Case number:** DRS 92-02714-U/Action No. 178/88

**Link:** https://merillionpress.com/cases/I-007.pdf

**Plaintiff (Respondent):** Jennifer Sheila SCHLAU aka Sunshine

**Defendants (Appellants):** Dennis BOYESKO and Sergio and Merine MASSOLIN (Third Parties)

**Opinion By:** PER CURIAM

**Prior History:** Jennifer Schlau was a passenger – along with several others – in a car driven by Sergio Massolin on April 3. 1983, when they collided with another vehicle driven by Dennis Boyesko, in Fort-Erie, Ontario. In the collision Jennifer sustained injuries to both her knees and was knocked unconscious for a couple of minutes. She was taken to a hospital, but released a few hours later. The next day she returned for additional medical tests and X-rays, all the while complaining of pain in the neck, back and legs. However, there were no fractures and the neurological examination turned up nothing unusual.

After 3 months of recovery she returned to work as an exotic dancer working the Niagara River circuit on both sides of the Canada-US border. Her usual dance routine was a mixture of acrobatic/ ballet/ country/ western style, which she felt, she could no longer perform. She adapted a less vigorous style, a comic routine, that wasn't well received by patrons of the bars. Unhappy customers hurled chicken bones on the stage, at which point her boss terminated her employment in May 1984.

The bar scene at the time was going through a transition. Her last employer described the conditions in the area as having approximately equal numbers of men and women as patrons. But now the patrons are almost all male and the emphasis is on nudity. Another of her employers opined, it was "the end of an era for that type of girl." She was "not like the other girls." Because of her "age (43), her body and the type of dance she did, the non-revealing." The inference drawn was that an era was coming to an end where entertainers disrobe to music, with minimum dancing and maximum disrobing.

Following her dismissal she returned to Canada and, continued to suffer various ailments. 46 months after the accident she launched her lawsuit against Boyesko. Her team of lawyers called on medical evidence, which was given by 8 practitioners including 3 psychiatrists and 2 orthopedic surgeons. The medical team had a lively debate when describing her condition: "emotional overlay, functional overlay, conversion disorder, conversion reaction." And finally agreeing on the term "chronic pain syndrome." It's easier for the patient to understand.

Not all medical experts were in agreement, as one on the defense team termed it "a widely believed but scientifically unsubstantiated view. The evidence that recovery of the so-called compensation or litigation neurosis regularly follows the settling of a case." After a 12-day trial the lower court found Boyesko entirely at fault for the collision and awarded C$ 338,000 in damages (US $700,000 today). This appeal follows.

**Before this Court:** Boyesko argues the trial judge erred in discharging the jury, finding him fully liable for Schlau's condition and that he did not satisfy the onus of establishing that her seat belt was not properly fastened at the time of the accident. The critical issue here was whether the trial judge accepted the evidence of the medical experts for the plaintiff or the defendant. The trial judge decided in favor of her experts and gave detailed reasons for it.

In our opinion, the trial judge considered all factors in deciding to award full compensation to her. He concluded that the award should not be reduced because of those factors and that the accident was the effective cause of the victim's condition.

**Verdict:** Appeal DISMISSED. The damages awarded were reasonable.

Boyesko appealed the decision in 1989 which he lost and appealed again in 1990 and lost again.

## 8-Blimp Shaped Balloon

**Court:** United States Court of Appeals for the Tenth Circuit

**Date:** 1984 APR 11

**Report:** 82-1234

**Case number:** 732 F. 2d 112

**Link:** https://merillionpress.com/cases/I-008.pdf

**Plaintiff (Respondent):** Michael D. GARNER

**Defendant (Appellant):** RAVEN Industries Inc.

**Opinion By:** William E. DOYLE, Circuit Judge

**Prior History:** Garner is an employee of Permian Ford, a car dealership in New Mexico. In May, 1978, the dealership purchased a helium-filled balloon for advertising purposes from Raven Industries. The balloon came with a user's manual, an inflation kit, a device for measuring pressure, and a rig for securing the balloon to the ground.

On May 6, 1978, the balloon escaped from its moorings. Permian contacted the Federal Aviation Administration to warn them of a possible hazard to air traffic. They also contacted Zip Franklin and requested that the balloon be followed in his airplane and he should attempt to shoot it down.

Meanwhile, Garner followed it in his truck.

Eventually it was shot down by Zip Franklin, but it took several hours before the partially deflated balloon landed in a field in Texas. Garner arrived at the scene about a minute after it hit the ground, but it kept moving across the field and he ran after it. He tried to stop it, but somehow became entangled in it and was severely injured as a result.

Garner maintained that the balloon's "automatic deflation device" failed to operate. The deflation feature is supposed to be activated to partially deflate an escaped balloon so that it will descend to the ground, preventing it from being a hazard to air traffic and to allow the owner to recapture it.

This personal injury action was brought against Raven Industries, alleging negligence in design and manufacture. At trial the jury found Permian Ford negligent, but not Raven Industries and Garner appeals.

**Before this Court:** Garner contends that the defective deflation device was itself unreasonably dangerous, that the balloon presented an unreasonable risk of injury to himself and the jury was improperly instructed concerning the chain of events.

Raven Industries' contention is that even if the balloon was unreasonably dangerous in the sky to air traffic, that condition did not exist at the time of his injury and that any defect in the balloon's deflation device could not be regarded as the proximate cause of his injury.

**Verdict:** Garner has failed to come forward with proof that the balloon was unreasonably dangerous to him and accordingly the trial court was correct in its decision. Based on the evidence, it is not shown how the alleged defective deflation device produced the injury. Trial court's decision UPHELD.

## 9-Drinking and Driving

**Court:** Supreme Court of Utah

**Date:** 1986 APR 11

**Report:** No. 19712

**Case number:** 717 P. 2d 1321

**Link:** https://merillionpress.com/cases/I-009.pdf

**Plaintiff (Respondent):** State of Utah

**Defendants (Appellants):** David A. BLOWERS and James J. SCHOFIELD

**Opinion By:** Michael D. ZIMMERMAN, Justice

**Prior History:** Schofield and Blowers spent the afternoon of April 23, 1983, drinking beer. At about 7:30 p.m., they rode their horses down a Kaysville street toward a summer pasture. Schofield's sister rode on Blowers' horse behind Blowers. Conflicting evidence indicates either two small boys frightened the horses or that Blowers and Schofield began racing. In any event, as the horses ran, Schofield's sister fell from Blowers' horse and suffered a severe concussion. Following a police investigation of the accident, Schofield was charged and convicted in circuit court of driving a vehicle while he was under the influence of alcohol.

The circuit court found that the Utah drunk-driving law applied to persons riding horses and convicted both men of driving under the influence of alcohol. Defendants appealed to the district court, which upheld Schofield's conviction but reversed Blowers' conviction and ordered a new trial.

Blowers and Schofield appeal their convictions.

**Before this Court:** We dismiss Blowers' appeal because this Court has no jurisdiction over the matter since no final judgment has been entered.

Schofield contends that his conviction denies him due process of law because the statute under which he was convicted did not give him adequate notice that being intoxicated while riding a horse was a crime.

A criminal statute "must be sufficiently clear and definite to inform persons of ordinary intelligence what their conduct must be to conform to its requirements and to advise one accused of violating it what constitutes the offense with which he is charged."

The statute, under which Schofield was convicted, prohibits operation of a "vehicle" while under the influence of alcohol. The motor vehicle code defines a "vehicle" as "every device in, upon, or by which any person or property is or may be transported or drawn upon a highway, except devices moved by human power or used exclusively upon stationary rails or tracks."

This definition cannot be legitimately read to include horses.

The State attempts to avoid this result by relying on a few cases from other jurisdictions where horses have been found to be included within the definition of the word "vehicles" for the purposes of applying specific statutes.

The State also attempts to uphold Schofield's conviction by arguing that the statute provides: "Every person riding an animal or driving any animal-drawn vehicle upon a roadway is subject to this chapter, except those provisions which by their nature can have no application."

This is a classic example of a criminal statute that is too vague in its prohibitions to survive due process challenge. It is impossible for anyone to determine, even upon thoughtful reflection, which portions of the vehicle code the legislature thought should apply to animals and animal-drawn vehicles and which should not. In fact, the very wording of the section suggests that the legislature had no firm idea as to what it meant.

**Verdict:** DISMISSED as to Blowers; REVERSED as to Schofield.

## 10-Mardi Gras Zulu Parade

**Court:** Court of Appeal of Louisiana for the Fourth Circuit

**Date:** 1976 APR 13

**Report:** No. 7291

**Case number:** 330 So. 2d 376

**Link:** https://merillionpress.com/cases/I-010.pdf

**Plaintiff (Appellant):** Carolyn T. SCHOFIELD

**Defendants (Appellees):** THE CONTINENTAL INSURANCE Company, et al.

**Opinion By:** Patrick M. SCHOTT, Judge

**Prior History:** Carolyn Schofield, accompanied by her son and several of his friends, was viewing the parade in a crowd of people at the intersection of Jackson and St. Charles Avenues in New Orleans. After several floats had passed with their riders throwing the usual Mardi Gras trinkets to the crowd, one of the floats stopped in front of them due to the uneven progress of the parade.

The uncontradicted testimony is to the effect that one of the riders on the stopped float picked up a decorated coconut (a traditional Zulu favor) and threw it in Schofield's direction. It struck her causing injuries to her face and mouth. At no time had she given any indication that she wanted a coconut, nor is there any reason to believe that the coconut was thrown to her rather than to the crowd generally.

She launched her action against the Zulu Social Aid and Pleasure Club and its liability insurer for damages for personal injuries she sustained while observing the parade on Mardi Gras day, 1974. The trial judge decided the case against her on the theory of assumption of risk. He found that she understood the tradition of Mardi Gras in general and was familiar with the Zulu parade in particular so that she "assumed the risk of those acts which would normally occur during the time of watching the Zulu parade."

She appeals.

**Before this Court:** At the outset it is emphasized that the coconut was thrown with force in Schofield's direction. It was not lobbed.

There is no evidence that she should know or understand that by attending this parade she incurred the risk of having a coconut thrown in her direction. There is no testimony that this had ever happened before. Indeed, the president of the Zulu organization testified that the riders are instructed to hand out the coconuts and "not to throw them because it could be dangerous throwing heavy coconuts throughout the route." He said that this had been the rule since 1949. It follows that she could not assume a risk which even the defendant disclaimed as an ordinary offshoot of its activities.

Defendants' argument as to Schofield's contributory negligence is likewise without merit. When she saw the object flying in her direction she ducked but was too late. Defendants would fault her for not moving faster or for not putting her hands up. We disagree. It would not be reasonable to insist that she perform like a baseball outfielder under these circumstances.

There is no proof of any negligence on her part.

**Verdict:** The judgment of the trial court is REVERSED and defendants jointly to pay $10,130.00 in favor of Schofield.

# 11-Saving Me, Suing You

**Court:** United States Court of Appeals for the Sixth Circuit

**Date:** 1996 JUL 10

**Report:** No. 95-5895

**Case number:** 89 F. 3d 268

**Link:** https://merillionpress.com/cases/I-011.pdf

**Plaintiffs (Appellants):** Donald CANTRELL; Dorla CANTRELL, his wife

**Defendant (Appellee):** USA, Department of the Army Corps of Engineers

**Opinion By:** Danny J. BOGGS, Circuit Judge

**Prior History:** Donald Cantrell went fishing on Fishtrap Lake in Pike County, Kentucky on October 25, 1992. His boat malfunctioned, and he ended up stranded on an isolated shore. When Cantrell did not return by nightfall, members of the Corps went searching for him.

They found him walking along the shoreline, picked him up, and proceeded to make their way back to the marina. It was dark, there was no moon, vapor had condensed on the windows of the boat, and the usual channels across the lake were narrowed by the winter drawdown. (The water table at the time of the accident was thirteen feet below the summer table.) The boat struck part of the newly-exposed shoreline and sank. Cantrell was trapped in the cabin of the boat and sustained serious injuries.

The United States Army Corp of Engineers (the Corps) uses the lake, as a flood control reservoir. Each September, the Corps lowers the water level of the lake by about thirty-two feet so that the lake will be able to store runoff from winter storms. The process of winter "drawdown" causes considerable changes in the size, depth, and navigability of the lake. The shoreline changes and features of the lakebed hidden in the depths during the summer emerge or lurk just below the surface.

After unsuccessfully seeking administrative remedies, Cantrell sued the United States in district court. In its defense the government claims that Cantrell's action was barred by the immunity clause of the Flood Control Act: "No liability of any kind shall attach to or rest upon the United States for any damage from or by floods or flood waters at any place." Cantrell responded by arguing that his injuries were caused by the negligence of the driver of the government's boat, not by its flood control activities.

The district court agreed with the government's defense and Cantrell appeals.

**Before this Court:** Looking at the nature of the particular cases, rather than the phrasing of the various standards, there does seem to be a clear category of cases in which immunity does apply, and a clear category of cases in which immunity does not. In most cases, a diver, swimmer, or boater — who are trying to make the government pay for its flood control policy choices— invariably lose.

If Cantrell had been driving the boat, we would affirm the judgment for the government without much hesitation. However, Cantrell seeks relief solely on the theory that the driver of the Corps boat was negligent. He does not allege that the drawdown was unreasonable, that the water level was dangerous, or that the government had a duty to make navigation easy. He has only one theory of liability: the pilot's negligence. Since the pilot's negligence was not part of government activity to control floods or flood waters, the immunity clause of the Flood Control Act is irrelevant to Cantrell's claim.

**Verdict:** The judgment is REVERSED, and the case REMANDED for further proceedings in light of this opinion.

## 12-Condition Is Real and Not Simulated (Anxiety Reaction)

**Court:** Supreme Court of Texas

**Date:** 1955 MAY 11

**Report:** No. A-4795

**Case number:** 279 S.W. 2d 315

**Link:** https://merillionpress.com/cases/I-012.pdf

**Plaintiff (Petitioner):** Emery E. BAILEY

**Defendant (Respondent):** AMERICAN GENERAL INSURANCE Company

**Opinion By:** Clyde E. SMITH, Justice

**Prior History:** In October of 1951, Bailey and another workman, while in the course of their employment, were at opposite ends of a movable scaffold which was supported by cables from the roof of a building. The end of the scaffold opposite that on which petitioner stood gave way, and the other workman fell to his death on the roof of another building eight stories below.

Bailey saw his co-worker strike the roof below and thought he himself was about to fall and be killed, but was caught in the cable in such manner that he did not fall. The wind was blowing and the scaffold swung away from the wall, but as it swung back he was released and was able to jump to the roof of another building which was about the same height as the scaffold. Bailey suffered a bruise on his leg and cable burn, but such injuries were minor in nature, were completely healed within a short time after the incident, and did not cause or contribute to any disability on his part.

He contends that the traumatic effect of the accident upon his nervous system directly resulted in a disabling neurosis, termed an "anxiety reaction" or "anxiety state" by both medical experts heard in the trial court, which has rendered it impossible for him to engage in the field of employment for which he is trained and upon which he depends for his livelihood. The majority of the Court of Civil Appeals sustained the insurance company's contention that Bailey's disability is not due to an injury within the meaning of the statutory definition of injury. With this conclusion we do not agree.

**Before this Court:** This is a workmen's compensation suit. The case was submitted to a jury upon special issues, resulting in a verdict and judgment for Bailey for 50% partial disability. That judgment has been reversed and rendered by the Court of Civil Appeals.

It is settled in this state that no recovery can be had for mere fright, where there is no physical injury inflicted. The distinction is clearly drawn; that is, that a recovery cannot be had for suffering from mere fright, but where physical injury results from the mental shock a recovery can be had."

**Verdict:** Therefore this cause is REVERSED and remanded to the Court of Civil Appeals for further proceedings consistent with this opinion, with two judges dissenting.

## 13-Risky Asset

**Court:** United States Court of Appeals for the Seventh Circuit

**Date:** 1995 JUN 29

**Report:** No. 94-3266

**Case number:** 58 F. 3d 1209

**Link:** https://merillionpress.com/cases/I-013.pdf

**Plaintiff (Appellant):** Roy CADEK

**Defendant (Appellee):** GREAT LAKES DRAGAWAY Inc.

**Opinion By:** Walter J. CUMMINGS, Circuit Judge

**Prior History:** Great Lakes operates a drag strip in Union Grove, Wisconsin. On July 17, 1992, Roy Cadek, a citizen of Illinois, paid a fee and signed a release in order to run his funny car, "Risky Asset," on the track. It was not a good run. His funny car collided with his own van which was parked by the side of the track. The damage from the collision itself was minor, but fuel leaked and an ensuing fire engulfed the funny car, the van and himself. Cadek's fire protective suit saved him from substantial injury. His funny car and van were not so fortunate, suffering combined damage of over $45,000.

Great Lakes Dragaway had a fire truck parked by the track which Cadek had seen on prior visits. Unfortunately for him, it was unmanned and its extinguishers were empty. Great Lakes' functional fire-extinguishing equipment consisted of a garden hose attached to an exterior spigot. Had the fire truck been operational, the fire could have been quickly extinguished and Cadek's damages greatly reduced.

On March 8, 1993, Cadek filed a five-count complaint against Great Lakes alleging breach of contract, negligent rescue, negligent misrepresentation, strict misrepresentation, and fraud and seeking $45,000 in compensatory and $150,000 in punitive damages. On various grounds the district court dismissed all his complaints and he appeals.

**Before this Court:** The dispute between the parties is over what Great Lakes' conduct – parking an inoperable fire truck by a drag strip –represented or misrepresented as the case may be.

Great Lakes argues that the presence of the fire truck and extinguisher at the race track "represents one fact and one fact alone: "there is a fire truck and fire extinguisher on the premises.' "That the truck is manned and the extinguisher is filled are, they argue, mere inferences and not representations, because the facts only represent the facts.

This is a very silly argument. The question is whether a reasonable person seeing a fire truck parked at a drag strip would believe that the truck was functional and there to fight fires or was a form of outdoor sculpture or home for wayward Dalmatians.

Great Lakes' conduct of placing the equipment on location, and keeping it there after it became dysfunctional, affirmatively misrepresented that the fire engine was manned and the extinguishers operational. Whether the track has a manned fire truck or a garden hose to fight fires is relevant to a reasonable person's decision whether to run his car at the track and whether to sign a liability release to do so. If Cadek produces evidence to support his allegations, the release should be held unenforceable and not bar his negligence claim.

Cadek pled sufficient facts to allege that Great Lakes had engaged in fraud by its misrepresentation, and that he was therefore entitled to punitive damages, thus enabling him to meet the amount in controversy requirement.

**Verdict:** The case is REMANDED to the district court for further proceedings consistent with this opinion with one dissent.

## 14-Bucking Brama Bull

**Court:** District Court of Appeal of Florida, Fourth District

**Date:** 1984 FEB 15

**Report:** No. 83-1087

**Case number:** 447 So. 2d 318

**Link:** https://merillionpress.com/cases/I-014.pdf

**Plaintiff (Appellant):** Sabina Van TUYN

**Defendants (Appellees):** ZURICH AMERICAN INSURANCE Co., a foreign corp., and Marr Investments, Inc., d/b/a Club Dallas

**Opinion By:** James H. WALDEN, Judge

**Prior History:** Van Tuyn, accompanied by a friend, went to the Club Dallas. On the Club premises was a mechanical device commonly known as "J.R.," a bull, which patrons were invited to mount. The device moved in a forward, backward and sideways direction, the object being to dislodge the rider.

She observed other patrons riding the bull for some fifteen or twenty minutes. It was her testimony that, having decided to ride the bull, she told the operator that she had never ridden before and asked that he go slowly. His response was something to the effect of, "Don't worry about it. We'll take care of it." Prior to mounting the device, plaintiff was asked to sign a written waiver. She signed, but did not read, the waiver.

She rode the bull for approximately ten to fifteen seconds before any problem arose. According to plaintiff's testimony, the operator suddenly started speeding up the bull very, very fast. She stated that, as the bull was moving left to right, the operator made the front of the bull come up at high speed. She testified that this was when she lost her balance and fell forward onto the head of the bull. She then fell off the bull, sustaining personal injuries.

She sued the defendants and this appeal followed.

**Before this Court:** Does the waiver signed by Van Tuyn bar her recovery and support the entry of her claims dismissed? We think not.

The waiver provided:

I fully understand that the mechanical Bucking Brama Bull known as "JR" is a dangerous amusement device.

I hereby voluntarily assume any and all risk, including injury to my person and property which may be caused as a result of my riding or attempting to ride this Bucking Brama Bull.

In consideration for CLUB DALLAS permitting me to ride such amusement device, I hereby voluntarily release, waive, and discharge CLUB DALLAS, Marr Investments, Inc., their lessors, heirs, successors and/or assigns from any and all claims, demands, damages and causes of action of any nature whatsoever which I, my heirs, my assigns, or my successors may have against any of them for, on account of, or by reason of my riding or attempting to ride this Bucking Brama Bull.

I also state that I am not under the influence of alcohol or any other intoxicant and execute this GENERAL RELEASE, WAIVER OF CLAIM AND ASSUMPTION OF RISK AGREEMENT of my own free will and accord.

The agreement being reviewed is devoid of any language manifesting the intent to either release or indemnify Club Dallas, Marr Investments, Inc., for its own negligence. Therefore, the agreement does not, as a matter of law, bar the Appellant's recovery.

Does this waiver shield the defendants from liability from its own negligence, as they contend? We think not. Particularly an issue is the conduct of the employee in his negligent or willful operation of the speed-regulating mechanism after being informed that plaintiff was a novice.

Van Tuyn's testimony is such that a jury could conclude that her injury was caused, not by any inherent characteristic of the mechanical device, but by either negligent or intentional conduct of defendants' employee.

**Verdict:** REVERSED and remanded.

## 15-Hot Coffee, Without the Stella Award*

**Court:** High Court of Justice, Queen's Bench Division, Royal Courts of Justice, London, England

**Date:** 2002 MAR 25

**Report: No.** HQ0005713

**Case number:** [2002] EWHC 490 (QB)

**Link**: https://merillionpress.com/cases/I-015.pdf

**Claimants:** Sam BOGLE and others

**Defendant:** McDonald's Restaurants Limited

**Opinion By:** Sir Richard A. FIELD LD, Justice

**Prior History:** This is the trial of a set of preliminary issues arising from the pleaded cases of a group of claimants suing for personal injuries caused by the spillage of hot drinks ( in two cases hot water) served by the defendant ("McDonald's"). It is a Group Litigation Order issued on 21 February 2001. There are presently 36 claimants in the group. The majority are children; at least 16 were aged 4 or under at the time the injury was sustained.

A fairly typical set of alleged facts is afforded by the case of Lamar Bartley who, aged almost 10 months, was taken by his mother, Gail McDonald, to a McDonald's restaurant in Nottingham. McDonald had her four other children with her as well as Lamar and was in the company of four other adults with seven other children. She bought three hot drinks and five cold drinks and carried them to a table. It is alleged that another customer put his tray on the same table and in so doing pushed her tray off the table spilling hot coffee onto Lamar who suffered serious scalding injuries requiring a skin graft under general anesthetic.

The exceptional case is that of Sam Bogle who, aged 15 months, was taken by his child minder to the McDonald's at Hinkley Town Centre. It is alleged that Sam attempted to drink a cup of hot coffee which had been left on a table with its lid removed, and in doing so spilled the contents onto himself, sustaining scalding injuries to his face, neck, chest, shoulders and back.

The group is claiming under 7 different theories, that McDonald's acted negligently, cups/lids were of unsound design and construction, inadequate warning, breach of duty of care and in breach of the Consumer Protection Act, because those hot drinks were "defective."

**Before this Court:** The claimants called six factual witnesses and an expert witness, Mr. Donald Ives. All of the factual witnesses were adults. Mr. Ives' 10 point presentation including the identification of 5 steps which in his opinion McDonald's should have taken to reduce the risk of scalding injuries to their consumers was not much of a revelation. If his reasoning stands, McDonald's should not have served drinks at any temperature.

The evidence is that tea or coffee served at a temperature of 65 C will cause a deep thickness burn if it is in contact with the skin for just two seconds. Thus, if McDonald's were going to avoid the risk of injury by a deep thickness burn they would have had to have served tea and coffee at between 55 C and 60 C. But tea ought to be brewed with boiling water if it is to give its best flavour and coffee ought to be brewed at between 85 C and 95 C. Further, people generally like to allow a hot drink to cool to the temperature they prefer.

Mr. Ives has no expertise in the field of selling hot drinks for consumption in restaurants. His view that the drinks should have been served at this temperature is therefore not supported by any relevant expertise on his part. He based his view on a paper published in Food Quality and Preference 10 (1999) 117-121 which reported the coffee drinking temperature preferences of 250 US students. In my judgment the article and the Automatic Vending Association codes of practice are a most insubstantial basis for Mr. Ives's conclusion and fall far short of providing a sound foundation for holding that McDonald's should have served tea and coffee at 70 C.

Is it right that the law of negligence and occupier's liability should be responsible for denying to the public a facility they want notwithstanding the known risk? In my opinion, the answer is plainly no. Although Mc-

Donald's owe a duty of care to those who visit their restaurants to guard against injury, that duty is not such that they should have refrained from serving hot drinks at all.

**Verdict:** The burns suffered by many of the claimants were serious, involving severe pain and skin grafts. However, for the reasons given above, I answer "NO" to all of the preliminary issues; the allegations contained in those issues that McDonald's are legally liable for these unfortunate injuries have not been made out.

* See the multimillion dollar landmark case *Liebeck v. McDonald's Restaurants, P.T.S. Inc.,* No. D-202 CV-93-02419, (Bernalillo County, N.M. Dist. Ct. August 18, 1994).

## 16-Career Enhancing Accident

**Court:** Supreme Court of British Columbia, Vancouver, B.C.

**Date:** 2015 JAN 07

**Report:** Nos. M103556/M103557

**Case number:** 2015 BCSC 10

**Link:** https://merillionpress.com/cases/I-016.pdf

**Plaintiffs (Respondents):** Alla AFONINA and Alissa AFONINA

**Defendants (Appellants):** Peter JANSSON and Her Majesty the Queen in Right of the Province of B.C.

**Opinion By:** Joel GROVES, Justice

**Prior History:** On August 9, 2008 Alla and Alissa Afonina (mother and her daughter) were travelling in a 2006 Toyota Tacoma owned and driven by Peter Jansson, Alla's former boyfriend. The trip took place on the Trans-Canada Highway from Tappen, B.C. towards Salmon Arm, B.C. Due to slippery road conditions and worn tires the small truck landed in a ditch on the side of the highway.

As a result of the impact Alla has suffered mild traumatic brain injury, while Alissa has suffered a moderate traumatic brain injury. The Afoninas allege Jansson's negligent driving caused the accident and are claiming damages for their personal injuries, sufferings and loss of future earnings.

**Before this Court:** Alla was 47 years old at the time of the accident; she arrived in Canada with her 2 kids in 2002 from Russia. She went through a number of entry-level jobs, several of them on a temporary basis, which were not terribly successful. She also enrolled in a number of courses in order to improve her job prospects. Based on the evidence these attempts didn't amount to much.

Her job at the time of the accident was with BC Housing and it was a series of renewable short-term contracts. When she recovered from her physical injuries and returned to work she felt foggy and had double vision, could not concentrate, was unfocused, and made a number of mistakes. She found multi-tasking difficult and found that the job she could handle effectively prior to the accident had become extremely difficult.

On February 29, 2009, her work with BC Housing ended and her contract was not renewed.

Prior to the accident and while in school Alissa sought out psychiatric help, and experimented in drugs and alcohol. She was on the other hand, able to identify her desired media-arts training program and successfully complete the pre-requisites for that program. She was a bright, engaging, young woman as described by her teacher.

After the accident, when her new school program began, she failed miserably and ultimately withdrew from school to complete her Grade 12 year from home. She became lethargic, disruptive, unable to follow course content, and socially isolated, before finally making the decision to withdraw due to the difficulties she was experiencing.

At some point prior to trial, Alissa began work as a professional female dominatrix under the pseudonym Sasha Mizaree, complete with extensive Social Media presence.

Jansson does not dispute that an accident occurred, but does dispute the extent of Alla's injuries. As for Alissa's claim, he suggests that she was a troubled youth with personal difficulties prior to the accident and would have struggled to succeed in life in any event.

**Verdict:** I have concluded that Jansson operated his vehicle in a negligent manner on August 9, 2008, causing the accident. I have assessed the damages suffered by Alla at C$943,889.36 and I have assessed the damages suffered by Alissa at C$1,525,404.77. (US $775,000 and $1.250, 000 respectively)

# CHAPTER II

# ANIMALS

*"I blame it on Walt Disney, where animals are given human qualities. People don't understand that a wild animal is not something that is nice to pat. It can seriously harm you." James F. Cameron is a Canadian filmmaker*

This collection is about animals one way or another connected to human beings. They can be best friends, though not always. Some might be hospitalized, obsessively cared for and cremated. You may chase them, or vice a versa. They can have rights and may even sue you, opening floodgates too vast to contemplate.

As long as a relationship exists a lawsuit can be pursued. The legal bone of contention is long-running, well established and seemingly - as all other segments - ever expanding.

## 1-Dead Cat, Instead of Dead Dog

**Court:** Civil Court of the City of New York, Queens County

**Date:** 1979 MAR 22

**Report:** No number in original

**Case number:** 97 Misc. 2d 530; 415 N.Y.S.2d 182

**Link:** https://merillionpress.com/cases/II-001.pdf

**Plaintiff:** Kay CORSO

**Defendant:** CRAWFORD Dog and Cat Hospital Inc.

**Opinion by:** Seymour FRIEDMAN, Judge

**Prior History:** On January 28. 1978, Ms. Corso brought her 15-year-old poodle into the Crawford Dog and Cat Hospital for treatment. After examining the dog, the Hospital recommended euthanasia and shortly thereafter the dog was put to death.

Both parties agreed that the dog's body would be turned over to Bide-A-Wee, a business specialized in animal welfare. Ms. Corso had arranged for an elaborate funeral for her dog including a head stone, an epitaph, and attendance by her two sisters and a friend. She also planned to visit the grave in the years to come.

A casket was delivered to the funeral which, when opened, revealed the body of a dead cat, instead of the body of her dead dog.

She felt wronged and started this action. During the nonjury trial she described her mental distress and anguish. She also indicated that she still feels distress and anguish, but sustained no special damages.

**Before this Court**: The question before us is twofold.

1-Is it an actionable tort that was committed?

2-If there is an actionable tort is the plaintiff entitled to damages beyond the market value of the dog?

Before answering these questions the court must first decide whether a pet such as a dog is only an item of personal property as prior cases have held. This court now overrules prior precedent and holds that a pet is not just a thing but occupies a special place somewhere in between a person and a piece of personal property.

In ruling that a pet such as a dog is not just a thing I believe the plaintiff is entitled to damages beyond the market value of the dog. A pet is not an inanimate thing that just receives affection; it also returns it. I find that Ms. Corso did suffer shock, mental anguish and despondency due to the wrongful destruction and loss of the dog's body.

She had an elaborate funeral scheduled and planned to visit the grave in the years to come. She was deprived of this right.

This decision is not to be construed to include an award for the loss of a family heirloom which would also cause great mental anguish. An heirloom while it might be the source of good feelings is merely an inanimate object and is not capable of returning love and affection. It does not respond to human stimulation; it has no brain capable of displaying emotion which in turn causes a human response. Losing the right to memorialize a pet rock, or a pet tree or losing a family picture album is not actionable. But a dog – that is something else. To say it is a piece of personal property and no more is a repudiation of our humaneness. This I cannot accept.

**Verdict:** Accordingly, the court finds the sum of $ 700 ($2,500 today) to be reasonable compensation for the loss suffered by Ms. Corso.

## 2-Hashish

**Court:** United States District Court, M.D. Florida, Tampa Division

**Date:** 1981 DEC 09

**Report:** Bankruptcy No. 80-561 Civ. T K.

**Case number:** 15 B.R. 884 (M.D. Fla. 1981)

**Link:** https://merillionpress.com/cases/II-002.pdf

**Plaintiff (Appellant):** Dr. Thomas A. GORNALL, III

**Defendants (Appellees):** Howard B. SADWIN and Linda P. SADWIN

**Opinion by:** Isaac B. KRENTZMAN, District Judge

**Prior History:** This is an appeal from a final judgment entered by the Bankruptcy Court on April 16, 1980. Dr. Gornall, a veterinarian, while treating the Sadwins' dog Hashish (means assassin in Arabic), was bitten by it in the lip area. Dr. Gornall sued the Sadwins in state court. The Sadwins failed to appear at trial, default judgment was entered as to liability and upon subsequent hearing damages were awarded in the amount of $77,829.00. The Sadwins sought and found relief in Bankruptcy Court and Dr. Gornall filed a complaint in that court, to determine whether the Sadwins' debt owed to him was dischargeable under the Bankruptcy Act. It was and Dr. Gornall appeals.

**Before this Court:** The issue is whether the Sadwins' liability is for "willful and malicious" injury to Dr. Gornall's person, and is therefore not dischargeable. The Bankruptcy Court held that the liability was dischargeable, finding from all the circumstances that it was not the result of the Sadwins' "willful and malicious" injury to Dr. Gornall.

To sustain a claim of dischargeability, Dr. Gornall must establish either that the Bankrupts actually harboured an ill will and malice toward him. And in furtherance of his hostility exposed the third party to the dog knowing, that the dog will bite the third party whether excited or not. Or the owner wilfully and knowingly put the dog in the position, in which he knew that there was a great likelihood that he would harm others. That court went on to find that the Sadwins did not know their dog was vicious, and even if they were aware of Hashish's "unpredictability," Dr. Gornall, as a veterinarian, assumed the risk of injury by agreeing to treat Hashish.

**Verdict:** This Court AFFIRMS the judgment of the Bankruptcy Court.

## 3-Hot Locks

**Court:** Michigan Court of Appeals

**Date:** 1987 JUL 21

**Report:** No. 91215

**Case number:** 161 Mich. App. 785; 411 N.W. 2d 859

**Link:** https://merillionpress.com/cases/II-003.pdf

**Plaintiff (Respondent):** Shila MORGANROTH

**Defendant (Appellant):** Susan WHITALL

**Opinion By:** David H. SAWYER, Judge

**Prior History:** Shila Morganroth appeals the trial court's decision dismissing her claims of libel and invasion of privacy by false light.

The article contested was written by reporter Whitall, which appeared in the Sunday supplement of the Detroit News on November 11, 1984. The article was entitled "Hot Locks: Let Shila burn you a new do."

The article was accompanied by two photographs, one depicting Morganroth performing her craft on a customer identified as "Barbara X" and the second showing Barbara X and her dog, identified as "Harry X," following completion of the hairdressing. Central to the article was the fact that she used a blowtorch in her hairdressing endeavours.

According to the article, plaintiff's blowtorch technique was dubbed "Shi-lit" and was copyrighted. The article also described two dogs, Harry and Snowball, the latter belonging to plaintiff, noting that the canines have had their respective coats colored at least in part. The article also indicated that the blowtorch technique had been applied to both dogs. Additionally, the article described plaintiff's somewhat unusual style of dress, including a silver holster for her blowtorch and a barrette in her hair fashioned out of a $100 bill. Much of the article devoted itself to plaintiff's comments concerning her hairdressing and the trend of what, at least in the past, had been deemed unusual in the area of hair styles.

In her brief complaint she alleges that the article, when read as a whole, is false, misleading and constitutes libel. More specifically, the article used the terms "blowtorch lady," "blowtorch technique" and the statement that she "is dressed for blowtorching duty in a slashed-to-there white jumpsuit." The complaint further alleges that the article falsely portrayed her as an animal hairdresser. In her appeal, she also takes exception to her being cast as an animal hairdresser and claims as inaccurate the portrayal in the article that she does "mutt Mohawks for dogs" and the reference to "two canines who have been blowtorched." She felt wronged and initiated this action.

**Before this Court:** Reading the article as a whole, we believe that it is substantially true; therefore Morganroth's complaint lacks an essential element of her defamation claim, namely falsity. In looking at her specific allegations of falsity, for the most part we find no falsehood. Considering as a group the various references to her using a "blowtorch" in hairstyling, we note that *The Random House College Dictionary, Revised Edition (1984)*, defines "blowtorch" as follows: A small portable apparatus that gives an extremely hot gasoline flame intensified by air under pressure, used especially in metalworking.

In looking at the photographic exhibits filed by defendants, we believe that the instrument used by Morganroth in her profession can accurately be described as a blowtorch. Accordingly, while the use of the term "blowtorch" as an adjective in connection with references to her or her hairdressing technique may have been colorful, it was not necessarily inaccurate and certainly not libellous.

As for the reference that she was "dressed for blowtorching duty in a slashed-to-there white jumpsuit," we have examined the photographic exhibits submitted by Whitall at the hearing and we conclude that reasonable minds could not differ in reaching the conclusion that Morganroth did, in fact, wear a jumpsuit "slashed-to-there."

For the above-stated reasons, we conclude that, when reviewing the article and accompanying photographs as a whole, the article was not libelous. In summary, although the manner in which the present article was written may have singed Morganroth's desire for obtaining favourable coverage of her unique hairdressing methods, we cannot subscribe to the view that it was libellous. We believe that the trial court aptly summarized this case when it stated that "this Court is of the Opinion that the Plaintiff sought publicity and got it."

**Verdict:** Lower court's decision AFFIRMED. Costs to defendants.

## 4-Cattle Unthriftiness

**Court:** District Court, D. Arizona

**Date:** 1953 JUL 14

**Report:** Civ. No. 1859

**Case number:** 114 F. Supp. 231

**Link:** https://merillionpress.com/cases/II-004.pdf

**Plaintiff:** GAINEY

**Defendant:** FOLKMAN

**Opinion By:** Leon R. YANKWICH, Chief Judge

**Prior History:** Gainey, a rancher in Paradise Valley, Arizona seeks to recover damages for injury to his cattle and injunctive relief against further "dusting" of cotton on Folkman's ranch, which lies across a road from his ranch. It is his contention that the dusting has caused some of the alfalfa on his ranch to become impregnated. As some of the cattle graze on this alfalfa he contends, that the poisoning from dusting is responsible for the "unthrifty" condition of his herd. This condition appeared only after the dusting in August of 1952. Injury, health conditions and annoyance to the employees of his ranch are also part of the complaint. Folkman has denied the allegations.

Gainey raises Hereford cattle chiefly for breeding purposes, although some are sold for beef. While there is disagreement as to the money value of the Hereford stock, all are in accord that it is a high-grade of cattle which, especially if registered, commands high prices for breeding purposes.

300 acres are planted to alfalfa, which is used to feed the cattle which are kept on the place. The surplus crop of alfalfa is very substantial and is sold to neighbouring ranches, including Mr. Folkman, bringing in between $20,000 and $25,000 each year.

**Before this Court:** Did enough chemicals from the spraying in 1952 drift over to Mr. Gainey's field so that, when ingested or absorbed by the cattle directly and impregnated in the alfalfa pastured by or fed to the cattle, they caused their unthriftiness? The only testimony in this respect which showed any direct effect is that of witnesses who testified that when near the dusting, the drift of some of the chemicals made their eyes smart. But every person giving such testimony readily admitted that the discomfort was temporary and disappeared quickly.

**Verdict:** The fact that some of the cattle were affected and the greater number not at all, convincingly indicate that the difficulties from which these young heifers were suffering may be traceable to the bull who sired them.

JUDGMENT for the defendant.

## 5-Stung by a Wasp

**Court:** United States Court of Appeals for the Eighth Circuit

**Date:** 1959 APR 29

**Report:** No. 16114

**Case number:** 266 F. 2d 935

**Link:** https://merillionpress.com/cases/II-005.pdf

**Plaintiff (Appellant):** Donald A. HEERMAN

**Defendant (Appellee):** Jessalynn BURKE

**Opinion By:** Charles J. VOGEL, Circuit Judge

**Prior History:** On the morning of July 17, 1956, Burke, an insurance adjuster, met Heerman, a shorthand reporter, at a prearranged location so that they could travel together to take statements of witnesses. After meeting, they proceeded together in Burke's automobile, him driving and Heerman riding in the front seat beside him. The windows in the car were open.

Burke was wearing a short-sleeved sport shirt and was driving with his left elbow resting on the ledge or sill of the left front window, with both hands on the steering wheel. As they were proceeding, an insect (wasp) flew into Burke's left shirt sleeve. He removed his right hand from the steering wheel and grabbed at his shirt in an attempt to imprison the insect. As he did so, it stung him in the armpit.

Burke stepped on the brakes and the combination of a sudden stop and the veering off to the right apparently resulted in Heerman being thrown forward and injured.

In the suit that followed Heerman obtained a jury verdict in the amount of $10,000 ($87,000 today) and Burke appeals on the grounds that the trial court erred in denying his request to have the jury specifically instructed on his theory of the case.

**Before this Court:** It was Burke's theory that he was acting with all due care, had complete control of his car, traveling at a proper and moderate rate of speed, when, through no fault of his own, the wasp entered his left shirt sleeve; that his natural, instinctive reaction was to try to contain it, stop the car and then remove the insect from his sleeve; that while he was so doing and was slowing down, the wasp gave him a sharp, sudden and very intense sting which startled, surprised and shocked him and caused him to involuntarily apply the brakes 'fairly hard' and bring 'the car to a stop quicker than I had intended'; that the wasp's entering his sleeve created an emergency for which he was not responsible and resulted in great mental stress or excitement, and that his actions should be judged by the emergency rule.

The evidence, as outlined, fully justified the submission of the legal excuse issue. It follows it was up to the jury to say whether the wasp's entering Burke's shirt sleeve created an emergency. If they found it did and the emergency was not of his making and he had not negligently contributed to it, they were then to measure his actions in the emergency by what a reasonable prudent person might do under like circumstances.

Baring in mind that one so confronted with a sudden emergency is not held to the same exercise of judgment and prudence as is required in calmer and more deliberate moments or when unraveled in the illuminating glare of hindsight.

**Verdict:** For refusal to specifically instruct on defendant's theory, this case must be REVERSED and remanded for a new trial.

## 6-Canine Utopia

**Court:** United States District Court Eastern District of Missouri

**Date:** 1960 FEB 11

**Report:** No. 58 C 18(3)

**Case number:** 186 F. Supp. 105

**Link:** https://merillionpress.com/cases/II-006.pdf

**Plaintiff:** AETNA Insurance Company

**Defendant:** Louis SACHS

**Opinion By:** Randolph H. WEBER, District Judge

**Prior History:** Sachs and his wife purchased in October 1957 a "French Poodle", which they appropriately and fascinatingly named "André." According to the Sachs, André was properly trained and "broke" and life was pleasant for all, until they went on a vacation and left André at a kennel for the duration. When they returned their first thoughts were of André and they promptly brought him back to their chateau, blissful in the reunion.

But the home-like serenity was soon shattered, for madam soon spied André with his leg hoisted in masculine canine fashion and his purpose had been, and was being, accomplished. Madam told him of the occurrence and he promptly surveyed the living room, dining room and hall and found signs of André's misfeasance. His next step was to notify his insurance agent and make claim under the "floater" provisions of the policy.

The law has always been a hard taskmaster and requires of its advocates a serious approach and stern visaged application. When it comes face to face with life, as it unfolds in the drama of the courtroom, the law sometimes reaches its serious, stern results from facts which have been compiled with humor. So – while the end results of the law are deadly serious – there is about the lawyer (and even judges, occasionally) a spark of the humor of life — and a need for it. So let it be with this opinion; for, while the end result is most serious to both plaintiff and defendant, what has brought about the necessity for the end result, is most humorous.

Our factual situation obviously had its inception when Sachs obtained the insurance policy from AETNA. If all had proceeded in the normal course of human events from that point on, this suit would never have been brought, for AETNA insured against and was prepared for the usual expectancies of fire, wind and rain. But, Sachs purchased, and AET-

NA issued, the rider, known commonly in the trade as a "floater." Now, "floater" provisions are covered by (and in this instance, rightly so) the rules of "maritime" law, for, the risks are sometimes unusual.

In any event, the policy in question provided generally for damages and loss to the furnishings and personal property of the defendant for reasons other than fire, wind and rain, to-wit, theft and other fortuitous circumstances. What subsequently transpired after issuance brings into play the "floater" provisions of this policy.

There was some dispute between the parties as to whether proper notice was given and claim made, but the Court is convinced that defendant gave notice within the terms and provisions of the policy and AETNA cannot escape liability on that point. An adjuster was sent to the premises to survey the effects of where André, the French Poodle, had popped in, piddled and popped out. In fact, he testified that André gave a "command performance" while he was there.

Also, a rug specialist was sent to the premises and he too made a survey. He found spots ranging in diameter from the size of a "dime" to nine inches, and in number from 75 to 80. He testified that one or two could have been repaired, but not that many, for it would have been impossible to match the yarn in the rug and the patches and repairs would have been as obvious as André's tell-tale marks. He also said that the spots would have been readily noticeable from the time they dried and that they extended throughout the living room, dining room, hall, and stairway and were on the rug, furniture and drapes; which gives rise to the conclusion that André had the run of the house.

The owner of the kennel, where André spent just two weeks, gave as his opinion that a dog with good habits would not lose them in two weeks; that he properly cared for the dog and had provisions for outside relief facilities for the dogs in his kennels; and, that four to five times a day would be a maximum amount of calls to nature for any dog, including André.

**Before this Court:** AETNA brought this suit to determine its liability for threatened prosecution by Sachs and contended that this was just too many incidents to be liable for. Sachs answered and denied, claiming surprise in André's change of habits and further contended that there were but four or five incidents and the rest of the spots were pure dribbles, and he counterclaimed for total loss of carpeting and for damages in the amount of $7,500 ($65,000 today).

At the rate of four or five calls per day, at best it would have taken André about sixteen days to make all the spots. But, on the theory that each incident is entitled to a dribble or two, it could probably be said, without fear of contradiction, that the spotting represents ten to twelve incidents and probably over a period of a week. In that length of time if the spots had not been seen, they at least should have been recognized by other sensory perception.

A review of the search books to the law reveals no cases in point. Either there never was a poodle as prolific as André, or, before such insurance, people caught them, put their nose in it and threw them outside. Thus, we have a case of first impression. The testimony is that André met his demise, by truck, some few weeks after his prolific, piddlin' propensities were discovered and he, therefore, can never be made aware of his place in history unless he rests in some Valhalla from whence he can eat, sleep and answer his calls to nature, while still permitted to glance back occasionally to review the results, devastation, chaos and the indecision caused by his handiwork.

The unprecedented problem requires some decision, for the law, right or wrong, must conclude litigation. I would conclude this episode in the following manner:

For one or two occasions of André's imprudence we might expect AETNA to be liable, even though it is stretching the credulity of any sage of the law to put permission and right upon liability where a person gives a canine pet the right to perambulate and pounce unrestrained throughout the house. Such privileges, even to a poodle, seem more the part of valor than of wisdom, especially where the play pen is a $7,500 rug and expensive furniture and drapes.

The law has always allowed each dog its first bite, for then the owner is put on notice of its dangerous tendencies. I would even go one or two better in incidents such as this and would have allowed recovery for two or three incidents. This would give the insured some opportunity, through sight or smell, to discover the occurrence, prevent its repetition and make claim for that which seems a fortuitous circumstance or event. But, to allow for such prolific indiscretions, ad infinitum, is beyond credulity and borders onto wanton recklessness and disregard for which a person should not be rewarded.

While André might not be expected to know the terms and conditions of AETNA's policy, it seems most fantastic that Sachs should be able to contend that André's indiscretion was fortuitous.

I would say that defendant, because of such gross negligence and indiscretion in permitting André to roam the house at will, hoisting his leg at random, probably yipping and yipping in his canine Utopia, should not be allowed to recover. Certainly, a dog can be controlled by his master, and while a master cannot expect perfection from a dog, even a poodle, he should be ever aware to keep him from expensive parts of the house where he might do damage with either end. Further, defendant here should not be allowed to collect for a total loss which he himself could have kept at a minimum by the exercise of a little discretion, observance or care.

**Verdict:** I am saying to the defendant, "You cannot recover"; to the plaintiff, "You may continue your policy in peace"; and to the beloved little French poodle, the proximate cause of this litigation and discourse, I say, "Paix á toi aussi, André."

## 7-Skittish Stallion

**Court:** Supreme Court of California

**Date:** 1997 AUG 05

**Report:** No. S049011

**Case number:** Super. Ct. No. EC 009 125

**Link:** https://merillionpress.com/cases/II-007.pdf

**Plaintiff (Appellant):** Darrell PARSONS

**Defendant (Respondent):** CROWN Disposal Company

**Opinion By:** Ronald M. GEORGE, Circuit Judge

**Prior History:** On December 2, 1991, at approximately 10:00 A.M., Parsons was riding his horse out of the Griffith Park Equestrian Center (Los Angeles) and turned left onto the dirt bridle path. As he did so, he looked to his right and saw Crown's garbage truck 10 feet away. The truck was stationary but the driver was in the process of emptying a trash bin behind a restaurant by lifting it with a pair of mechanical forks over the top of the vehicle. The trash bin was just six inches from the bridle path, with a chain link fence between.

Parsons had restrained his horse to a walking pace. After seeing the trash truck, he almost immediately sensed his horse beginning to tense up.

Meanwhile, the driver lifted the trash bin to the level of the truck's windshield and proceeded to shake the bin up and down, apparently to settle the contents of the bin. As the noise increased, the horse began to spin and bolt. At his point, Parsons saw the driver in the truck's side view mirror and thought to himself, "Oh, my God. You know, shut it down, you're scaring my horse to death."

The driver did not stop but proceeded to lift the bin above the truck, producing "the loudest noise" as bottles and cans fell from the bin into the truck. Parsons' horse then bolted spinning and bucking. He was thrown off the horse and he landed on the concrete pavement of an adjacent street, sustaining injuries.

Parsons' complaint for damages alleged, as the basis for Crown's liability, that it "negligently operated a trash collection vehicle so as to scare his horse, causing him to be thrown from the horse to the ground and to proximately and legally cause injuries and damages to plaintiff. . . ."

**Before this Court:** For more than 150 years courts have recognized that a defendant breaches no duty of care merely by operating socially beneficial machinery in a manner that is regular and necessary, even if such ordinary operation happens to frighten a nearby horse and, as a result of the horse's reaction, some injury or damage ensues.

This long-standing line of authority establishes that although defendant had a duty to conduct its garbage collection activity in a prudent fashion (and to use due care to avoid making unusual noises unnecessary to accomplish its task), it had no duty to avoid making the regular noises that were a normal incident to its operations merely because of the possibility that these ordinary operations might happen to frighten a horse that was in the vicinity of its truck.

Once the scope of defendant's duty of care is properly understood, we believe it is clear that the record in this case discloses no evidence that Crown breached its duty of care to Parsons, and thus that the trial court properly entered judgment in Crown's favor.

The present unfortunate encounter falls within a centuries-long continuum of contacts between horses and machinery. Whatever the standards of the leisure classes, as exemplified by the sentiment attributed to Mrs. Patrick Campbell ("My Dear, I don't care what they do, so long as they don't do it in the street and frighten the horses"), the courts long have recognized that the needs of a modern, industrial society often conflict with and generally must prevail over the delicate sensibilities of horses.

But under the circumstances here presented, there is no basis on which to conclude that defendant breached the limited duty of care it owed to plaintiff. There is no evidence that Crown operated its garbage truck in anything but the regular and necessary manner of a garbage truck acting like a garbage truck.

**Verdict:** We conclude that the trial court properly dismissed Parsons' claims and, accordingly, we REVERSE the judgment of the Court of Appeal. (With two judges dissenting.)

## 8-Resident Cat

**Court:** Supreme Court of Montana

**Date:** 1997 JAN 28

**Report:** No. 96-381

**Case number:** 931 P. 2d 717

**Link:** https://merillionpress.com/cases/II-008.pdf

**Plaintiff (Appellant):** Embernetta D. SMITH

**Defendant (Respondent):** Krayton KERNS, d/b/a Beartooth Veterinary Clinic

**Opinion By:** W. William LEAPHART, Justice

**Prior History:** Smith and her husband arrived at Beartooth Veterinary Clinic to drop off the family dog. While Smith's husband waited in their vehicle, she entered the clinic through the front door which closed behind her by way of a mechanical closing device. After handing her dog to the receptionist, Smith walked back toward the front door to leave. As she walked toward the door, she stopped to move Dr. Kerns' "resident" cat which was sitting in front of the door. Smith placed the cat to the side of the door and continued exiting the building.

As she was exiting through the doorway, she looked back at the cat and fell on her right shoulder and left hand. As a result of this fall, she suffered a fracture of the shoulder/greater tuberosity, and other injuries.

Smith brought this action in District Court to recover damages for the injuries she incurred as a result of her fall. She alleged that the cat interfered with her safe exit from the building. The District Court dismissed her suit, holding that Smith had failed to establish that Dr. Kerns had breached his duty to use ordinary care to maintain his premises in a reasonably safe condition or to show that Dr. Kerns' cat was the cause of her injuries. Smith appeals this judgment.

**Before this Court:** In the present case, there is a genuine issue as to whether Dr. Kerns breached his duty towards Smith by allowing the cat to remain in proximity to the doorway and leaving his clients in doubt as to whether the cat was going to bolt for the exit.

The District Court's conclusion is wrong in two regards.

First, there is clearly a dispute in the testimony as to whether the cat remained stationary or exited the door at the same time as Smith. Although a moving cat is presumably more distracting than a stationary cat, it appears from the record that no contact occurred between Dr. Kerns' cat and Smith. Dismissal of the case was not appropriate as reasonable minds could still differ as to whether Dr. Kerns' cat was the cause of Smith's injuries.

Secondly, the District Court assumed that, in order to establish causation, Smith would have to show that the cat tripped or contacted her thus causing her fall. The court's rationale, however, is too narrow an interpretation of her claim. She alleges in her complaint that the cat "interfered with her safe exit...." She testified in her deposition that, as she held the door open to exit, "I turned around to look to see if the cat was following me out the door."

In dismissing the suit because the cat did not touch or trip Smith, the court ignored the fact that, although the cat may not have tripped or contacted her, it may have constituted a distraction causing her to fall.

In a case such as this, the jury may reasonably infer that Dr. Kerns was negligent in allowing the cat to roam freely about the premises and distract patrons who are negotiating the stairway exit. The jury is in the best position to determine the reasonableness of Smith's claim.

**Verdict:** Accordingly, we REVERSE and remand.

# 9-Big Game Hunting and Risk

**Court:** United States District Court, District of Minnesota

**Date:** 2004 NOV 18

**Report:** None in original

**Case number:** 03-CV-2872 (JMR/FLN)

**Link:** https://merillionpress.com/cases/II-009.pdf

**Plaintiff:** Rolf ROHWER

**Defendants:** FEDERAL Cartridge Co. et al.

**Opinion By:** James M. ROSENBAUM, Chief District Judge

**Prior History:** On August 11, 2000, Rolf Rohwer led a Tanzanian lion-hunting safari, during which a participant shot a lion wounding its paw. Being a professional big game hunter, Rohwer knew a wounded animal presented a serious threat. Beyond this, allowing an injured animal to suffer a non-lethal wound is inhumane and violates the tenets of the profession. He then, tracked the beast for three hours, intending to kill it.

When he located and confronted the injured lion, it charged toward him and he waited until it was seven meters away before firing a single shot. He claims he aimed at, fired at, and hit the lion's left shoulder. To his surprise, the animal absorbed the impact and continued to charge. It then pounced less than a second later, mauled him, walked away, lay down, and died of its wounds. Rohwer was airlifted to a hospital.

In this adventure he used a Federal Premium 500 grain Trophy Bonded Bear Claw ("Bear Claw") bullet manufactured by Federal Cartridge Co. As Rohwer tells that in nearly 40 years of hunting, he has personally killed more than 100 lions, including four charging him at close range. According to him, this was the first time he used a Bear Claw bullet to do so.

Three members of Rohwer's hunting party examined the lion's carcass. Each avers that the shoulder entrance and abdominal exit wound appeared to be the same size. These were neither measured, nor photographed. The lethal bullet was not recovered and the carcass was not preserved.

**Before this Court:** Rohwer contends the Bear Claw bullet was defective because it was manufactured with a hard casing. He further claims a hard cased bullet properly expands after striking a thick-skinned animal, but does not expand when used on thin-skinned animals, such as lions. The Bear Claw bullet has been in use since 1985 and prior to this action, there have been no reports of failure. The bullet has expanded in all tests conducted for this litigation.

It almost goes without saying that there is no empirical evidence, conducted under controlled circumstances, concerning such an event. Scientists simply do not kill wild animals to prove differing theories of bullet performance, or best-wounded-animal killing methods. Even if a jury would credit Rohwer's reports of his own experiences at close range with three other wounded and charging lions, his statements cannot suffice. His statements are nothing more than his own anecdotal observations. There is no replicable evidence concerning the state of these other animals' wounds, their condition, how long after the injury they charged, or any other way to correlate their behavior – even if it could be fully articulated – with the lion in the present circumstance.

The Court does not doubt Rohwer's sincere belief that his shot was perfect and entered the lion's body through its left shoulder. But his observation is based on his own perception of a shot at a charging animal which would maul him in the next split-second. His testimony and beliefs must be balanced against the testimony of three witnesses who examined the beast's body, each of whom did so post-the animal's-mortem, while the he was receiving medical care or recuperating from his wounds.

**Verdict:** Rohwer's consolidated claims of negligence, design defect, breach of warranty, and failure-to-warn cannot stand, because the lion's behavior could not be attributable to a bullet defect without precise evidence of the bullet's path and other variables associated with an unfortunate accident.

Accordingly, the complaint must be DISMISSED.

## 10-A Dog's Life

**Court:** Appellate Division of the Supreme Court of the State of New York, First Department

**Date:** 2003 FEB 27

**Report:** No. 304 A.D.2d 74

**Case number:** 758 N.Y.S. 2d 276

**Link:** https://merillionpress.com/cases/II-010.pdf

**Plaintiff (Appellant):** Jon H. HAMMER

**Defendants (Respondents):** AMERICAN KENNEL CLUB et al.

**Opinion By:** David B. SAXE, Judge

**Prior History:** Through the years, the American Kennel Club (AKC) and its member breed clubs have set breed standards for dogs entering various competitions sponsored by that organization. For each of the 146 separate breeds recognized by the AKC, distinct breed standards are established, initially by the national parent breed club, and then submitted to the AKC for approval.

For some breeds, the standard involves the cropping, or clipping, of the dogs' ears to a certain size or shape. For certain other breeds, the standard involves docking, or amputation, of all or part of the dog's tail. The standard promulgated by defendants for judging the breed of dog known as the Brittany, or the Brittany spaniel, in sponsored competitions, includes the provision that "any tail substantially more than four inches shall be severely penalized."

Jon Hammer is the owner of a purebred Brittany spaniel which has a natural, undocked tail approximately 10 inches long. He contends that tail docking is a form of animal cruelty, and that the practical effect of AKC's tail standards for Brittany Spaniels is to effectively exclude his dog from meaningfully competing in AKC shows unless he complies with what he perceives as an unfair and discriminatory practice.

Specifically, he seeks a declaratory judgment that the complained-of standard (1) unlawfully discriminates against him by effectively precluding him from entering his dog in breed competitions, (2) is arbitrary and capricious, (3) violates Agriculture and Markets Laws and he further seeks an injunction prohibiting defendants from applying, enforcing or utilizing the standard.

On February 28, 2002 the Supreme Court of New York County dismissed his action and he appeals.

**Before this Court:** The word "cruelty" is defined in section 350 of the Agriculture and Markets Law as an act causing unjustifiable physical pain. The statute does not prohibit causing pain to animals, but unjustifiably mutilating or causing unjustifiable pain.

In addition, Hammer has no individual right to seek civil enforcement of Agriculture and Markets Law statutes. Those portions of his complaint seeking a declaration that AKC's tail standard for Brittany Spaniels violates the statute and is null and void, and seeking an injunction prohibiting defendants from applying, enforcing or utilizing the standard, must be dismissed.

Hammer's allegations, even accepted as true, fail to establish a right to a declaration that defendants' promulgation of standards for canine tail length constitutes illegal discrimination or arbitrary and capricious conduct.

**Verdict:** The judgment of the Supreme Court of New York County is AFFIRMED, with one dissent.

## 11-Boomer and the Invisible Fence

**Court:** Court of Appeals of Ohio, Second District, Montgomery County

**Date:** 2003 OCT 03

**Report:** No. 19614

**Case number:** 154 Ohio App.3d 744, 2003-Ohio-5333

**Link:** https://merillionpress.com/cases/II-011.pdf

**Plaintiffs (Appellants and Cross-Appellees):** PACHER et al.

**Defendants (Appellees and Cross-Appellants):** INVISIBLE FENCE OF DAYTON et al.

**Opinion By:** James A. BROGAN, Judge

**Prior History:** The animal in this case, "Boomer," is a golden retriever belonging to Andrew and Alyce Pacher. When they acquired Boomer in December 1997, they began to investigate invisible fences as a method of restraint. Ultimately, they purchased a "Top Dog" package from IFD in July 1998. This package included installation of a fence (up to one acre), a platinum computer collar, a one-year computer-generated battery plan, and five visits for personal training assistance, for a total price of $1,527.80.

The IFD invisible fence uses buried antenna wire, a transmitter (located in this case in the garage), and a dog collar. If the dog attempts to break the plane of the fence, an electric "correction" or shock is delivered. The transmitter's job is to emit a radio signal through the antenna wire buried in the yard, and the collar delivers the actual "correction." The collar is a snap collar with ends that clip together. It also has metal prongs that make contact with a dog's neck. Knobs on the transmitter adjust how close a pet can come to the wire before the collar activates. However, the amount of correction can be increased only by adjusting dials in the collar. This is not something customers can access; instead, IFD personnel carry miniature computers for that purpose.

Unfortunately, Boomer was never successfully contained by the invisible fence. Over the next two and a half years, IFD made many service calls to the Pacher home to deal with containment issues. IFD claimed that many calls were the Pachers' fault because they accidentally cut the wire, did not properly secure the collar, or improperly installed the collar's battery.

In December 2000, the Pachers called IFD after yet another incident when the fence failed to contain Boomer. This time, IFD suggested a new idea, called the "sandbag technique." Basically, this involved attaching a gym bag filled with 50 pounds of sand to the dog. The bag would slow the dog down, causing him to receive a greater "correction" when passing through the signal field. The Pachers rejected this idea because they felt that it was ludicrous and was potentially cruel to the dog.

The ongoing dispute came to a boiling point on February 5, when Andrew Pacher noticed while petting Boomer that his hand had become wet. After removing Boomer's collar, he discovered dark black wounds, a lot of irritation, and pus. The next morning, they took Boomer to the veterinarian, who prescribed a two-week antibiotic. After that date, the Pachers never again used the invisible fence or collars.

They launched their suit and the case was tried on both the negligence and contractual claims. After a bench trial, the court awarded a judgment of $1,714.85 against IFD for negligence and breach of contract. The Pachers claim the trial court erred and abused its discretion by dismissing their complaint regarding the emotional distress (non-economic damages) suffered by Boomer's pet guardians and Boomer himself as a result of IFD's negligence and breach of contract, hence their appeal.

**Before this Court:** The trial court dismissed these claims before trial, finding, that the Pachers failed to state a claim for negligent infliction of serious emotional distress because they were not bystanders to the injury. The trial court next addressed Boomer's direct claim for emotional distress. The court noted that despite Boomer's fine qualities as a dog, his status as "personality" deprived him of the legal capacity to sue.

Without in any way discounting the bonds between humans and animals, we must continue to reject recovery for noneconomic damages for loss or injury to animals.

While the complaint does request punitive damages, the allegations refer only to negligence and breach of contract, not misconduct. Furthermore, the evidence fails to suggest misconduct or anything bordering on intentional injury. The fact that IFD may have negligently injured the dog does not mean that it intentionally did so, or that a "deterrent" measure is required.

**Verdict:** On all counts the judgment of the trial court is AFFIRMED.

## 12-Menacing Puppy

**Court:** Court of Appeals of the State of Mississippi

**Date:** 2011 APR 26

**Report:** No. 2009-CA-01324-COA

**Case number:** Not citable

**Link:** https://merillionpress.com/cases/II-012.pdf

**Plaintiffs (Appellants):** PENNY PINCHERS and William B. JOHNSON D/B/A Penny Pinchers

**Defendant (Appellee):** Lenetra OUTLAW

**Opinion By:** Kenny GRIFFIS, Presiding Judge

**Prior History:** Cindy Scott was the manager of Penny Pinchers, a discount grocery store located in West Point, Mississippi. She was also the owner of a four-month-old daschund puppy named Sophie, which weighed four pounds and one ounce. Scott took Sophie to work with her every day.

On August 16, 2006, Outlaw entered Penny Pinchers. She said hello to Scott, who was having a conversation with a customer. Outlaw testified that she started walking down an aisle when she heard a dog bark. Because she is terrified of dogs, she started running down the aisle toward the back of the store. She said that she could hear the claws of the dog hit the floor as the dog chased her down the aisle. When she turned to see how close the dog was, she ran into a freezer at the back of the store. She then tried to jump on top of the freezer to get away from the dog.

When Outlaw saw how small the dog was, she began to laugh and tell Scott about her extreme fear of dogs. Outlaw then went on with her shopping. Outlaw testified that she began to feel a severe pain in her hip as she continued to shop.

Scott's testimony of the events surrounding Outlaw's injuries was markedly different. She testified that it only took a moment for her to pick up Sophie after she heard the bark. By then, Scott said that Outlaw was already thirty feet away at the back of the store.

When Outlaw returned to the counter, she began to sob. Scott said that she could not understand Outlaw because of the sobbing. She called Johnson, the owner of Penny Pinchers, who came to the store. He called an ambulance, and Outlaw was transported to the hospital.

Outlaw had extensive health problems before including hip replacement and had to have a second revision surgery in 2006 following her collision with the freezer.

Outlaw filed suit against Penny Pinchers, Johnson, and Scott. The jury found Penny Pinchers 70% liable and Outlaw 30% liable for Outlaw's injuries. Outlaw was awarded $130,000. Penny Pinchers now appeals.

**Before this Court:** It was undisputed that, as a customer of Penny Pinchers, Outlaw was classified as a business invitee. A business owner owes a business invitee a duty of ordinary care to keep the business premises in a reasonably safe condition. However, the owner is not an insurer against all injuries that may occur on the premises.

There was no proof that Sophie had previously exhibited any of the behaviors that Outlaw alleged.

Scott took Sophie with her to Penny Pinchers on a daily basis. Sophie had never barked or chased any of the other customers. We must also consider that Sophie was a four-pound puppy at the time of the incident.

We find that Outlaw failed to prove that Sophie created a dangerous condition.

**Verdict:** The judgment of the circuit court is REVERSED, and judgment is rendered in favor of Penny Pinchers.

# 13-JUSTICE,
## AN AMERICAN QUARTER HORSE

**Court:** Circuit Court of the State Of Oregon for the County of Washington

**Date:** 2018 MAY 01

**Report:** None in original

**Case number:** Not citable

**Link:** https://merillionpress.com/cases/II-013.pdf

**Plaintiff:** JUSTICE, an American Quarter Horse, by and through his Guardian, Kim Mosiman

**Defendant:** Gwendolyn VERCHER

**Opinion By:** John KNOWLES, Judge

**Prior History:** This case involves Justice, a horse who suffered extreme pain, distress, and permanent injury due to the criminal neglect of Defendant Gwendolyn Vercher. Disregarding the requirements of Oregon law, Vercher denied Justice adequate food and shelter for months, abandoning him to starve and freeze. As a result of this neglect, Justice was left debilitated and emaciated. He continues to suffer from this neglect, including a prolapsed penis from frostbite. These injuries will require special and expensive medical care for the remainder of his life.

On July 10, 2017, Vercher pled guilty to neglect of Justice and agreed to pay restitution to Sound Equine Options for the costs of Justice's care incurred prior to July 6, 2017. She failed to pay the restitution by the deadline and her plea agreement does not include restitution for the cost of Justice's care after July 6, 2017.

Finding a permanent home for the horse is more difficult, if not impossible, due to the substantial additional costs caused by Vercher's neglect. On August 22, 2017, Mosiman created the Justice Equine Trust, of which Justice is the sole beneficiary. Mosiman created the trust in order to provide for Justice's care from July 6, 2017 until the end of Justice's life, with any funds obtained in this action against Vercher.

**Before this Court:** As a result of Vercher's negligence, Justice has incurred noneconomic damages for pain and suffering in an amount to be determined at trial. Mosiman seeks economic damages for past costs of care incurred from July 6, 2017 to present and future costs of care in an amount to be determined at trial but not less than $100,000; Non-economic damages for pain and suffering in an amount to be determined at trial; Reasonable attorneys' fees as permitted by law in an amount to be determined at trial; Its costs and disbursements; and all such other and further relief as the Court may deem just, proper, and equitable.

**Verdict:** The court finds that a non-human animal such as Justice lacks the legal status or qualifications necessary for the assertion of legal rights and duties in a court of law. Such a finding would likely lead to a flood of lawsuits whereby non-human animals could assert claims we now reserve just for humans and human creations such as business and other entities.

## 14-People Eating Tasty Animals

**Court:** United States Court of Appeals for the Fourth Circuit

**Date:** 2001 AUG 23

**Report:** None in original

**Case number:** 263 F. 3d 359

**Link:** https://merillionpress.com/cases/II-014.pdf

**Plaintiff (Appellee):** PEOPLE for the Ethical Treatment of Animals

**Defendant (Appellant):** Michael T. DOUGHNEY

**Opinion By:** Roger L. GREGORY, Circuit Judge

**Prior History:** In 1999 People for the Ethical Treatment of Animals ("PETA") sued Michael Doughney ("Doughney") after he registered the domain name peta.org and created a website called "People Eating Tasty Animals." PETA alleged claims of service mark infringement, unfair competition, service mark dilution and cybersquatting.

PETA is an animal rights organization with more than 600,000 members worldwide. PETA "is dedicated to promoting and heightening public awareness of animal protection issues and it opposes the exploitation of animals for food, clothing, entertainment and vivisection."

Doughney is a former internet executive who has registered many domain names since 1995; at the time these proceedings started he owned 50-60 domain names.

After registering the peta.org domain name, Doughney used it to create a website purportedly on behalf of "People Eating Tasty Animals." Doughney claims he created the website as a parody of PETA. A viewer accessing the website would see the title "People Eating Tasty Animals" in large, bold type. Under the title, the viewer would see a statement that the website was a "resource for those who enjoy eating meat, wearing fur and leather, hunting, and the fruits of scientific research."

The website contained links to various meat, fur, leather, hunting, animal research, and other organizations, all of which held views generally antithetical to PETA's views. Another statement on the website asked the viewer whether he/she was "Feeling lost? Offended? Perhaps you should, like, exit immediately." The phrase "exit immediately" contained a hyperlink to PETA's official website.

PETA did not seek damages, but sought only to enjoin Doughney's use of the "PETA" Mark and an order requiring Doughney to transfer the peta.org domain name to PETA.

Doughney responded to the suit by arguing that the website was a constitutionally protected parody of PETA.

The district court rejected Doughney's parody defense, explaining that only after arriving at the "PETA.ORG" web site could the web site browser determine that this was not a web site owned, controlled or sponsored by PETA. Therefore, the two images: (1) the famous PETA name and (2) the "People Eating Tasty Animals" website was not a parody because they were not simultaneous.

**Before this Court**: Doughney appeals the district court's decision in favor of PETA's claims and in turn, PETA cross-appeals the district court's denial of its attorney's fees and costs.

Looking at Doughney's domain name alone, there is no suggestion of a parody. The district court reviewed the factors listed in the statute and properly concluded that

(I) Doughney had no intellectual property right in Peta.org;

(II) Peta.org is not Doughney's name;

(III) Doughney had no prior use of peta.org in connection with the bona fide offering of any goods or services;

(IV) Doughney used the PETA Mark in a commercial manner;

(V) Doughney "clearly intended to confuse, mislead and divert internet users into accessing his web site which contained information antithetical and therefore harmful to the goodwill represented by the PETA Mark";

(VI) Doughney made statements on his web site and in the press recommending that PETA attempt to "settle" with him and "make him an offer";

(VII) Doughney made false statements when registering the domain name; and

(VIII) Doughney registered other domain names that are identical or similar to the marks or names of other famous people and organizations.

PETA sought attorney fees of more than $276,000. The district court denied it, holding that Doughney did not act maliciously or deliberately because "he thought that he had a legitimate First Amendment right to express himself this way" and "to create a parody of the plaintiff's organization."

**Verdict:** Finding no error in the district court's reasoning, we AFFIRM.

# CHAPTER III

# BLAMESTORMING

*"We are taught you must blame your father, your sisters, your brothers, the school, the teachers - but never blame yourself. It's never your fault." Katharine H. Hepburn (1907 – 2003) was an American actress*

These cases are all tied to the fundamental principle: "It's not my fault." The once "reasonable man" standards no longer apply. A bewildering variety and volume of safety regulations suffocate everyday life for most. Yet, ignorance or just using plain common sense is too much for some. But, as the following cases show, wounded entitlement radiates and as soon as a legal limb can be attached – the billable-hours trade springs into action – all barriers are removed and lawsuit(s) follow.

## 1-Watched Football on Television

**Court:** Court of Special Appeals of Maryland

**Date:** 1994 APR 07

**Report:** 1306

**Case number:** 100 Md. App. 60 (1994) 639 A.2d 223

**Link:** https://merillionpress.com/cases/III-001.pdf

**Plaintiff (Respondent):** Tawana HAMMOND, et al.

**Defendant (Appellant):** BOARD OF EDUCATION OF CARROLL COUNTY, MARYLAND.

**Opinion By:** J. Frederick MOTZ, Judge

**Prior History:** On August 25, 1989, Tawana Hammond, the first female high school football player in Carroll County history, was injured in her team's initial scrimmage. Three years later, she and her mother filed suit in the Circuit Court for Carroll County against the Board, seeking $1.25 million in compensatory damages. The Hammonds asserted (1) that the high school authorities negligently failed to warn them of the potential risk of injury inherent in playing football and (2) had they been so warned she would not have chosen to play football and her mother would not have permitted her to do so.

Prior to her injury, the then 16 year old girl had watched football on television from an early age, but she had never observed any "really serious" injuries in these televised games, only a "twisted ankle or something." She knew football was a "physical contact sport" and determined she wanted to play it because "it was different." She and her father also signed a school release form which specifically warns that "We do our very best to avoid accidents, but we realize that in the normal course of events, some occur."

Circuit court Judge Beck dismissed the suit as baseless.

**Before this Court:** The Hammonds' appeal states, that the school board had a duty to warn them of the severe injuries that might result from voluntarily participating on a varsity high school tackle football team, is one that, as far as we can determine, has never been adopted by any court in this country.

The playing of football is a body-contact sport. The game demands that the players come into physical contact with each other constantly; frequently with great force ... the ball-carrier ... must be prepared to strike the ground violently. Body contacts, bruises, and clashes are inherent in the game. There is no other way to play it. No prospective player need be told that a participant in the game of football may sustain injury. That fact is self-evident.

**Verdict:** Lower court's decision AFFIRMED.

## 2-Bad Driver

**Court:** District Court of Appeal of Florida, Third District

**Date:** 1987 APR 07

**Report:** 84-2813

**Case number:** 505 So. 2d 560

**Link:** https://merillionpress.com/cases/III-002.pdf

**Plaintiff (Appellant):** VIC POTAMKIN CHEVROLET, Inc.

**Defendant (Appellee):** Junie HORNE

**Opinion By:** James R. JORGENSON, Judge

**Prior History:** Nora Newry went to Vic Potamkin Chevrolet to buy a car. She had a restricted driver's license which requires that a licensed driver be present when she is driving. When Newry took a test drive, she had difficulty handling the car. At one point, the salesman riding with her grabbed the wheel to avoid an accident. The salesman told her that she should bring someone back with her when she came to pick up the car.

Later that afternoon, Newry returned to complete the sale and pick up the car and met Junie Horne, an old friend who happened to be at the lot. Horne, who is a licensed driver, ended up driving home with Newry. The salesman who had accompanied Newry on the test drive predicted to a fellow employee that Newry would not drive one block without causing an accident. As Newry was driving west on MacArthur Causeway, she lost control of the car and hit a tree. Horne suffered injuries in the accident and sued Potamkin and others. The case against Potamkin went to the jury on a theory of negligent entrustment. The jury returned a verdict against Potamkin for $195,000, and this appeal followed.

**Before this Court:** The issue presented on appeal is whether this court should extend the law of negligent entrustment to include negligent sales. Horne argues that sellers have a duty to protect the world against incompetent product users. The creation of a duty on the part of the seller to guarantee the acts of a buyer would be manifestly unreasonable. We think it sufficient for a dealer prior to delivery of a car to determine that a buyer has a valid license. We think it inappropriate to further burden car dealers with an additional obligation of determining that every customer is a safe driver.

**Verdict:** For these reasons, the judgment of the circuit court is REVERSED and we certify the above question to the Florida Supreme Court for its consideration.

## 3-Pilot's Operating Handbook

**Court:** United States Court of Appeals for the Fifth Circuit

**Date:** 1985 DEC 10

**Report:** No. 84-1086

**Case number:** 777 F. 2d 1072

**Link:** https://merillionpress.com/cases/III-003.pdf

**Plaintiff (Appellant):** J. E. REHLER, Independent Executor of the Estate of James A. Rehler, Deceased

**Defendant (Appellee):** BEECH Aircraft Corporation

**Opinion By:** William L. GARWOOD, Circuit Judge

**Prior History:** In this suit, J. E. Rehler seeks compensation for the wrongful death of his father, James A. Rehler, who died, when the Beech Baron, model 95-B55, aircraft he was piloting crashed outside Jarrell, Texas, on March 21, 1979. Rehler's Baron, a light twin-engine airplane was manufactured by Beech Aircraft Corporation in 1974.

Rehler departed from Georgetown Municipal Airport in his airplane on the afternoon of the fatal accident. Approximately one hour after Rehler took the Baron into the air three bystanders observed that the plane was spinning to the left. One of the witnesses testified at trial that the airplane was at a low altitude prior to the spin and that the airplane's "nose was pitched down." The Baron subsequently crashed, nine miles north of its point of takeoff.

The case was tried to a jury. Under products liability theory Rehler alleged that Beech was liable for defective design and for failure to adequately warn consumers, that the aircraft had a tendency to enter into a flat spin. Under a misrepresentation theory he alleged that Beech had falsely represented the spin recovery procedure contained in the *Pilot's Operating Handbook and FAA Approved Airplane Flight Manual* would correct a flat spin. In addition, he sought exemplary damages on the ground that Beech had shown a conscious indifference to the safety of persons flying the Baron.

The jury subsequently returned a special verdict finding that there was neither defective design of the aircraft, nor any failure by Beech to give adequate warnings and instructions for its safe use and that pilot negligence was the cause of the accident. The district court entered judgment in favor of Beech.

**Before this Court:** On appeal, J.E. Rehler argues that the district court refused to submit to the jury the following important issues:

1-The spin recovery procedure outlined in the Pilot's Operating Handbook would bring the airplane out of "any" spin the airplane might enter into, when in fact the procedure would not correct a flat spin.

2- The manual failed to distinguish between flat spins and steep (normal) spins, since the manual obliquely states that the procedure is applicable "if a spin is entered."

3- By suggesting falsely that the procedure will correct "any" spin, the passage in Beech's manual constituted a misrepresentation.

As the proceedings clearly show, the district court provided the following definition to the jurors:

"Adequate warnings and instructions" means warnings and instructions sufficient to convey to the reasonably prudent pilot the nature and extent of the dangers involved in the use of the aircraft and how to avoid the dangers.

We reject Rehler's arguments that the district court's failure to provide additional instructions misled the jury. The jury was told that for a warning to be adequate it had to be "sufficient to convey" both the *"nature"* and *"extent"* of the "dangers" involved; instructions had to sufficiently convey *"how to avoid the dangers."* This adequately encompasses the several concepts urged by Rehler in this connection so that the charge presents no reversible error in this respect.

**Verdict:** For the above reasons, the district court's judgment is AFFIRMED.

## 4-Subaru Brat

**Court:** United States District Court For the District Of Kansas

**Date:** 1988 APR 13

**Report:** No. 85-2621-S

**Case number:** 684 F. Supp. 1567

**Link:** https://merillionpress.com/cases/III-004.pdf

**Plaintiff (Respondent):** Luther Kevin CUNNINGHAM

**Defendant (Appellant):** SUBARU of America, Inc., et al.

**Opinion By:** Dale E. SAFFELS, United States District Judge

**Prior History:** On July 16, 1983 Cunningham and two of his friends went out for a bit of "four-wheeling," in the country in a 1979 Subaru "Brat," a vehicle resembling a small pick-up that included two rearward-facing seats in the bed. As per his testimony the vehicle went over a series of bumps on a dirt road at a speed somewhere between 20 and 45 miles per hour, causing his body to be bouncing up and down. He also testified that other articles such as lawn chairs and beverage coolers were being thrown around, all "like a rag doll."

The only other witnesses to the alleged incident, Kevin Jones and Rebecca Stack, were riding in the cab of the Subaru Brat. Their testimony is consistent and diametrically opposed to Cunningham's. At no time was the vehicle going faster than 20-25 miles per hour. They neither saw nor heard the other articles in the back bouncing or rattling around. In all respects, the ride was extraordinarily calm and uneventful.

Shortly after the ride, he began complaining of back pain and subsequently developing an acute compression loading of the lumbar spine, creating a burst fracture and a partial spinal cord injury.

A law suit followed and this product liability action was tried to a jury in September and October, 1987, resulting in an award for $ 467,710 in actual damages (reduced to $ 374,168 based on his own comparative fault of 20%) and $ 1.5 million in punitive damages. The jury found defendant Fuji Heavy Industries Ltd., the manufacturer of the vehicle, to be 50% at fault and liable for $ 1 million in punitive damages, and defendant Subaru of America, Inc., the importer and distributor, to be 30% at fault and liable for $ 500,000 in punitive damages.

Subaru and Fuji appeal.

**Before this Court:** There are several dubious matters concerning the mechanics of how and when the injury was produced. Several medical experts gave testimony and although they may not be in total agreement, but the injury complained of may have taken place well before July 16, 1983.

**Verdict:** The court empathizes with Cunningham but it is bound in concluding that the jury verdict was against the weight of the evidence. A new trial on all issues is appropriate.

# 5-Golfing Gizmo "Bolo" Effect

**Court:** Supreme Court of California

**Date:** 1975 APR 28

**Report:** L.A. No. 30216

**Case number:** 14 Cal. 3d 104; 534 P.2d 377

**Link:** https://merillionpress.com/cases/III-005.pdf

**Plaintiffs (Respondents):** Fred E. HAUTER, JR., a Minor, etc., et al.

**Defendants (Appellants):** Rudy C. ZOGARTS et al.

**Opinion By:** Mathew O. TOBRINER, Judge

**Prior History:** On July 14, 1967, Fred Hauter was seriously injured while using a "Golfing Gizmo" a training device designed to aid unskilled golfers to improve their games. Rudy C. Zogarts, who does business as House of Zog the manufacturer and Miles Kimball Company the seller.

Its catalogue states that the Gizmo is a "completely equipped backyard driving range." In 1966, Louise Hauter purchased a Gizmo from the catalogue and gave it to Fred Hauter, her 13 1/2-year-old son, as a Christmas present.

The user stands by the ball in order to hit his practice shots. The instructions state that when hit correctly, the ball will fly out and spring back near the point of impact; if the ball returns to the left, it indicates a right-hander's "slice"; a shot returning to the right indicates a right-hander's "hook." If the ball is "topped," it does not return and must be retrieved by the player. The label on the shipping carton and the cover of the instruction booklet urge players to "drive the ball with full power" and further state: "Completely Safe Ball Will Not Hit Player."

On the day of the accident Fred took his normal swing with a seven-iron. The last thing he remembers was extreme pain and dizziness. After a period of unconsciousness, he staggered into the house and told his mother that he had been hit on the head by the ball. He suffered brain damage and, in one doctor's opinion, is currently an epileptic.

The parents then filed suit on his behalf, claiming false representation, breach of express and implied warranties and strict liability in tort. The trial court returned a verdict favorable to Fred on all counts and the defendants appeal.

**Before this Court:** The bone of contention is whether they can escape liability by limiting the scope of their warranties by pointing to a drawing in the instructions depicting a golfer "correctly" using their product. Fred Hauter was not "playing golf." He was home on his front lawn learning to play the game with the aid of a supposedly danger-free training device. His injury stemmed from a risk inherent in defendants' product, not a risk inherent in the game of golf.

A device, which states in the catalogue: "You may be a duffer and divot digger but just give yourself a few hours with this and you'll be challenging Jack Nicklaus! . . . Practice with the Gizmo and you'll have even your golf pro watching admiringly."

**Verdict:** We conclude that Fred Hauter reasonably believed he could use the Gizmo with safety and agree with the trial court that they established all the elements of a cause of action for misrepresentation. We AFFIRM the order and remand the case to the trial court for the purpose of ascertaining damages.

## 6-Just Looking

**Court:** Court of Appeals of Texas

**Date:** 1973 DEC 19

**Report:** No. 15157

**Case number:** 505 S.W. 2d 682

**Link:** https://merillionpress.com/cases/III-006.pdf

**Plaintiff (Appellant):** Larry L. DAVIS

**Defendant (Appellee):** GIBSON Products Co., d/b/a Gibson Discount Store

**Opinion By:** Carlos C. CADENA, Justice

**Prior History:** Larry L. Davis' minor son Mark, 13-years old at the time and a couple of his friends of the same age walked into a Gibson Discount Store, a Texas based retailer. After Mark had purchased some gum and one of the other boys had bought some popcorn, the boys went to the sporting goods department. While they were in the vicinity of an archery display, Ralph Schoenfeld, the manager of the department, asked if he could help them and was told that they were "... just looking." According to Schoenfeld, one of the boys upset a box of arrows, and Schoenfeld "... remarked at the time it wasn't a playhouse and they should cut it out."

Schoenfeld testified that the boys then proceeded down the aisle to the machete display, where one of the boys picked up a machete. He was joined by two other boys, and "... they were all handling them, fooling around." Schoenfeld said that when one of the boys "... acted like he was going to fence," Schoenfeld told him, "That's about enough now. Why don't you just put them back and leave?"

While Schoenfeld was attending to other customers, Mark cut his hand. According to the petition, he picked up a machete on display, which was encased in a cloth sheath, to examine it. As he pulled it out, the blade cut through the bottom of the sheath, Mark suffered lacerations on the third and fourth fingers of his left hand. They sued the store seeking damages on the basis of "strict liability" and on several alleged negligent acts on the part of Gibson Discount Store.

The jury found: The store negligently failed to inspect the machete and the protective sheath, but such negligence was not the cause of the injury and denied compensation.

**Before this Court:** Davis appeals the lower court's decision. We have reviewed the evidence concerning the sharpness and the thinness of the sheath. While we concluded that the evidence was insufficient to establish the existence of a dangerous condition, it is sufficient to support the conclusion that, considering the sharpness of the blade, the sheath was improperly designed. Because of such defective design, it was unreasonably dangerous when put to one of its intended uses.

There is nothing in the record to suggest that Mark assumed the risk. Since the machetes were encased in sheaths, it was impossible to discover the sharpness of the blades without withdrawing the machetes from the sheaths.

**Verdict:** The judgment of the trial court is REVERSED and a new trial is ordered.

## 7-In the Obituaries Tomorrow

**Court:** United States Court of Appeals for the Seventh Circuit

**Date:** 1993 JUL 28

**Report:** No. 92-2742

**Case number:** 1 F. 3d 537

**Link:** https://merillionpress.com/cases/III-007.pdf

**Plaintiff (Appellant):** Todd KRUEGER

**Defendants (Appellees):** City of Algoma, Wisconsin, Police Department, et al.

**Opinion By:** Daniel A. MANION, Circuit Judge

**Prior History:** In 1988, the City of Algoma faced an epidemic of underage drinking. Todd Krueger, then a senior at the local high school, had been cited at least five times. On two of those occasions he required medical treatment. On December 20, 1988, Krueger attended a high school basketball game.

As he was leaving the parking lot after the game he hung out of the passenger window of the car he was in and yelled to Officer Todd Haltaufderheid, who was directing traffic, "why don't you direct that G- D- traffic?" Officer Haltaufderheid got into his police car and tracked down the vehicle in which Krueger was a passenger. The car sped away, while the officer questioned him. Officer Haltaufderheid issued an underage drinking citation and took Krueger to the Algoma police station.

While at the police station, Krueger told the officer that "If I get this ticket, you'll be reading about me in the obituaries tomorrow." When Krueger's mother came to pick him up at the police station Officer Haltaufderheid released him into his mother's custody and she and her son went home.

The next morning, Krueger's father then went to the police station to report that his son and his shotgun were missing from the family home. He suggested to Chief Marvin DeQuaine that no police officer should have contact with his son until he (the father) had been called to calm him down.

Later that morning, Officer Zahn saw a car speeding and disobeying traffic signals in the city he gave chase; he did not know at the time that Krueger was driving the car. When Krueger noticed that Officer Zahn had activated his siren and flashing lights, he "accelerated hard" in an attempt to flee. Krueger continued to flee at high speed until he reached the Bruemerville Dam. Once there, he got out of his car brandishing the shotgun he had taken from his house. He pointed the gun at Officer Zahn, who ducked behind his car. Officer Zahn warned Krueger to put down the gun. He then heard a shot. When Officer Zahn looked around the car which was shielding him, he saw Krueger lying on the ground bleeding from the chest. Krueger had attempted suicide, which he survived but with major injuries.

On December 1, 1989 he sued the City of Algoma and several police officers, claiming they violated his civil rights by arresting him and that the alleged violations somehow caused his suicide attempt. In a well-reasoned judgment the district court dismissed his suit and he appeals.

**Before this Court:** The district court noted that "there comes a point when human beings must be required to accept responsibility for their voluntary actions rather than being permitted to impose legal liability or moral blame on other individuals or on society in general." It is tragic when an 18-year-old attempts suicide. But who is responsible for this tragedy?

Krueger's theory that the arrest was improper is partly based on his belief that because his father advised the police that his son should not be approached until the father had a chance to talk with him; the police were required to follow this advice. Police officers, however, do not commit constitutional violations by failing to follow the tactical advice of non-police officers. Police officers have discretion to arrest even in contravention of such advice. Officer Zahn had good reasons to arrest Krueger.

**Verdict:** The judgment of the district court is AFFIRMED.

## 8-Four Abrasive Strips Instead of Seven

**Court:** United States Court of Appeals for the Third Circuit

**Date:** 1996 APR 26

**Report:** No. 95-5462

**Case number:** 82 F.3d 69

**Link:** https://merillionpress.com/cases/III-008.pdf

**Plaintiff (Appellant):** Elizabeth FEDORCZYK

**Defendants (Appellees):** CARIBBEAN CRUISE LINES Ltd. et al.

**Opinion By:** Robert E. COWEN, Circuit Judge

**Prior History:** Fedorczyk sailed from Miami aboard the Sovereign, a cruise ship operated by Royal Caribbean. While on board she went to the pool area, then returned to her cabin to take a shower. She turned on the water, stepped into the middle of the bathtub, at which time she slipped and fell onto the floor of the tub.

The tub in her cabin was about five and one-half feet long and two-feet, four-inches wide. It had four anti-skid strips, each running from the middle to the back of the tub. She has no recollection whether her feet were on or off the abrasive strips at the time of her fall. The tub was also equipped with a grab rail which she made a failed attempt to reach when she fell. After the accident she returned to the bathtub to ascertain the cause of the accident. She re-entered the tub and discovered that there was sufficient space between the abrasive strips so that her feet could just fit in between them. However, she does not know where her feet were at the time of the accident.

Fedorczyk's expert, an architect, testified that at the time he examined the bathtub, there were seven as opposed to four abrasive strips. Even with the seven abrasive strips, according to the expert, Royal Caribbean failed to provide a sufficiently large area of non-slip surface to permit its safe use. He based his finding on the fact that the tub failed to comply with the Consumer Products Safety Commission's standard for slip-resistant bathing facilities.

The district court held that she did not provide any evidence to support her claim that Royal Caribbean's failure to provide adequate abrasive strips in its bathtub was the proximate cause of her injuries and dismissed her claim.

**Before this Court:** In this appeal for Fedorczyk to prevail on her negligence claim, in addition to proving that Royal Caribbean was negligent, she must also prove that the Royal Caribbean's negligence caused her injury. Her expert testified that a person may fall in a bathtub under ordinary circumstances and the presence of bath oil and soap are "great variables" that could have caused the fall. She could have fallen in the bathtub for reasons other than Royal Caribbean's negligence.

She has not provided any direct evidence that the lack of abrasive surface in the bathtub caused her accident. Instead, she relies on "a preponderance of probabilities according to the common experience of mankind."

**Verdict:** We conclude that she was standing between the strips at the time of the accident, because her feet could fit between the strips, is not an appropriate inference to be drawn. The possibility of the existence of an event does not tend to prove its probability. We AFFIRM the June 26, 1995 order of the district court.

## 9-Swimming and Bodysurfing

**Court:** United States Court of Appeals for the Third Circuit

**Date:** 1995 DEC 26

**Report:** Nos. 95-5067, 95-5078

**Case number:** 72 F. 3d 385

**Link:** https://merillionpress.com/cases/III-009.pdf

**Plaintiffs (Appellants):** Roman KOWALSKY and Gary PETRILLO et al.

**Defendants (Appellees):** Long Beach TOWNSHIP et al.

**Opinion By:** Anthony J. SCIRICA, Circuit Judge

**Prior History:** During mid-afternoon on September 2, 1990, Roman Kowalsky entered the ocean to go swimming at Spray Beach in Long Beach Township, New Jersey, an area protected at the time by municipal lifeguards. After swimming and "bodysurfing" in the water for twenty minutes, he decided to return to the beach. "Bodysurfing" to shore, he was caught between two waves and driven into the sand. Although a lifeguard quickly reached Kowalsky and summoned an ambulance, he had already suffered a broken neck, resulting in permanent paralysis below the waist.

Kowalsky said that when he arrived at the beach the surf looked normal and no different from other visits; he contends the water conditions were hazardous, resulting from Hurricane Gustav, 1000-1200 miles offshore. He maintains that because of the hurricane, an unusually high number of rescues occurred over that Labour Day weekend. Both the lifeguard on duty and the beach supervisor testified the weather was sunny and dry, the surf normal for that time of year and there was no reason to close the beach or prohibit bodysurfing.

His complaint alleged that various municipal entities and certain municipal employees: (1) negligently supervised the beach; (2) failed to warn of a dangerous condition; and (3) failed to properly train beach patrol personnel.

They all denied negligence asserting immunity. The district court agreed and dismissed his case.

A day earlier on September 1, 1990, Gary Petrillo was swimming and "bodysurfing" in the ocean at the 12-14th Street Beach in Surf City, New Jersey. After forty minutes he became cold and decided to head ashore. While hip-deep in the water he was struck from behind by a wave that knocked him face first into the sand. Realizing he could not move, he remained lying on his back in the water. The attending lifeguard called for assistance and Petrillo was taken by ambulance and helicopter to a hospital. As a result of his injury Petrillo remains paralyzed from the neck down and has lost his speech abilities.

His complaint is similar to Kowalsky's and his case was also dismissed by the district court.

**Before this Court:** These cases were brought separately but decided by the same district court, and were consolidated on appeal.

The central issue presented by these appeals is the nature and scope of immunity conferred upon defendant municipal entities and municipal employees. The New Jersey Tort Claims Act sets forth the parameters of immunity for government officials and government acts, specifically; "the area within which government has the power to act for the public good is almost without limit and therefore government should not have the duty to do everything that might be done."

The tragic facts are that the injuries to Roman Kowalsky and Gary Petrillo were caused by ocean waves-acts of nature, which are a "natural" condition of unimproved public property. The key issue here is the difference between improved and unimproved property.

Both Kowalsky and Petrillo submitted reports prepared by beach experts, which chronicled "beach nourishment/modification" projects and the placement of "permanent shore protection structures," such as stone jetties, along the beaches of the region where the accidents occurred. The thrust of the report was that the beaches of the area "did not constitute a natural system" and that the beach configuration on the day of their injuries "would not have been possible without substantial man-made modifications to the natural system."

Yet the experts did not offer any evidence of "water motions" or "beach characteristics" at the site of the injuries or the immediate surrounding area. We also hold that, human modifications do not necessarily result in "improved" property.

**Verdict:** We AFFIRM the district court's dismissal in favour of all defendants.

## 10-Junk Science in the Courtroom

**Court:** United States Court of Appeals for the Seventh Circuit

**Date:** 1993 SEP 10

**Report:** No. 92-3594

**Case number:** 4F. 3d 537

**Link:** https://merillionpress.com/cases/III-010.pdf

**Plaintiffs (Appellants):** Ljubomir and Nevenaka ANTEVSKI

**Defendants (Appellees):** VOLKSWAGENWERK AKTIENGESELLSCHAFT et al.

**Opinion By:** Joel M. FLAUM, Circuit Judge

**Prior History:** Ljubomir Antevski was driving his 1983 Audi 5000 ST south along U.S. Route 41 outside of Lake Village, Indiana on the evening of April 30, 1988 when he was involved in a single-car accident. As his car approached a curve in the road, the right front and right rear wheels dropped four to five inches off the pavement and onto the gravel shoulder. Antevski's car proceeded straight, notwithstanding the curve, for approximately two car lengths before coming back onto the highway. At that point, the car went into a slide across the southbound lanes. While crossing the median, the car flipped over and came to rest in a northbound lane of the highway.

Antevski maintains that his accident was caused by a sudden unintended acceleration of his Audi 5000. According to his testimony, he pulled his car off to the side of the highway shortly after passing through Lake Village. After putting the transmission into park and turning off the engine, he exited the car in order to relieve himself.

Then he lit a cigarette and got back into the car. After starting the engine, he placed his foot on the brake prior to shifting the transmission from park to drive. Once the engine had engaged, the car began to accelerate rapidly and unexpectedly. Allegedly, the sudden acceleration of the car, despite his attempts to brake, caused his accident and serious injuries.

When Antevski arrived at the hospital that night, he was alert and oriented. During a conversation with Linda Decker, the emergency room nurse, he explained that the accident occurred when he lost control of his car while attempting to light a cigar (which was probably her abbreviation for cigarette). John Cifaldi, a former business associate of his, testified that he went to see Antevski after receiving a phone call from the hospital. Antevski told him that the accident occurred after he dropped his cigarette and lost control of the car when he reached down to pick it up.

Following the accident, Antevski and his wife brought suit, alleging that the Audi 5000, being defective and unreasonably dangerous, causing his accident. Specifically, the Antevskis' experts developed the theory that when three particular valves in the transmission body become jammed, unintended acceleration results. However, the engineering expert conceded that there was absolutely no physical evidence that any valve was jammed in the car the night of the accident. Additionally, Robert Lang, Audi's engineering expert, testified that the transmission in the car was not defective and that unintended acceleration could not occur in the manner the Antevskis' experts had hypothesized.

With respect to the brakes, neither side disputes that as a general proposition Audi's brakes are stronger than the engine and will always prevail over the engine.

The jury, after hearing the lengthy testimony, returned a verdict in favor of Audi's parent company on the issue of liability. The Antevskis demanded a new trial based on legal, rather than technical grounds, which the district court denied and this is their appeal.

**Before this Court:** Although the Antevskis would have us believe that the defendants' case rose and fell with Cifaldi's testimony, and his questionable credibility, the hefty trial record suggests otherwise. And as the Antevskis' lawyer acknowledged at oral argument, they presented only a theory of how an accident might have occurred. They did not actually present any conclusive evidence that any of the valves in question did stick.

Moreover, both the emergency room nurse and at least one of the attending physicians explicitly corroborated Cifaldi's testimony regarding

Antevski's preliminary explanation of the accident, namely that he was attempting to light a cigarette when he lost control of the car.

**Verdict:** Consequently, we are unable to discern any reason to upset the jury's verdict, its decision AFFIRMED.

## 11-Neglected to Switch Off

**Court:** United States Court of Appeals for the Seventh Circuit

**Date:** 1994 MAR 09

**Report:** No. 93-2595

**Case number:** 18 F. 3d 474

**Link:** https://merillionpress.com/cases/III-011.pdf

**Plaintiff (Appellant):** Milton DONALD

**Defendant (Appellee):** LIBERTY MUTUAL INSURANCE Company

**Opinion By:** Walter J. CUMMINGS Jr., Circuit Judge

**Prior History:** On June 25, 1990, Milton Donald severely injured his right arm when he attempted to remove his clothes from laundry equipment that he had neglected to switch off. He sued the University of Evansville, Indiana, which owned the equipment, and Daryl Buente, an employee of the University who had given Donald permission to use the equipment, alleging negligence.

The parties settled that claim and it is not at issue here. In addition, he also sued the University's insurer, Liberty Mutual Insurance Company, alleging breach of contract on account of its refusal to pay him $5,000 in benefits (Complaint Count Two), and alleging that Liberty Mutual breached a duty to deal with him in good faith (Complaint Count Three).

The district court dismissed both counts of Donald's complaint and he appeals.

**Before this Court:** After the accident Donald's attorney and representatives of Liberty Mutual corresponded by mail and over the telephone. It was clear that Donald was exploring the possibility that the University and Buente might be liable in tort for his injuries; if they were, then Liberty Mutual would be required to pay the amount of that liability. Liberty Mutual took the position that there was no negligence on the part of the

University or Buente, and that Donald's claim to the contrary was very weak.

Donald also inquired whether the University's contract of insurance provided for any medical payment benefits. In this context Donald's lawyer referred to Donald as an "insured," apparently meaning by this that Donald would be eligible for any medical payment benefits included in the University's policy. This precipitated confusion on the part of Liberty Mutual's representatives, who were of the opinion that Donald probably was not an "insured" under the policy. They refused to release a copy of the policy to Donald's lawyer. However, he continued to refer to Donald as an "insured," unaware that by the terms of the policy any "insured" was by definition not covered.

During these negotiations Liberty Mutual forwarded a "Release and Settlement of Claim" form:

For the sole consideration of FIVE THOUSAND DOLLARS ... the undersigned hereby releases and forever discharges UNIVERSITY of EVANSVILLE and all other persons, firms and corporations from all claims and demands, rights and causes of action of any kind the undersigned now has or hereafter may have on account of ... an occurrence which happened on or about JUNE 25, 1990.... This release expresses a full and complete SETTLEMENT of a liability....

Donald's lawyer refused this offer but did offer that Donald would execute a release of Liberty Mutual's liability for medical payment benefits in exchange for the $5,000. Liberty Mutual refused.

We hold that Donald, a third party beneficiary of the medical payment provision of the University's contract with Liberty Mutual, may sue to enforce that provision in Count Two of his Complaint, and that he may sue Liberty Mutual in Count Three for breaching a duty to deal with him in good faith.

The district court decided in favour of Liberty Mutual on Count Two (breach of contract) of Donald's Complaint because it held that under Indiana law an injured person not party to the contract of insurance cannot sue the insurer directly to recover for his losses. Because this aspect of Indiana law only applies in a tort context, while Donald is suing Liberty Mutual in contract, the district court misapplied Indiana law to Donald's suit.

**Verdict:** The district court's decision in Liberty Mutual's favour must be REVERSED.

# 12-Another Smoker

**Court:** United States Court of Appeals for the Seventh Circuit

**Date:** 1996 MAR 11

**Report:** No. 95-3064

**Case number:** 78 F. 3d 316

**Link:** https://merillionpress.com/cases/III-012.pdf

**Plaintiff (Appellant):** Raymond ROSEN

**Defendant (Appellee):** CIBA-GEIGY CORPORATION

**Opinion By:** Richard A. POSNER, Chief Judge

**Prior History:** Rosen, a heavy smoker all his adult life, had his first heart attack in 1987, followed by quadruple bypass surgery.

He was told to stop smoking, but did not. He experienced chest pains and other cardiac symptoms in the following years, indicating a progression of his coronary artery disease. His previous heart attack, high blood pressure, cholesterol count, age (60 in 1992), and continued smoking placed him at high risk of having another heart attack.

In June of 1992 his treating cardiologist, prescribed the Habitrol (manufactured by CIBA-GEIGY) patch and told him not to smoke while wearing it. Rosen affixed the patch to his arm but continued smoking, as, we are told, 75% of patch wearers do.

Upon awakening on the morning of the third day of wearing the patch, Rosen smoked two cigarettes and then took a bath. During the bath he removed the patch and immediately felt a numbing sensation in the same arm. Later that morning he experienced discomfort in his chest, went to the hospital, and was diagnosed as having had another heart attack. He later resumed smoking and has since had two more heart attacks.

In his suit Rosen claims that CIBA-GEIGY was negligent in developing, marketing, and selling the Habitrol patch. What exactly the negligence is believed to consist in is unclear. Rosen seems to believe either that the warnings of possible harm to people with coronary artery disease are inadequate or that the product is unreasonably dangerous, perhaps because the product is sold to addicts who can be expected to disregard any warnings.

The district court dismissed his case and he appeals.

**Before this Court:** When an unusual event follows closely on the heels of another unusual event, the ordinary person infers a causal relation; so it was natural for Rosen to assume that the heart attack he experienced in June of 1992 was caused either by wearing or removing the patch. The inference is reinforced by the fact that nicotine is a principal ingredient of cigarette smoke, which is known to be a cause of coronary artery disease, and by the fact that the manufacturer of the patch had warned that it might have bad effects on persons who already have the disease.

But lay speculations on medical causality, however plausible, are a perilous basis for inferring causality; and though Rosen refers to newspaper accounts of "an epidemic of heart attacks to patch users who smoked" while wearing the patch, we do not understand him to be quarreling with the proposition that without scientific evidence of a causal relation between the nicotine patch and his heart attack, as distinct from journalistic reports, he cannot prevail in this suit.

His expert's deposition, while expressing what may be an insightful, even an inspired, hunch concerning the cause of the heart attack that Rosen experienced in June of1992, lacks scientific rigor. The deposition offers neither a theoretical reason to believe that wearing a nicotine patch for three days, or removing it after three days, could precipitate a heart attack. Shoveling snow can precipitate a heart attack, but it cannot cause coronary artery disease. But decades of relentless smoking can.

**Verdict:** For the forgoing reasons the district court's decision is AFFIRMED.

## 13-Far-Fetched for Now

**Court:** Superior Court of New Jersey, Appellate Division

**Date:** 2012 OCT 27

**Report:** No. A-1234-11T4

**Case number:** Not citable

**Link:** https://merillionpress.com/cases/III-013.pdf

**Plaintiffs (Appellants):** Scott SIMON, an Incompetent, by his Guardians, et al.

**Defendants (Appellees):** Harding Pharmacy, Inc., Kinray Inc., et al.

**Opinion By:** PER CURIAM

**Prior History:** Since 1996, Harding Pharmacy (Harding) purchased prescription drugs, including controlled dangerous substances (CDS) such as Xanax, from Kinray, a large-scale drug wholesaler and distributor.

On September 22, 2007, Mark Malajian an employee of Harding stole a partially-full, open bottle of Xanax from a shelf in the pharmacy department. Later that evening, he went to a party at his friend Scott Simon's house. There, Malajian gave seventeen-year-old Scott the stolen Xanax, even though he observed that Scott seemed "messed up" and despite knowing Scott's reputation for getting "a little crazy [with drugs] at times." The party, which was attended by dozens of teenagers, was loud, and an adult on the premises told Scott to shut the party down. Instead of complying, Scott arranged to move the party to another teenager's house; that teen's parents were not at home, and the unsupervised revelry continued into the early hours of September 23, 2007.

The next morning, Malajian found Scott lying unresponsive, with shallow breathing and blue-tinged skin. Instead of calling an ambulance, he called a friend, who, unable to resuscitate Scott, drove him to the hospital. Scott was eventually revived, but suffered catastrophic injuries that left him in a coma.

Scott's Guardians filed suit against Kinray, Harding, Harding's owners, Malajian and numerous other parties. To the tune of $4.1 million all those sued settled or otherwise resolved their claims against all of the defendants except Kinray. The trial court dismissed Scott's claims reasoning that Kinray owed no common law duty to Scott; a third party with whom it had no special relationship. Scott Simon and Arnold Simon appeal that decision.

**Before this Court:** Having reviewed the record, we conclude that the Simons' appellate arguments are completely without merit. Judge Harz addressed the issues in her comprehensive written opinion, and they require little further discussion here.

As Judge Harz concluded, even viewing the evidence in the light most favorable to the Simons, no jury could reasonably conclude that Kinray's acts or omissions were a proximate cause of Scott's injury. In her decision, the judge found that "plaintiffs have failed to establish any connection between the delivery of Kinray drugs to Harding and the theft of the Xanax which is the known cause of Scott's drug overdose."

The Simons' remaining arguments amount to an assertion that Kinray had a duty to exercise extensive oversight and regulation of its wholesale pharmacy customers, including periodically inspecting their premises and demanding criminal background checks of all their employees. We reject that argument for the same reasons as Judge Harz. It would be burdensome and impractical for Kinray to exercise that level of detailed oversight of the thousands of pharmacies to which it sold its products.

**Verdict:** Plaintiffs' complaint against Kinray was far-fetched and unsupported by evidence, and the lower court's judgment is AFFIRMED.

## 14-Too Hot to Handle

**Court:** Supreme Court of the State of New York, New York County

**Date:** 2013 OCT 03

**Report:** No. 152423/13

**Case number:** 2013 NY Slip Op 32402(U)

**Link:** https://merillionpress.com/cases/III-014.pdf

**Plaintiff:** Frank DIETL

**Defendants:** Dr. Mehmet OZ, M.D., Zoco Productions, Sony Pictures Television, et al.

**Opinion By:** Saliann SCARPULLA, Judge

**Prior History:** According to the allegations of the complaint, on April 17, 2012, 76 year old Dietl was watching an episode of the Dr. Oz Show, in which Dr. Oz was providing viewers with an at-home remedy to cure sleeplessness due to cold feet. Specifically, Dr. Oz suggested that viewers could put uncooked rice into a pair of socks, warm the socks in a microwave, and then place the socks on their feet and go to bed.

Dietl tried the at-home remedy, and fell asleep. He suffers from neuropathy and diminished sensation in his lower extremities due to diabetes, and suffered second and third degree burns on both of his feet. In his complaint, Dietl alleged that defendants breached their duty to instruct the audience as to the proper procedure for the at-home remedy, and breached their duty to warn against any reasonably foreseeable risk of harm to a person attempting such home remedy.

Dietl commenced this action in March 2013 in which he avers that he trusted Dr. Oz as if he was his own physician. He maintains that if Dr. Oz had advised that viewers who suffered from conditions involving the feet should not try this at-home remedy, he would have taken extra precautions or not tried the remedy at all. Dietl maintains that he and Dr. Oz had a quasi-physician-patient relationship. He argues that the defendants breach their duty of care owed to the audience by providing negligent medical advice.

The defendants ask to dismiss the complaint, first arguing that a television talk show and its host do not owe a duty of care to a general television audience, and in any event, Dr. Oz properly warned viewers by stating that they should not let the rice get "too hot, just warm." They next argue that they did not owe a specific duty to warn Dietl, and, in any event, he was aware that he could be susceptible to injury due to his medical condition.

**Before this Court:** The court finds that the complaint does not state a cause of action for negligence against the defendants. Specifically, there is no factual basis for Dietl's claim that defendants breached a duty of care allegedly owed to him. There was no direct or quasi physician-patient relationship between Dr. Oz and Dietl, sufficient to establish a duty of care.

He has pointed to no authority that would lead this court to find a duty of care between a television talk-show host and his vast home-viewing audience, and Dietl fails to convince this court that creating such a duty would be sound public policy. While the injuries sustained by him were serious and unfortunate, there is no basis alleged for his claim against the defendants.

**Verdict:** The complaint is DISMISSED and this constitutes the decision and order of the court.

## 15-Insufficient Height of Fence

**Court:** Supreme Court of Queensland, Court of Appeal, Brisbane, Australia

**Date:** 2003 FEB 14

**Report:** Appeal No 6596 of 2002

**Case number:** [2003] QCA 29

**Link:** https://merillionpress.com/cases/III-015.pdf

**Plaintiff (Appellant):** Benjamin K. MILLER

**Defendants (Appellees):** Council of the Shire of LIVINGSTONE & ANOR, State of Queensland

**Opinion By:** Bruce H. MCPHERSON, Judge

**Prior History:** Ben and Mark Miller, two brothers arrived at the Railway Hotel in Yeppoon at 6.30 pm with Mark's wife Rhonda, then his fiancée and another male friend. They stayed there until about 9.30 pm. Ben, who had a cold, drank about three 'mid-strength' beers. From the Railway Hotel the brothers went to the Marsden Tavern to play pool. They remained there until about 11.00 pm and drank about six half rum and Cokes each.

From the Marsden Tavern they went next door to a nightclub where they had another half rum and Coke. They then returned to the Marsden Tavern where they played pool and had another 'couple' of half rum and Cokes before deciding at about midnight to return home on foot, as they had often done before. They jogged to Appleton Drive. When they reached it Ben was in front. They slowed to a walk and crossed the road to the concrete footpath. Ben began jogging again, then walking, leaving him 20m ahead of Mark.

As one travels south the pathway turns to the left just before the culvert. The corner was blind because there were mangroves growing near the water-course. Ben was hidden from Mark's view, but ten or fifteen seconds after Mark last saw Ben he heard a thud. Mark came around the bend but saw no sign of his brother. He called out; 'Come on, Ben. Stop mucking around. Get up.' Soon after, Mark found Ben lying face down on the culvert apron, seriously injured.

There were no eye witnesses of the event and Ben himself has no recollection of it, or of how or why he fell. Miller sued the Council and the State claiming that the fence along the edge of the footpath was not sufficiently high to present an effective barrier to guard against the risk that someone might fall over the fence into the culvert. His case was dismissed and he appeals.

**Before this Court:** In the absence of evidence, speculation is not enough. It was necessary for the plaintiff to prove how or why he fell. Inference from proved facts will do, but not mere hypothesis. The circumstantial evidence in the present case does not support an inference that Miller's injuries resulted from the negligence of the defendants or either of them in installing or maintaining a fence that was too low rather than from some other cause that is inconsistent with negligence on their part. To conclude that on this occasion he suffered a mishap in a most particular way – incidentally the way most favourable for his case for compensation. But it could reasonably be concluded, I think, that the brothers' history of safe returns suggests something other than the condition of footpath, ground, and fence as the cause of the fall.

**Verdict:** Appeal DISMISSED with costs.

# CHAPTER IV

# CRIME

*"A thief who has broken into a bedroom claims his sense of shame had been outraged, and by threatening the occupants with exposure of an immoral act he blackmails them into not bringing charges for burglary." Karl Kraus (1874-1936) was an Austrian journalist*

This part is composed of mostly pathetic criminals, bungled robberies and the myriad and lame excuses as the guilty try to weasel out of their predicament. The common thread running is "I pleaded guilty because I was guilty. But my confession was under duress and as the saying goes felony stupid." Blaming accomplices, face-saving absurdities the main gist of which could be condensed to: "I've been caught, but the penalty is too severe, and of course the verdict handed out is somehow unconstitutional."

## 1-An Arrow in the Back

**Court:** Court of Appeals of California, Second Appellate District, Division Six

**Date:** 1987 JUN 10

**Report:** B020018

**Case number:** 193 Cal. App. 3d 196; 238 Cal. Rptr. 82

**Link:** https://merillionpress.com/cases/IV-001.pdf

**Plaintiff (Respondent):** The PEOPLE

**Defendant (Appellant):** Kelsey Dru GLEGHORN

**Opinion by:** Steven J. STONE, Presiding Judge

**Prior History:** This case is a parable of the dangers of weaponry in the hands of unreasonable powers who become unduly provoked over minor irritations. Melody Downes shared her house with several persons, including Gleghorn. She rented her garage to Michael Fairall for $150 per month. She believed he was to give her a stereo as part of the rent. He believed her intent was only to borrow it. He asked for the return of the stereo; she said she sold it.

Fairall, a man of obvious sensitivity, smashed all the windows of her automobile, slashed the tires and dented the body. Not quite mollified, he kicked in her locked door, scattered her belongings in the bedroom, and broke an aquarium, freeing her snake. (It was scotched, not killed. See Macbeth, W. Shakespeare). Ms. Downes advised Gleghorn of Fairall's behavior; he apparently took umbrage. On the fateful night in question, Fairall, having quaffed a few, went to the garage he called home and then to bed, a mattress laid upon a lofty perch in the rafters. He was rudely awakened by a pounding on the garage door accompanied by Gleghorn's request that he come out so that he might kill him. Fairall wisely advised him that they could exchange pleasantries in the morning.

Undeterred, Gleghorn opened the garage door, entered with stick in hand and began beating on the rafters, yelling for Fairall to come down. In the darkness, Fairall claimed he could see sparks where the board hit the rafters. Gleghorn said that if Fairall did not come down, he would burn him out. No sooner said than done, he set a small fire to some of Fairall's clothes.

Fairall, who happened to have secreted a bow and quiver of arrows in the rafters to prevent its theft, loosed one but did not see where it landed. Abandoning his weapons, he swung down from the rafters and was immediately hit from behind. He yelled for someone to bring a hose and attempted to extinguish the fire with his hands. Meanwhile, Gleghorn, in an ill humour from the gash in his back caused by the arrow, continued to beat him, causing a two-inch-wide vertical break in Fairall's lower jaw, tearing his lips, knocking out six to ten teeth, mangling two fingers, and lacerating his arm, stomach and back. Fairall also suffered burns on the palms of his hands.

Fairall testified under a grant of immunity concerning the vandalism of the car. The jury found Gleghorn guilty on two counts:

1-Simple assault by means of force likely to incur great bodily injury.

2-Battery with the infliction of serious bodily injury.

**Before this Court:** He appeals the guilty decision contending, that since the jury found his acts prior to being shot constituted only simple assault, Fairall was not justified in replying with deadly force. Since the victim responded with deadly force, he continues, he was entitled to defend himself with deadly force. Ergo, he could not be convicted of battery with the infliction of serious bodily injury.

We disagree both with Cleghorn's contentions. Even though if a person is mistaken in judgment as to the actual necessity for the use of extreme measures, if he was misled through no fault or carelessness on his part and defends himself correctly according to what he supposed the facts to be, his act is justifiable.

Here, the jury could reasonably infer from the evidence that: (1) Fairall acted reasonably upon the appearances that his life was in danger or (2) even if Fairall acted unreasonably in shooting him in the back with the arrow and Cleghorn was justified in responding with deadly force, Cleghorn continued to beat his attacker long after the attacker was disabled. If a person attacked defends himself so successfully that his attacker is rendered incapable of inflicting injury, or for any other reason the danger no longer exists, there is no justification for further retaliation.

The evidence supports a finding that Fairall did not threaten or take any action against Cleghorn after Fairall descended from the loft. On the other hand, if the jury found, as it could have, that Fairall was justified in reasonably fearing for his life on the appearances of Cleghorn's actions, he never obtained the right of self-defence in the first place. We find no error.

Stone, P. J.: "May a person who enters the habitat of another at 3 o'clock in the morning for the announced purpose of killing him, and who commences to beat the startled sleeper's bed with a stick and set fires under him, be entitled to use deadly force in self-defence after the intended victim shoots him in the back with an arrow? Upon the basis of these bizarre facts, we hold that he may not, and instead, must suffer the slings and arrows of outrageous fortune (with apologies to William Shakespeare and Hamlet, Act III, sc. 1)."

**Verdict:** The judgment is AFFIRMED.

# 2-A Very Bungled Robbery

**Court:** Supreme Court of Minnesota

**Date:** 1972 MAR 10

**Report:** 42326

**Case number:** 195 N.W.2d 583

**Link:** https://merillionpress.com/cases/IV-002.pdf

**Plaintiff (Respondent):** State of Minnesota

**Defendant (Appellant):** Michael J. MCGLYNN

**Opinion By:** C. Donald PETERSON, Justice

**Prior History:** McGlynn was the mastermind of a blundered fur robbery on December 12, 1968. At about noon of that day, he borrowed a blue 1963 Oldsmobile from Herbert Wroge, a used-car salesman, on the pretense of taking it to his wife for approval. This automobile was later identified by others as the getaway vehicle. At about 2:30 p. m. McGlynn and Raymond Stanley Smith (an accomplice who did not testify as state's witness) approached Antell, who was walking with his girlfriend, Gail Dubak, and asked whether he "wanted to go on a score."

Although Antell initially refused, he reconsidered after McGlynn assured him that the "score was real easy." Dubak did not hear the conversation since, at Antell's suggestion; she had continued walking to a nearby store to wait for him. Shortly thereafter, Antell and Mrs. Dubak accompanied defendant and Smith to Mary Anderson's apartment, which Smith shared with Anderson, a divorcee.

At the apartment Antell, at McGlynn's direction, shaved off his beard and mustache and put on clothes supplied by McGlynn. He also gave Anderson a blond wig to wear in the robbery, a wig similar to that which he gave for safekeeping to his downstairs neighbor, Colleen Clark, a few days after the robbery. At the same time he handed a loaded .22-caliber revolver to Antell and supplied Antell and Smith with nylon hosiery with which to bind the persons to be robbed and laundry bags in which to carry the stolen furs.

Smith, Antell, and Anderson then proceeded to execute the robbery of the Gershkow Fur Company at 1013 West Broadway, Minneapolis. Smith and Anderson, who had previously visited the Gershkow store pretending to look at furs, entered first. As Anderson was trying on a fur jacket, Antell entered twirling the revolver on his finger, and at some point he shot his own finger, an injury later observed by others.

After tying up Gershkow and his wife with the nylon hosiery, Antell and Smith filled the laundry bags with furs, but they had tied Gershkow so ineffectually that he immediately escaped after they had left the store. Gershkow observed the blue Oldsmobile getaway car and ran to it, grabbing the door handle. This so startled the robbers that they rear-ended another automobile. They drove away, but Gershkow noted the license number and reported it to the police.

The errant trio returned to the Anderson apartment. Antell proceeded to place the laundry bags loaded with stolen furs into a panel truck which McGlynn had stated would be parked there for that purpose. However, the truck proved to be an exterminator's van, and Smith ran back from the apartment to assist Antell in carrying the loot into the apartment.

McGlynn came to the apartment later to pick up the furs. Dubak and Kathleen LaFore, a babysitter for Anderson's children, observed him moving laundry bags in the apartment, and Mrs. Dubak also saw him leave the premises carrying two large white bags which "looked like they were full of something." These bags were like those McGlynn supplied to Antell and Smith prior to the robbery.

Antell did not deliver all of the stolen furs to McGlynn, but hid one fur coat under the bed before he arrived. He later offered to sell the coat to one Tim Janzen who, having read of the Gershkow fur robbery turned the fur coat over to the police. McGlynn himself sold one of the furs to his neighbor, Colleen Clark, who likewise turned the coat over to the police. Mrs. Gershkow subsequently identified one of the fur coats for the police from hand embroidery she had done on the inside of the coat.

**Before this Court:** McGlynn, appealing from his conviction of aggravated robbery, challenges the constitutional propriety of testimony against him by two of his accomplices, Franklin J. Antell and Mary Anderson, both of whom had pleaded guilty to the offense but had not been sentenced, and the sufficiency of non-accomplice testimony to corroborate the Antell-Anderson testimony.

**Verdict:** No authority has been cited for this claim that there is a constitutional impediment to the state's use of witnesses who, under expectancy of leniency, testify for the state. The credibility of such a witness is, naturally, suspect, but the issue of credibility is for the jury. The inherent corruptness of a confessed criminal is the very reason for the statute's requiring that an accomplice's testimony be corroborated.

Judgement AFFIRMED.

## 3-Trespassory Re-entry

**Court:** Supreme Court of Nevada

**Date:** 1990 OCT 25

**Report:** No. 20444

**Case number:** 799 P. 2d 550

**Link:** https://merillionpress.com/cases/IV-003.pdf

**Plaintiff (Appellant):** The State of Nevada

**Defendant (Respondent):** Bill Aaron MCNICHOLS

**Opinion By:** PER CURIAM

**Prior History:** Bill Aaron McNichols lost his house at 60. Logan Street, Las Vegas, through foreclosure. Three and four day notices of unlawful detainer were served, as well as an order of summary eviction. The eviction was carried out sometime between the 15th and 20th of September, 1988.

Responding to reports that the former occupants had re-entered the premises with a weapon, police officers and an agent of the mortgagee went to 60. Logan Street on November 15, 1988. The lock and court seals had been removed, and someone had entered the residence via the back door.

The police officers entered the house and found a small amount of marijuana above a headboard in the northwest bedroom, and a methamphetamine laboratory spread throughout the house and garage. The police took samples of suspected contraband, and ultimately the state charged McNichols with trafficking in a controlled substance.

On October 2, 1989, McNichols filed a motion to suppress evidence in the district court, alleging that the warrantless entry into 60. Logan Street was unreasonable and the evidence derived from the entry should be suppressed. The district court granted the motion to suppress and dismissed the case. The state appeals.

**Before this Court:** The state contends that the district court erred by dismissing the case. Specifically, the state contends that at the time of the search, McNichols no longer had a reasonable expectation of privacy in the 60. Logan Street residence. The state maintains that his subsequent re-entry was a trespass and did nothing to restore a reasonable expectation of privacy.

Although he may have had a subjective expectation of privacy in the premises, this expectation was not one that society is prepared to recognize as reasonable. He lost his legal interest in the property when it was foreclosed. He lost his possessory interest in the property when he was evicted. The new owner changed the locks, and the constable's office placed court seals on the entryway.

**Verdict:** We REVERSE the district court's order and remand for further proceedings consistent with this opinion.

## 4-Soldier of Misfortune

**Court:** United States Court of Appeals for the Fifth Circuit

**Date:** 1989 AUG 17

**Report:** No. 88-2499

**Case number:** 880 F. 2d 83058 USLW 2142, 16 Media L. Rep. 2148

**Link:** https://merillionpress.com/cases/IV-004.pdf

**Plaintiffs (Appellees):** Marjorie A. EIMANN, Individually, as Next Friend of Gary Wayne BLACK, and as Representative of the Estate of Sandra Kay BLACK, Deceased, and Glenn G. EIMANN

**Defendants (Appellants):** SOLDIER OF FORTUNE Magazine, Inc. and Omega Group Inc.

**Opinion By:** W. Eugene DAVIS, Circuit Judge

**Prior History:** John Wayne Hearn shot and killed Sandra Black at the behest of her husband, who offered to pay Hearn $ 10,000 for doing so. Robert Black contacted Hearn through a classified advertisement that Hearn ran in Soldier of Fortune Magazine, Inc. (SOF), a publication that focuses on mercenary activities and military affairs.

The ad read: EX-MARINES – 67-69 'Nam Vets, Ex-DI, weapons specialist – jungle warfare, pilot, M.E., high risk assignments, U.S., or overseas. (404) 991-2684.

Between early 1982 and January 1984, Black had asked at least four friends or coworkers from Bryan, Texas to kill Sandra Black (to collect on her life insurance) or help him kill her. All four refused.

Black called Hearn in October 1984 after seeing his ad in SOF. After several contacts Hearn killed Sandra Black on February 21, 1985. By this time Hearn also had killed two other people within a 6-week span and was sentenced to concurrent life sentences.

Sandra Black's son, Gary Wayne Black, and her mother, Marjorie Eimann, sued SOF and its parent, Omega Group, Ltd., for wrongful death under Texas law on the theory that SOF negligently published Hearn's classified ad. The jury awarded Eimann $1.9 million in compensatory damages and $7.5 million in punitive damages. SOF appeals.

**Before this Court:** SOF argues first that the criminal activities of Hearn and Robert Black, rather than Hearn's ad, were the proximate cause of Sandra Black's murder. SOF also argues that tort liability here contravenes first amendment protection for commercial speech because (1) the judgment imposed a duty on publishers to investigate its advertisers and their ads; and (2) allowed the jury to penalize SOF for the mercenary and military focus of the magazine's articles and other ads.

**Verdict:** The standard of conduct imposed by the district court against SOF is too high. The burden on a publisher to avoid liability from suits of this type is too great: he must reject all such advertisements. The range of foreseeable misuses of advertised products and services is as limitless as the forms and functions of the products themselves. Without a more specific indication of illegal intent we conclude that SOF did not violate the required standard of conduct by publishing an ad that later played a role in criminal activity.

The judgment of the district court is REVERSED and RENDERED.

The Brauns and SOF magazine settled the wrongful-death lawsuit for $200,000. One consequence of the lost lawsuits was the magazine's suspension of publication of classified advertisements for mercenary work either in the U.S. or overseas.

# 5-Murder She Wrote

**Court:** Court of Special Appeals of Maryland

**Date:** 1990 MAR 30

**Report:** No. 1007, September Term, 1989

**Case number:** 82 Md. App. 294 (1990); 571 A. 2d 850

**Link:** https://merillionpress.com/cases/IV-005.pdf

**Plaintiffs (Appellees):** Lucille MICHAELS, et al.

**Defendant (Appellee):** Carol Joann NEMETHVARGO

**Opinion By:** Rosalyn B. BELL, Judge

**Prior History:** The Michaelses sued Carol Nemethvargo for the loss of their son's services and companionship as a result of his current imprisonment. In the spring of 1986, Nemethvargo employed Tony, their, son and three other young men to kill her husband. In return, she promised to pay Tony $6,000 for murdering her husband. The plan to kill the husband failed and Tony was ultimately tried as an adult and found guilty of attempted first degree murder. He was sentenced to six years imprisonment, while Nemethvargo was placed on probation for her role in the plot.

The Michaelses filed suit on July 10, 1987. Nemethvargo countered, alleging that the Michaelses had no cause of action because her contract with Tony was illegal. The trial judge ruled in favor of Nemethvargo and dismissed the case. This appeal followed.

**Before this Court:** The Michaelses complain: as parents of a minor child, they have a cause of action where they were deprived of the services of their minor child and lost the child's companionship, and sustained other losses, as a result of Nemethvargo's employing the minor child to murder her husband without obtaining the parents' consent to the employment. One who contributes to the delinquency of a minor by inducing the minor to enter into an attempted first degree murder is liable in tort to both the minor and the parents.

An essential element of a parent's cause of action is that the requested compensation flow from a personal injury for which, under the law, the child would be entitled to recover.... If the child is not entitled to recover, the parent cannot recover. We observe that juvenile proceedings are not criminal in nature; they are, rather, an attempt to rehabilitate the juvenile. In this case, Tony was sentenced to six years imprisonment for attempted first degree murder. He was treated as an adult and neither he nor his parents can maintain an action.

The parental claims in this case were not "bad guys," and can pursue a cause of action for loss of their minor son's services. Their child, however, cannot make the same claim: he is not entitled to recover for his injuries. Where the parents' cause of action is totally separate, as with the common law right to services and necessary expenses, they can maintain their claim. But where the parents' claim stems from the child's, and the child could not collect, neither can the parents.

**Verdict:** The judgment is AFFIRMED in part and REVERSED in part.

## 6-Suitcase Left Behind

**Court:** United States Court of Appeals for the Seventh Circuit

**Date:** 1993 JAN 26

**Report:** No. 92-1672

**Case number:** 984 F. 2d 806

**Link:** https://merillionpress.com/cases/IV-006.pdf

**Plaintiff (Appellee):** United States of America

**Defendant (Appellant):** David REM

**Opinion By:** Daniel A. MANION, Circuit Judge

**Prior History:** On May 28, 1991, a Chicago police officer assigned to the Drug Enforcement Administration (DEA) Task Force received a telephone call from the police in Kansas City, Missouri, regarding a suspicious person on the Amtrak train. The Kansas City police told the officer that they had arrested two people on the train's sleeper car 0430 in an unrelated drug investigation.

They had learned from train employees that another passenger on sleeper car 0430, traveling under the name of David Reilly, bought his ticket in Los Angeles with a large amount of cash; kept his suitcase with him in his compartment; stayed in the sleeper car, having meals brought to him; and would not allow the car attendant to come in and make his bed.

David Rem boarded a train in Los Angeles destined for Chicago. He departed the train during a stop outside Chicago, but left his suitcase containing 18 kilograms of cocaine on the train. After all passengers got off in Chicago, the police obtained the suitcase and opened it without a search warrant. The suitcase contained 18 brick shaped packages of cocaine. They carried the suitcase to officer Kinsella's office in the train station.

Ten minutes after Kinsella brought the suitcase to his office, several Amtrak employees came in to report that they had just seen "Reilly," although his clothing was different. Kinsella and another officer left the office and entered the station's lobby area, where they saw Rem talking on a pay telephone; he "appeared very excited," waving his hand in the air. The officers approached him and asked if they could speak with him. He nervously attempted to hang up the telephone. When asked, Rem, his hands shaking, produced a New York driver's license in the name of David Rem.

Rem pleaded guilty to possession of a controlled substance with intent to distribute but claims the evidence against him was illegally obtained. The district court found that the suitcase was abandoned, leaving Rem with no expectation of privacy and he appeals.

**Before this Court:** Rem urges this court to focus on his own subjective desire to regain possession of the suitcase as proof of his expectation of privacy. This obviously will not work. His subjective "intent" could be any hindsight excuse that fits the situation. We must instead examine the objective facts as the various agents encountered them.

Rem never checked his bag with Amtrak. Instead, he chose to place the suitcase, which had no identification on it, in a public luggage rack on the train, and then abruptly and mysteriously left the train without it before reaching his destination. Rem's failure to pick up the luggage along with several other factors indicated that he had abandoned the luggage and retained no legitimate expectation of a privacy interest in it.

Rem also argues that he only stepped away from the train for a few moments to make a telephone call. The trial court found this testimony to be incredible. The district court believed that Rem was nervous about the Kansas City drug-related arrests made in his car on the train, "jumped off the train" in Chillicothe, Illinois, carrying only a backpack in order to distance himself from the cocaine-laden suitcase, and later thought better of the idea, fearful of his supplier's response to news of the intentionally abandoned crack cocaine.

In addition, the police were aware that prior to leaving the train, Rem had acted peculiarly, raising the suspicions of the train crew. He had also showed unusual concern about the Kansas City arrests. Other facts known about Rem's trip, such as his paying over $700 cash for the ticket just before departure and giving a wrong telephone number, fit the profile of a drug courier. He also took one of his bags when he "jumped off" the train, yet left the bag which held the cocaine in a common area with no identification attached.

**Verdict:** We AFFIRM the district court's decision.

## 7-Fake Policeman

**Court:** United States Court of Appeals for the Seventh Circuit

**Date:** 1990 JUL 03

**Report:** No. 89-2530

**Case number:** 906 F. 2d 284

**Link:** https://merillionpress.com/cases/IV-007.pdf

**Plaintiff (Appellee):** United States of America

**Defendant (Appellant):** Randy L. REIS

**Opinion By:** James T. MOODY, District Judge

**Prior History:** On the afternoon of March 7, 1989, Milwaukee County Sheriff Detectives Richard Blakney and John Hepp were on duty in an unmarked police car, driving on Green Bay Avenue in Milwaukee, Wisconsin, when they pulled up at a stoplight next to a white Dodge Diplomat automobile. Because the Dodge Diplomat had two spotlights attached to it, one on each side of the windshield, and because it was similar to the unmarked police cars used by the City of Milwaukee, the detectives assumed the driver of that car was a police officer working a "special" (i.e., undercover) assignment.

When the light changed, the detectives proceeded forward onto Interstate 43. Once on the freeway, Detective Blakney, who was driving, noticed the Dodge Diplomat was following only two car lengths behind him. Blakney, thinking perhaps the driver wanted to pass him, changed lanes several times. The Dodge Diplomat, however, remained on the detectives' tail, mimicking each of their lane changes and maintaining a distance of only two car lengths behind them.

Blakney, somewhat aggravated, told Hepp that he was going to see what that other driver was up to. They were driving in the right hand lane at the time, and Blakney suddenly veered onto an entrance ramp and hit his brakes. The Dodge Diplomat passed on by. Blakney accelerated and caught up with the Dodge Diplomat, at which point the Dodge Diplomat pulled over into an emergency lane and stopped. The detectives pulled up behind the Dodge Diplomat.

Reis, who was driving the Dodge Diplomat, placed a "fireball" (a rotating red light of the sort used by police officers) on the dashboard of his car and activated it. Reis then stepped out of his car and, in an aggressive and assertive manner, approached Detective Hepp, who had by then gotten out of the other car. According to Hepp's testimony, the following exchange occurred between the two:

Reis: What's your problem?

Detective Hepp: Well, I'm not the driver of the vehicle, but the driver does not appreciate the fact that you are tailgating him so.

Reis: I wasn't tailgating you. You guys made an illegal turn off of Capitol Drive and you're speeding.

Detective Hepp: Who are you?

Reis: Who the fuck are you?

Detective Hepp: Sheriff's Department.

Reis: Show me your identification.

As Hepp reached into his pocket to produce his badge, he ordered Reis to show his own identification.

Upon seeing Hepp's detective's badge and identification, Reis wilted, lost his assertive and aggressive manner, and meekly replied "I'm nobody." He produced his driver's license and, in response to questions from Hepp about the fireball, he stated that he needed it for his work as a private security officer. Hepp walked Reis back to his car.

When Reis got in and deactivated the fireball, Hepp looked into the car and saw a billy club with a side handle sticking out from between the seats and, in a holder on the door, a black "mag" flashlight of a type typically used by police officers. Hepp returned to his car and after running a license check on the car and on Reis (which disclosed no outstanding warrants and also disclosed that Reis was not the registered owner of the car), the officers allowed Reis to leave.

The next day the investigators visited Reis at his home, questioned him for about 10 minutes and searched his car. The detectives found, among other things, a .38 caliber Colt Diamondback revolver. The detectives told Reis he was under arrest. They patted him down, handcuffed him, and returned him to the police car.

This revolver, which had been in a brown paper bag in the glove compartment, led to Reis' indictment on a charge of possession of a firearm by a convicted felon. After a two day trial, a jury found Reis guilty of possession of ammunition and possession of a firearm by a felon.

**Before this Court:** According to the evidence, the detectives had ample reason to believe Reis had violated Wisconsin law, which makes it a crime to "impersonate a peace officer with intent to mislead others into believing that the person is actually a police officer."

The government and Reis each filed objections to the portions of the recommendation that were unfavorable to their respective positions. The district court agreed with the magistrate's findings on the existence of probable cause for arrest and the court also determined that probable cause existed to search the car.

**Verdict:** We find no error in the district court's decision and its verdict is AFFIRMED.

## 8-Playing with Stolen Dynamite

**Court:** Supreme Court of Virginia

**Date:** 1940 FEB 26

**Report:** 2155

**Case number:** 175 Va. 62; 7 S. E. 2d 119

**Link:** https://merillionpress.com/cases/IV-008.pdf

**Plaintiffs (Respondents):** Lillian V. DAUGHERTY, Administratrix, et al.

**Defendants (Appellants):** Jack HIPPCHEN, Who Sues, Etc.

**Opinion by:** Herbert B. GREGORY, Justice

**Prior History:** This case arose out of an injury sustained by Jack Hippchen from the explosion of a dynamite cap procured by him from property owned by Theodore B. Daugherty. Daugherty died while the case was pending in the trial court, and the trial was concluded in the name of his administrators.

Daugherty had leased a piece of property in Arlington, Virginia, to Ella S. Waters, reserving to himself the use of a tool house located near the rear of the property.

Upwards of a dozen children lived in the immediate neighborhood, and were accustomed to romp and play throughout the nearby property. Waters, and her daughter, in the interest of peace and quiet, had occasionally asked them to go elsewhere. Daugherty knew that the children played there, but gave them no warning to stay away.

This shed was used as a repository of various building materials and supplies, including dynamite and dynamite fuse caps. The door of the tool house was left open nearly all the time. The lot on which the shed stood was not fenced on either side, and had only a dilapidated chicken-wire fence at the back. Hence the children had no difficulty in gaining access to the area.

On September 6, 1936, Jack Hippchen eight years of age, his younger brother (7), and another child (5), were playing in the grove and he went into the tool house through the open door. He noticed a tin box on the floor, opened it, and carried away several of the bright metallic objects it contained. These objects were dynamite caps, but their nature was unknown to any of the children.

Jack gave several of them to his playmates and took the rest home. That evening at his home he was picking at one of the caps with a pin when it exploded, causing serious injury. Extensive medical treatment was necessary, including amputation of all fingers on the left hand except the index finger.

Hippchen sued Daugherty and the jury determined that defendant was negligent and that plaintiff was free of contributory negligence. Daugherty appeals.

**Before this Court:** The general rule, even if an immature child is a trespasser, one who stores explosives or has control of other dangerous instrumentalities is not relieved of the duty of exercising a proper degree of care for his protection. If the one who keeps explosives is negligent in leaving them in a place accessible to children who he knows or should know are accustomed to play nearby, the fact that the child is a trespasser will not relieve the owner from liability.

**Verdict:** Finding and no error of law appearing, we must AFFIRM the judgment.

## 9-Self-Inflicted Injury with Stolen Gun

**Court:** United States Court of Appeals for the Fifth Circuit

**Date:** 1992 JUN 15

**Report:** No. 90-6036

**Case number:** 964 F. 2d 376

**Link:** https://merillionpress.com/cases/IV-009.pdf

**Plaintiff (Appellee):** James YARBROUGH, Individually and as Next Friend of R. YARBROUGH, a Minor

**Defendant (Appellant):** STURM, RUGER & Co.

**Opinion By:** Jerry E. SMITH, Circuit Judge

**Prior History:** Robert Yarbrough was thirteen years old when he and fourteen-year-old Rusty Cowart stole a number of guns and other property from at least two houses in their neighborhood. One of those guns was a .44 caliber Sturm, Ruger single action revolver ("the revolver"). Yarbrough and Cowart carried the firearms around in a paper bag, apparently playing with them and attempting to sell them. Although the boys had found the revolver unloaded, they obtained ammunition and carried it fully loaded, with the hammer forward over a live cartridge.

A few days after the theft, while Yarbrough and Cowart were, ironically, walking past the house from which they had stolen the revolver, after failing to sell the stolen firearms, one boy began to hand the bag to the other. The bag either dropped or gave way. The revolver hit the pavement and discharged, wounding Yarbrough in the leg, which eventually was amputated above the knee.

He and his family brought a products liability action against the gun's manufacturer alleging that the gun was defectively designed. After an initial trial in which the jury returned an inconsistent verdict and, upon further consideration, pronounced itself unable to agree on a resolution of the suit, the district court, over Sturm, Ruger's objections, accepted the jury's findings as to liability and impaneled a second jury to determine damages.

The jury returned an initial verdict stating that the revolver was defectively designed and that the defect caused Yarbrough's injuries. It found Sturm, Ruger 60% liable and Yarbrough 40% liable for those injuries awarding a total of $400,000 to Yarbrough.

The district court determined that the inconsistency between the finding of liability and the various damage awards were "inconceivable" and "absolutely unbelievable." The jury deliberated for another four hours before informing the court that it was "unable to agree on a resolution of this lawsuit." The jury foreman stated as follows: On the money that was awarded, everybody has sort of agreed to that particular figure. But there were arguments on how that figured down the line. I mean, that was our argument on the liability end and on the negligence, injury and pain . . . . I think we were trying to come up with a dollar figure that would be reasonable to get him to an even start in life now with perhaps something to give him a boost so he can go on with his life.

Sturm, Ruger appeals, arguing that the jury verdict represented an impermissible compromise.

**Before this Court:** This case may lack the strong examples of improper judicial behavior or juror confusion that were present in some of the cases in which we have found impermissible compromises. Nevertheless, the record reveals substantially more facial evidence that the verdict was compromised, i.e., that the jurors had agreed on an amount of damages they wanted to award Yarbrough and then reached their liability finding based upon that.

The district court sanitizes Yarbrough's conduct, and Sturm, Ruger was deprived of the opportunity to have any fault attributed to it compared to the fault of Yarbrough. In such a context, we cannot say that permitting the introduction of the evidence would unduly prejudice Yarbrough, and hence such evidence should be admitted in the new trial.

**Verdict:** We thus VACATE the judgment and remand for a new trial on all issues.

# 10-Mugger Turned Victim and Millionaire

**Court:** Court of Appeals of the State of New York

**Date:** 1993 APR 05

**Report:** None in original

**Case number:** 81 N.Y. 2d 923

**Link:** https://merillionpress.com/cases/IV-010.pdf

**Plaintiff (Respondent):** Bernard MCCUMMINGS

**Defendant (Appellant):** New York City Transit Authority

**Opinion By:** MEMORANDUM

**Prior History:** On June 28, 1984, McCummings was one of the muggers who attacked Jerome Sandusky, 72 years of age, in the 96th Street-Eighth Avenue line subway station. A team of on-duty undercover transit police officers responded to Sandusky's cry for help and witnessed McCummings rummaging through Sandusky's pockets, as another mugger held him down in a choke hold. Concededly, Sandusky suffered serious injury.

McCummings was caught in the act of committing an all-too-common subway attack on a particularly vulnerable target. He broke off from the attack only to avoid arrest by attempting to flee the crime scene after an alert from his lookout. Officer Rodriguez, who fired his weapon and seriously wounded the perpetrator-turned-plaintiff, testified that McCummings and another of the muggers, only several feet away, lunged at him when he rushed into the crime scene. The officer's attempt to rescue the victim and arrest the culprits consumed only seconds.

As a defendant in the criminal proceedings, McCummings pleaded guilty to attempted robbery.

In his civil action against the City Transit Authority a jury awarded $4.3 million for personal injuries sustained by McCummings, who was permanently paralyzed from the mid-chest down. His spinal cord was severed by a bullet fired by Officer Rodriguez, an employee of the New York City Transit Authority.

McCummings' theory is that Officer Rodriguez was negligent in employing deadly physical force and did not exercise the degree of care which would reasonably be required of a police officer under similar circumstances. The City Transit Authority appeals the lower court's decision.

**Before this Court:** Here the evidence presents sharp factual issues. The key question — whether Rodriguez saw a violent crime in progress — is disputed. McCummings testified that he was unarmed at the time and running away from Officer Rodriguez when he fired, hitting him twice in the back.

While this case approaches the surreal zone involving split-second decisions by public safety employees made in the most dangerous circumstances, the crucial fact is that Officer Rodriguez did not see a mugging and did not know, whether a violent crime had been committed. Deadly force of course may be appropriate in some circumstances to prevent the flight of a violent felon. However, the record in front of us does not support that conclusion.

**Verdict:** Lower court's decision of awards is UPHELD with two sharp dissents.

# CHAPTER V

# FAITH MARKET

*"There's no reason to bring religion into it. I think we ought to have as great a regard for religion as we can, so as to keep it out of as many things as possible." Sean O'Casey (1880-1964) was an Irish dramatist*

The imbroglios in this part are about faith, more often than not, discovered in prison. The issues are complex because from the beginning of time most leading religious teachings forbid sins of any kind. A convicted murderer is not only guilty of a crime, but also violates the basic tenets of a religion. Once locked up, excessively fond attachment to one's faith, its artifacts and rituals become somewhat hypocritical. Cases in this genre avoid this fact with a precision that has to be deliberate.

## 1-No Lawyers Please

**Court:** United States Court of Appeals for the Ninth Circuit

**Date:** 1989 OCT 31

**Report:** 88-3148

**Case number:** 888 F.2d 636

**Link:** https://merillionpress.com/cases/V-001.pdf

**Plaintiff (Respondent):** United States of America

**Defendant (Appellant):** Larry TURNBULL

**Opinion By:** Robert R. BEEZER Circuit Judge

**Prior History:** The United States asserted its authority over Turnbull in matters temporal by charging him with failing to render unto Caesar that which was due, in willful violation of the Internal Revenue Code.

At Turnbull's initial appearance before the magistrate in Fairbanks, Alaska his arraignment was continued for a week. Turnbull then filed pleadings in the district court stating that he did not waive his right to counsel, but that his religious beliefs precluded him from using the services of any member of the bar. Turnbull stated his belief that the teachings of Jesus require him to avoid associating with lawyers.

Turnbull requested that lay persons who shared his beliefs be appointed as his co-counsels. At his arraignment, Turnbull appeared without counsel and stood mute when asked to plead. The court entered a plea of not guilty on his behalf.

Since Turnbull declined to waive his right to counsel, but was unwilling to be represented by anyone the court could appoint, the magistrate appointed Federal Public Defender Michael Karnavas as Turnbull's "standby counsel," who would be available to Turnbull should he desire assistance, and who would be able to take over the defense should Turnbull be unable to continue it himself.

Karnavas did the best he could in the nightmarish position of representing a client who objected to his very presence on religious grounds, and refused to cooperate with him in any way. The jury convicted Turnbull of all the charges, and he was sentenced to one year of imprisonment, probation, costs of prosecution, and special assessments.

**Before this Court:** Turnbull timely appeals his conviction claiming, that the district court's appointment of Karnavas, and its failure to appoint lay counsel, violated his sixth amendment right to the effective assistance of counsel and his first amendment right to the free exercise of religion.

A defendant has a constitutional right to represent himself. A district judge may allow "hybrid representation," in which the accused assumes some of the lawyer's functions. In this case, although Turnbull had the opportunity to participate, he did not.

The court did all it could do under the circumstances to ensure a fair trial. We hold that the state's compelling interest in a fair and orderly trial outweighs Turnbull's objection to counsel. All of his tax protestor arguments were thoroughly considered and correctly rejected in the magistrate's ruling on pre-trial motions. Turnbull's sixth amendment rights were not violated. His right to the free exercise of his religion was burdened, but the burden was excused by a compelling state interest.

**Verdict:** The conviction is AFFIRMED, but the special assessments are VACATED.

## 2-Inmate Starving

**Court:** Commonwealth Court of Pennsylvania

**Date:** 1990 AUG 14

**Report:** None in original

**Case number:** 134 Pa. Commonwealth 415 (1990) 580 A.2d 887

**Link:** https://merillionpress.com/cases/V-002.pdf

**Plaintiffs (Petitioners):** Pennsylvania, DEPARTMENT of PUBLIC WELFARE et al.

**Defendant (Respondent):** Joseph KALLINGER

**Opinion By:** Daniel PELLEGRINI, Judge

**Prior History:** Kallinger, a convicted murderer wants to starve himself to death. On June 22, 1990, he stated, as a result of his vision of Christ in a toilet bowl telling him to join him, that he would refuse to eat or drink, and that he desires to "meet his maker." On June 30, 1990, he agreed to be transferred to Wayne Memorial Hospital in Wayne County, Pennsylvania, in order to have intravenous fluids, including antibiotics, administered to him. However, he continued in his refusal to accept nutrition and other medical treatment.

The Department offered testimony and evidence that if Kallinger is allowed to starve to death, this would have major negative repercussions on the prison and mental health systems; that his death would trigger others to "copy-cat" his actions.

**Before this Court:** We note at the outset that Kallinger is committed to Farview, a mental hospital for the criminally insane. We also recognize that through this action, he may be attempting to manipulate the system in order to stay at the hospital, rather than return to Huntingdon prison. His authorization of his attorneys to enter appearances on his behalf, one to say that he has the right to die, the other to say the state had an obligation to make him stay alive is certainly part of that manipulation.

While Kallinger is sufficiently competent to make a decision to starve himself to death, this is not a "right to die" case in the usual sense. By asking the Commonwealth to stand by and watch him die while it has custody and control over him, he is asking it to aid and abet his suicide.

The Commonwealth of Pennsylvania has an overwhelming interest in the orderly administration of its prison system.

The Commonwealth must maintain prison security, order and discipline. It must also fulfill its duty to provide proper medical care to the inmates, thus preserving life and preventing suicide. These vital interests clearly outweigh any diminished right to privacy held by Kallinger.

**Verdict:** We ORDER that Farview can and must continue to provide appropriate nutrition through a nasogastric tube and appropriate medical care to Joseph Kallinger so long as he continues to refuse nutrition and medical treatment. Kallinger shall remain committed to Farview until such time as the medical and psychiatric staff feel it's appropriate for him to return to a State Correctional Institution.

## 3-Female Chaplin and Male Offenders

**Court:** Court of Appeal, Third District, California

**Date:** 1974 SEP 24

**Report:** No. 14303

**Case number:** 41 Cal. App. 3d 1000; 116 Cal. Rptr. 562

**Link:** https://merillionpress.com/cases/V-003.pdf

**Plaintiff (Appellant):** Louise LONG

**Defendant (Respondent):** California State Personnel Board

**Opinion By:** George E. PARAS, Associate Justice

**Prior History:** Louise Long is an ordained Methodist minister and was denied a position at the DeWitt Nelson Youth Training Center, a facility of the California Youth Authority located in Stockton, California. She indicated an interest in the position of Protestant Chaplain at DeWitt Nelson, but her request was denied due to a 'male-only certification' given that position by the California State Personnel Board.

The DeWitt Nelson Training Center is an institution administered by the California Department of Youth Authority for the purpose of rehabilitating up to 400 young males who are committed there for a broad range of criminal offenses, including rape and other sex crimes. The average age of the inmate population is 19 1/2 years (the spread is 18 to 23 years).

Long challenges the validity of the male-only certification on a number of specific grounds, all focusing upon the concept of sex discrimination in employment.

**Before this Court:** Under the facts of this case, does the male-only certification violate the equal protection clauses of the Federal and California Constitutions? There is no doubt that it discriminates against members of the female sex.

The question narrows down to whether the board has demonstrated a compelling state interest in restricting the job of chaplain at DeWitt Nelson Youth Training Center to men and not women. We conclude that such interest has indeed been demonstrated.

In considering the validity of the classification, there are three separate and distinct interests which must be taken into account.

First there is the interest of a woman who is being discriminated against in presumptive contravention of the equal protection clause of the United States and California Constitutions. This is a most vital interest, and it will not be lightly interfered with, particularly under the guise of 'romantic paternalism.'

'The desire to protect women from the general hazards inherent in many occupations cannot be a valid ground for excluding them from those occupations. . . . Women must be permitted to take their chances along with men when they are otherwise qualified and capable of meeting the requirements of their employment. We can no more justify denial of the means of earning a livelihood on such a basis than we could deny all women drivers' licenses to protect them from the risk of injury by drunk drivers. Such tender and chivalrous concern for the well-being of the female half of the adult population cannot be translated into legal restrictions on employment opportunities for women.'

A second interest is that of the wards at the institution. These are young men who find themselves in difficulty with the penal laws of this state for one reason or another.

The third interest is that of the administrators of DeWitt Nelson who are representatives of the people of this state; more appropriately, the public.

How are these three interests affected by the male-only classification? To analytically answer this question, we assume first that such classification did not exist and that women would be eligible to act as chaplains at DeWitt Nelson. What would the consequences be?

It could reasonably be expected to have three consequences: interference with privacy of the wards, inability to control and discipline the wards, and danger of sexual attack.

We now consider the effect of these consequences upon the three interests concerned with our problem. Is the effect such that constitutionally there is a compelling state interest in making the position unavailable to women, thus eliminating the consequences?

The interests of the public and those of the inmates are substantially different from those of Long and the members of her class. The former interests are so overwhelming as to constitute a compelling state interest in the male-only certification, thus satisfying equal protection standards. The classification is clearly necessary to further this interest.

Long's interest, although itself very important, must yield.

**Verdict:** The judgment is AFFIRMED (With two dissents).

## 4-The Ten Commandments

**Court:** United States District Court, W.D. Wisconsin

**Date:** 1987 JUN 22

**Report:** No. 85-C-850-C

**Case number:** 663 F. Supp. 606

**Link:** https://merillionpress.com/cases/V-004.pdf

**Plaintiffs (Respondents):** FREEDOM FROM RELIGION FOUNDATION Inc., et al.

**Defendants (Appellants):** Patrick ZIELKE, individually and as Mayor of the City of LaCrosse, WI et al.

**Opinion By:** Barbara B. CRABB, District Judge

**Prior History:** LaCrosse City owns and maintains Cameron Park, a public park located within its corporate boundaries. Within that park, the city has displayed a tombstone-like monument on which appear tablets that traditionally symbolize one of the versions of the Bible's Ten Commandments. Written on the tablets is an English translation of one of the versions of the Ten Commandments.

The land comprising Cameron Park was purchased by the city in 1899. The park occupies approximately one acre of land near the downtown area of the city, directly across the street from the building housing the Fraternal Order of the Eagles. The park contains no man-made structures other than the monument and some benches. It has no playground equipment or picnic tables.

In September 1964, representatives of the Eagles approached the City of LaCrosse Park Commission with a proposal to donate a monolith bearing the Ten Commandments, to be located in Cameron Park and to be lighted at night from the roof of the Eagles' building across the street. The park accepted the gift and it now stands a short distance from the sidewalk, plainly visible to anyone. The monolith contains symbols representative of the Jewish and Christian religions.

Freedom From Religion Foundation, Inc. is a Wisconsin non-profit corporation based in Madison, Wisconsin, with a nationwide membership. Its purpose is the promotion of separation of church and state. Together with LaCrosse residents Phyllis Grams, Annie Laurie Gaylor, and Anne Nicol Gaylor they suggest the statue be removed.

They claim the Ten Commandments do not accord with their own religious beliefs and view the existence of the monolith deeply offensive under city auspices as a mandate from the city to them as private citizens, telling them what religious beliefs they should hold.

**Before this Court:** The threshold question in this case is whether plaintiffs have standing to challenge the continued presence of the Ten Commandments monolith. The City contends that none of the individuals has established a distinct and palpable injury that would entitle them or the Foundation to standing.

The fact that the plaintiffs do not like a cross to be displayed on public property—even that they are deeply offended by such a display — does not confer standing, for it is not by itself a fact that distinguishes them from anyone else in the United States who disapproves of such displays. To be made indignant by knowing that government is doing something of which one violently disapproves is not the kind of injury that can support a federal suit.

Accordingly, I find that plaintiffs do not have standing to sue because they have failed to establish any injury other than their belief that the presence of the monolith in the city park violates the Establishment Clause.

**Verdict:** It is ordered that this action is DISMISSED for lack of standing.

## 5-Pipe Ceremony

**Court:** United States Court of Appeals for the Ninth Circuit

**Date:** 1987 SEP 08

**Report:** No. 86-3805

**Case number:** 827 F. 2d 563

**Link:** https://merillionpress.com/cases/V-005.pdf

**Plaintiffs (Appellants):** Earl ALLEN, Donald BARKLEY

**Defendant (Appellees):** Thomas G. TOOMBS, J.C. KEENEY et al.

**Opinion By:** Warren J. FERGUSON, Circuit Judge

**Prior History:** Earl Allen and Donald Barkley are Native Americans presently incarcerated in the Oregon State Penitentiary. OSP is a maximum security prison located in Salem, Oregon. It currently houses about 2000 prisoners, of whom 80-100 are Native Americans. OSP includes the Disciplinary Segregation Unit which is a separate building some distance from the cell block in which the general prison population is housed. Inmates confined in the DSU are those who constitute the greatest security risk, but are allowed a limited number of trips outside the unit to confer with lawyers, for visits with wives or girlfriends, and for medical purposes. DSU staff accompany the inmates on all such trips.

While confined in the DSU, Allen and Barkley repeatedly requested that they be allowed to participate in the ceremonies of their religion: they asked that a Pipe Bearer be allowed to come to the DSU to perform the Pipe Ceremony in front of their cells, and that DSU inmates be allowed access to the Sacred Sweat Lodge. These requests were either ignored or summarily denied. DSU inmates who were adherents of other faiths had access to the rituals of their religion as OSP permitted priests, ministers, and spiritual leaders to perform religious rituals in the unit and allowed inmates to participate in them.

On May 21, 1985, Allen and Barkley filed their complaint. In it they alleged that prison policies denied DSU inmates any opportunity to attend and participate in either the Pipe Ceremony or the Sacred Sweat Lodge, and that these policies therefore abridged their constitutional rights to free exercise of their religion and to equal protection of the laws. The district court dismissed the suit and they appeal.

**Before this Court:** Several well-settled principles govern the court's consideration of constitutional challenges to prison regulations. Incarceration, however, necessarily brings about the withdrawal or limitation of many of the privileges and rights available to non-prisoners. Allen and Barkley ask that inmates confined in the DSU for more than one month be allowed monthly access to the Sweat Lodge.

Prison officials contend, however, that the prohibition on access to the Sweat Lodge is necessary to maintain security in the DSU. In particular, they note that the ceremony requires the use of an axe to chop wood for a fire, red hot stones to heat the lodge, and a pitchfork to transport the stones from the fire to the lodge interior. They argue, that the use of these materials necessarily involves a substantial security risk every time the ceremony is held anywhere in the OSP.

**Verdict:** Since the prison administration is not under an affirmative duty to provide each inmate with the spiritual counselor of his choice, and since the OSP permits outside religious leaders to enter the DSU to address the religious needs of Native American inmates, we conclude that the OSP policy provides a reasonable opportunity for the plaintiffs to exercise their faith, and does not violate the equal protection clause. The decision of the district court is AFFIRMED.

## 6-Clothes Made of a Single Fabric

**Court:** United States Court of Appeals for the Ninth Circuit

**Date:** 1993 JUL 30

**Report:** 91-15427

**Case number:** 1 F. 3d 873

**Link:** https://merillionpress.com/cases/V-006.pdf

**Petitioner (Appellant):** Jason McKinley WARD

**Respondent (Appellee):** Jessie WALSH, Associate Warden of Programs

**Opinion By:** Diarmuid O'SCANNLAIN, Circuit Judge

**Prior History:** Jason McKinley Ward is the only Orthodox Jewish prisoner at Ely State Prison in Ely, Nevada. He brought this suit, arguing that the prison infringes upon his First Amendment right to exercise freely his religion by not providing him with a kosher diet, clothes made of a single fabric, or an Orthodox rabbi; by not allowing him to have candles in his cell; and by refusing to guarantee that he will not be transported on the Sabbath. The district court handed down judgment in favor of the warden after a bench trial and he appeals.

**Before this Court:**

1-Ward argues that he must be allowed to have candles in his cell to observe certain rituals of his religion. The warden asserts that candles pose a significant fire hazard, and thus under no circumstances are prisoners allowed to have them in their cells.

2-Ward argues that the warden violated his First Amendment rights when it transferred him to Ely on the Sabbath. He asks for an injunction to prevent the prison from transporting him on any Sabbath or Jewish holiday, comprising eighty-eight days in the year. He does not contend that the prison intends to transfer him on *every* Sabbath. Because he can observe most Sabbaths, we conclude that he has alternative means of exercising his religion.

3-Ward has requested that the prison provide him with an Orthodox rabbi. He is the only Orthodox Jewish prisoner in the institution, it does not have a rabbi on staff and there were no Orthodox Jewish rabbis within a one hundred mile radius of the prison. Since Ely is the only maximum security institution in the state and Ward is a maximum security prisoner his request to transfer to another prison is moot.

4-Ward argues that the prison has an affirmative obligation to provide him with clothing that is made with only one fiber. The prison has refused to do so, but has informed Ward that he may provide his own clothing, as long as it conforms to the prison dress code. All prisoners are required to wear solid blue denim clothing. We conclude prisons don't have such clothing obligations.

5-Ward argues that the prison is obliged to provide him with a strict kosher diet at the prison's expense "that is certified or deemed religiously acceptable by an outside independent Orthodox Jewish Organization.

The warden provides a pork-free diet to inmates who request it, but complying with every precept of the Kashruth, the Jewish dietary law, may involve significant expense. However, we suggest, it may be possible to comply with the laws in substantial part at minimum cost.

**Verdict:** AFFIRMED in part, REVERSED in part and REMANDED

## 7-Religious Diet in Jail

**Court:** United States Court of Appeals for the Fifth Circuit

**Date:** 1987 JAN 15

**Report:** No number in original

**Case number:** 805 F. 2d 1218

**Link:** https://merillionpress.com/cases/V-007.pdf

**Petitioner (Appellant):** Ed UDEY

**Respondents (Appellees):** B.C. KASTNER, Warden, et al...

**Opinion by:** PER CURIAM

**Prior History:** Ed Udey, a prisoner in the Federal Correctional Institution in Texarkana, asked to be provided with a diet consistent with his sincerely held religious beliefs; he primarily requested organically grown produce washed in distilled water. The federal prison officials declined, he refused to eat the nutritionally adequate food provided, and has since been force-fed through nasal tubes.

The district court found that the inmate's religious beliefs were not sincerely held. In addition, Judge Hall determined, that an undue burden would be imposed on the prison system and that it was not required to do so. He based his findings on four independent grounds:

1 - Total accommodation costs in excess of $15,000.00 per year for *one* person

2 - Hostility from other inmates, theft or "pilferage" of specialty foods, and the potential creation of a black market in such items might result, causing security problems

3 - Administrative costs of providing would include problems of determination, procurement, preparation, health standards, and storage, requiring three or more hours of additional staff time

4 - The potentially disruptive effect on prison order and discipline (from the probable proliferation of claims for specific individual religious dietary requirements)

**Before this Court:** It elects not to review the trial judge's determinations except as regards the potential for proliferation of false claims and the burdens potentially imposed by many individuals on the prison system (4).

When a court can recognize a free exercise claim without inviting numerous additional claims, focusing on the particular consequences of the ruling in the case at bar is appropriate. But when recognizing the claim will predictably give rise to further claims, many of which will undoubtedly be fraudulent or exaggerated, the situation is different.

When numerous claims are likely, recognizing some while rejecting others unavoidably forces courts to pick and choose among religions and to draw subtle distinctions on the basis of criteria with which no governmental unit should ever be entangled.

The trial judge cited testimony stating that the potential for proliferation was a "very strong likelihood" and that the number of religious dietary requests has "grown by leaps and bounds."

**Verdict:** We thus AFFIRM the trial court's decision on this ground only.

## 8-Infringements of Religious Liberty

**Court:** United States Court of Appeals for the Seventh Circuit

**Date:** 1996 APR 03

**Report:** 95-1331 & 94-1849

**Case number:** 80 F. 3d 1175

**Link:** https://merillionpress.com/cases/V-008.pdf

**Plaintiff (Respondent):** John MACK, John L. LIPSCOMB-BEY

**Defendant (Appellant):** Michael F. O'LEARY, Howard A. PETERS, III et al.

**Opinion By:** Richard A. POSNER, Chief Judge

**Prior History:** John Mack and John L. Lipscomb-Bey, two Illinois State prisoners sue prison officials in which they seek damages for alleged infringements of religious liberty.

According to Mack's complaint, during Ramadan in 1992 and 1993 (a 30-day ritual fasting from sunrise to sunset) prison officials refused to accommodate his religious needs and other Muslim inmates of Stateville prison.

The Muslims were forced to have their dinner in the prison's mess hall immediately after the rest of the prison population had had its dinner and the hall was left filthy. As a result the Muslims were unable to prostrate themselves for prayer during the prayer intervals in their meal.

Also, the tables in the mess hall were bolted to the wall, and made it impossible for the diners to sit facing Mecca or to pray in the prescribed close formation. The mess hall also lacked running water; the diners could not perform ritual purification (Wudu), which might become necessary if a diner defiled himself during the meal, for example by breaking wind.

According to Lipscomb-Bey's complaint he belongs to a religious sect known as the Moorish Science Temple of America. "Moors," as the adherents to the sect are known, celebrate January 8, the birthday of their founder, Drew Ali, with a Prophet's Day banquet. The Moors imprisoned in Menard prison requested, but were refused permission to have such a banquet.

Both suits have been dismissed by a district court.

**Before this Court:** We have consolidated the two appeals, which require us to consider the meaning of the key term "substantially burden a person's exercise of religion."

There is a danger of putting judges into the awkward position of taking sides in religious schisms, for it requires the court to separate center from periphery in religious observances. A court should be able to figure out which religious practices are important to their practitioners and which are not, without having to determine who in the religion is authorized to lay down dogma and what the content of that dogma is.

In Mack's case it is fairly obvious that tables in prison mess halls have to be bolted to the floor, since they would be formidable weapons in a prison riot. His other claim, that the Muslim prisoners' equal protection of the law were violated by officials (by being much more accommodating of the needs of Christian prisoners) is valid.

In Lipscomb-Bey's case an evidentiary hearing and the national leader of the Moors, Grand Sheikh Robert Love-El, testified that a Prophet's Day banquet was an important but not a required rite of the Moorish

Science Temple. Officials of Menard testified that it would be utterly impractical to allow each of the 300 denominations to have its own feast day. Menard cannot sponsor 300 banquets a year, or even 100.

Its grouping of the denominations into four umbrella groups for purposes of festal occasions is all that the law could reasonably be thought to require of so religiously heterogeneous a prison.

**Verdict:** The judgment in Mack's case (No. 95-1331) is AFFIRMED in part (the part based on the Eleventh Amendment), but is otherwise REVERSED and his case remanded for further proceedings consistent with this opinion. The judgment in Lipscomb-Bey's case (No. 94-1849) is AFFIRMED in its entirety.

## 9-Spiritual Injuries

**Court:** Superior Court of New Jersey, Appellate Division

**Date:** 2011 APR 18

**Report:** A-3059-09T2

**Case number:** A-3059-09T2

**Link:** https://merillionpress.com/cases/V-009.pdf

**Plaintiffs (Appellants):** Durgesh GUPTA et al.

**Defendant (Respondent):** ASHA ENTERPRISES, L.L.C. d/b/a Moghul Express & Catering Co.

**Opinion By:** Edith K. PAYNE, Judge Advocate Division

**Prior History:** On August 10, 2009 Durgesh Gupta and Sharad Agarwal placed an order for vegetarian samosas at Moghul Express, a restaurant located in Edison, New Jersey. When they placed the order they advised Mogul Express's employee that they required vegetarian samosas, because they were being purchased for a group of sixteen individuals who were strict Hindu vegetarians.

The two men were informed that they should not be concerned because the restaurant did not make meat-filled samosas. One-half hour later, the men returned to the restaurant to pick up their order and were handed a tray that had written on its top "VEG samosas," and they were again assured of the vegetarian nature of the food.

After munching on some of the samosas, some members became concerned that the samosas might contain meat. Although they continued eating for a time, eventually they returned the remaining samosas to Moghul Express for verification. Once there, Moghul Express's employee advised them that the samosas, indeed, contained meat. As a consequence of eating the meat-filled samosas, they were spiritually injured.

Hindu vegetarians believe that if they eat meat, they become involved in the sinful cycle of inflicting pain, injury and death on God's creatures, and that it affects the karma and dharma, or purity of the soul. Hindu scriptures teach that the souls of those who eat meat can never go to God after death, which is the ultimate goal for Hindus.

The Hindu religion does not excuse accidental consumption of meat products. One, who commits the religious violation of eating meat, knowingly or unknowingly, is required to participate in a religious ceremony at a site located along the Ganges River in Haridwar, Uttranchal, India, to purify himself.

The damages sought by the group included compensation for the emotional distress they suffered, as well as economic damages they would incur by virtue of having to participate in the required religious cleansing ceremony in India.

The lower court judge dismissed the claims and they appeal.

**Before this Court:** Plaintiffs claim that they have sufficiently pleaded ascertainable loss by seeking damages in the amount of the cost of a trip to India to undergo a purification ritual. However, what they are seeking is the cost of cure for an alleged spiritual injury that cannot be categorized as either a loss of moneys or property. In fact they have not pled or provided evidence of any "loss of moneys or property." Indeed, it would be difficult for them to do so, since unrefuted evidence demonstrates that, following recognition by the restaurant of its mistake, Moghul Express furnished an order of conforming samosas to them without cost.

We next address claims of negligence resulting in spiritual injury and negligent infliction of emotional distress. Those claims were dismissed by the motion judge and we agree. The judge determined that she would "not create new laws that protect religious dietary concerns when there is no precedent for such an act."

We decline to address at this time Moghul Express's argument that any liability on its part is limited to the claims of the person who placed the order for the samosas, regarding the resolution of that matter to be dependent on future discovery.

**Verdict:** AFFIRMED in part; REVERSED in part and remanded.

# CHAPTER VI

# FREQUENT FILERS

*"Listen, we all have to agree that there is too much litigation going on in this world. But every year it seems to multiply tenfold. Why can't we stop it? Well, it's because the lawmakers in Congress and the Senate are almost all lawyers, too!" James Belushi is an American humorist*

Adorning the next pages are examples of pure legal hedonism, as a caricature of the justice system. The practice of filing assembly-line complaints by the legally infatuated – most, if not all – come from prisons. The skimpiest of complaints coupled with dogged determination to clog the system. And given enough time and there is plenty of that, it's a chance to be in the record books. The karmic beauty, of course, is that for little or no cost, the filer will be known the world over for fifteen minutes of dubious glory.

## 1-Serial Litigant Disbarred

**Court:** Supreme Court of Illinois

**Date:** 1982 DEC 17

**Report:** 56759

**Case number:** 93 Ill. 2d 450 (1982); 444 N.E. 2d 143

**Link:** https://merillionpress.com/cases/VI-001.pdf

**Plaintiff (Complainants):** ADMINISTRATOR of the Attorney Registration and Disciplinary Commission

**Defendant (Respondent):** Syed M.J. Iqbal JAFREE

**Opinion By:** PER CURIAM

**Prior History:** Jafree was admitted to practice law in Illinois in 1972, and within a short time was appointed an assistant Attorney General for this State. His employment was terminated in 1973, at which time he filed a civil rights action against the former Attorney General, William Scott. The suit was eventually dismissed for want of prosecution.

Subsequently, he filed a number of appeals and other lawsuits in Federal courts, naming as defendants William Scott, certain judges, lawyers, lay people, and a former President of the United States. He sued both in his own name and on behalf of others. He also sued unnamed parties under the fictitious name "Judgeso N. Thetake."

On the basis of these facts and the numerous exhibits introduced into evidence, the Commission found that he filed approximately 30 frivolous lawsuits, 15 groundless appeals, and numerous vexatious claims before State agencies. Some of them:

1- Financially Poor People ex rel. Jafree, Asian American Community Legal Aid Clinic and Trees of the United States of America v. Executive Committee of the United States District Court and the United States of America minus Jafree et al.

2- He sued several individuals for breaching the United States Treaty of Friendship with Pakistan.

3- He filed a complaint against William Scott with the Pollution Control Board alleging pollution of the mind and contamination of the air with character assassination.

In 1977, this court granted the Administrator's motion for an order requiring Jafree to submit to a mental examination. He refused and was suspended from the practice of law until such time as he complied with the order. He eventually submitted to the examination and was permitted to resume his legal practice.

**Before this Court:** The Administrator of the Attorney Registration and Disciplinary Commission filed a three-count complaint before the Commission charging Syed Jafree with professional misconduct. The complaint alleged that Jafree instituted numerous defamatory and frivolous lawsuits, appeals and administrative actions. The Hearing Board recommended that he be disbarred, and the Review Board adopted that recommendation.

**Verdict:** We cannot help but conclude that Jafree is incapable of conforming his conduct to an acceptable standard. His unprofessionalism is an abuse of the privilege to practice law and clearly tends to bring the judicial system and legal profession into disrepute. Accordingly, we adopt the recommendations of the hearing panel and Review Board and ORDER that Jafree be disbarred.

## 2-Can't Take No for an Answer

**Court:** United States Court of Appeals for the Seventh Circuit

**Date:** 1986 FEB 25

**Report:** No. 85-1987

**Case number:** 784 F. 2d 777

**Link:** https://merillionpress.com/cases/VI-002.pdf

**Plaintiff (Appellant):** Geraldine G. CANNON

**Defendants (Appellees):** LOYOLA University of Chicago, et al.

**Opinion By:** William J. BAUER, Circuit Judge

**Prior History:** Mrs. Cannon applied for admission to the 1975 entering class at seven Illinois area medical schools. Each of the schools denied her application.

The present appeal marks the thirteenth time she has been before the court to obtain judicial relief from the decisions of the universities not to admit her to medical school ten years ago. Her claims run the gamut of sex-discrimination, age-discrimination (she was 39 years-old at the time), courts lacking jurisdiction, violations of equal protection clause and others.

Her filing of the suits against the universities range from 3-5 years and the district court found that these were inexcusable delays showing at least a lack of diligence.

**Before this Court:** Mrs. Cannon's ten year history of litigation demonstrates her penchant for harassing the defendants. The interest of a medical school in selecting its student body is well established. Academic freedom, though not a specifically enumerated constitutional right, long has been viewed as a special concern of the First Amendment. The freedom of a university to make its own judgments as to education includes the selection of its student body.

Where a violation of Rule 11 (suit is filed in good faith) occurs, the court is expressly given the power to award the opposing party his costs, including attorney fees, incurred by reason of the violation. It is only fair that Mrs. Cannon bear the attorney fees and costs plus, the costs of this appeal that her propensity for litigation has caused non-profit institutions of higher learning for far too long.

**Verdict:** For the foregoing reasons the judgment of the district court is AFFIRMED.

## 3-Breaking the Laws of God

**Court:** United States Court of Appeals for the Fourth Circuit

**Date:** 1997 FEB 04

**Report:** No. 96-6089

**Case number:** 106 F. 3d 553

**Link:** https://merillionpress.com/cases/VI-003.pdf

**Plaintiff (Appellant):** Danny Alan VESTAL

**Defendants (Appellees):** Bill CLINTON; James B. HUNT

**Opinion By:** PER CURIAM

**Prior History:** Danny Alan Vestal is before us as plaintiff/appellant for the seventh time within a year. All of Vestal's claims in the past have been totally frivolous. This appeal is no exception. Vestal now argues that the President of the United States and the Governor of North Carolina are "breaking the Laws of God" by swearing oaths on the New Testament upon taking office.

Vestal concludes that, as a result of this action by President Clinton and Governor Hunt, Vestal is "suffering undue punishment and distress because the defendants are breaking the Law of God in speaking and conspiring against the Holy Commandments resulting in plagues upon this nation and my situation." (Internal Biblical citations omitted).

Vestal adds, for good measure, that "the defendants should be visiting the prisons." Because of the utter frivolousness of this appeal, we impose sanctions upon Vestal pursuant to Federal Rule of Appellate Procedure 38.

Vestal began his pro se legal career claiming that during his incarceration at Davidson Correctional Center in Lexington, North Carolina, he was subjected to cruel and unusual punishment because he was denied his request to visit his terminally ill grandmother. Vestal claimed that these alleged violations entitled him to $3,000,000 in damages.

Next, he brought an action claiming that understaffing at the Davidson Correctional Center created stress and overwork for guards.

Followed by his next challenge, claiming the amenities enjoyed by other state and federal inmates, such as better televisions, computers for personal use, private rooms, and air conditioning are superior to conditions he currently enjoys.

Vestal later claimed that as a member of the prison road squad he was denied access to certain educational programs which were available to other prisoners, thus leaving his rehabilitation needs unsatisfied.

**Before this Court:** Vestal's current effort to obtain adjudication of "God's Law" in this court is another example of his disregard for the limited resources (and limited jurisdiction) of this court. Despite the repeated and consistent holdings by this court and the district court that Vestal's claims are frivolous, he continues to file such suits.

**Verdict:** Because of the utter frivolousness of this appeal, we impose the following sanctions upon Vestal: We award the amount of $500 to the appellees, as we have frequently done in similar circumstances.

## 4-Prison Nurses Said "No"

**Court:** United States Court of Appeals for the Fourth Circuit

**Date:** 1997 FEB 04

**Report:** No. 96-6116

**Case number:** 105 F. 3d 952

**Link:** https://merillionpress.com/cases/VI-004.pdf

**Plaintiff (Appellant):** Robert Lee BROCK, a/k/a Two Souls Walker

**Defendant (Appellee):** Ronald ANGELONE

**Opinion By:** PER CURIAM

**Prior History:** Robert Lee Brock, a.k.a. Two Souls Walker, a Virginia inmate, lodged twenty-nine appeals before this court in 1995-96 alone, making him one of, if not the most frequent litigants in this circuit.

Brock has a history of filing frivolous appeals in an apparent effort to undermine the legal system that incarcerated him. Over the course of his litigious history, Brock has complained about all aspects of his legal treatment and prison conditions including; food, clothing, access to and the poor condition of the prison's law library, mail delivery, hot water, and improper placement of a mirror for the handicapped, phones, canteen needs, art supplies, mental stress, and the price of coffee.

One of Brock's earlier appeals, filed when Brock only had 30 claims pending in various courts, requested "$1 million dollars for mental cruelty and cruel and unusual punishment" because the prison nurses said "no" when Brock requested that his meals contain "extra meat" or "vitamins in place of vegetables."

Brock's current claim is typical of the claims with which he has burdened the courts of this circuit over the past several years. Here, Brock alleges that he is "either being poisoned or experimented on" because one of the ingredients listed on the side of the bottle of pancake syrup served at his prison is propylene glycol, which petitioner notes is also used in deodorant and antifreeze. Brock attempted to evade the pre-filing judicial review imposed on him by the District Court in the Eastern District of Virginia by filing his action in the Western District of Virginia. This, even though Brock stated in his complaint that he was aware the Western District did not have jurisdiction over his claim.

Even though Brock's claim on its face is at best fanciful or delusional, and more likely simply a deliberate affront to the judicial system, the district court thoroughly researched Brock's claim and found it to be frivolous. Still, he appeals.

**Before this Court:** None of Brock's allegations have ever been found by any court to have any merit. Because Brock's repeated, frivolous claims have placed a significant burden on this court, as well as on the district court. We ordered Brock on May 16, 1996, to explain us why he should not be sanctioned for filing this most recent appeal.

**Verdict:** Having reviewed his response, we hereby impose sanctions upon Brock; we AWARD the amount of $500 payable to the Warden of the Haynesville Correctional Center. Additionally, he is barred from filing any further civil appeals in this court until these monetary sanctions are paid, and unless a district court judge certifies that his claim is not frivolous.

# 5-Weighty Issues

**Court:** United States Court of Appeals for the Fourth Circuit

**Date:** 1997 FEB 04

**Report:** No. 95-8587

**Case number:** 106 F. 3d 556

**Link:** https://merillionpress.com/cases/VI-005.pdf

**Plaintiff (Appellant):** Frederick Lynwood FOLEY

**Defendants (Appellees):** Ms. C. FIX; Sergeant SANTIAGO; Ms. SWISHER

**Opinion By:** PER CURIAM

**Prior History:** Foley, an inmate in the Augusta Correctional Center (ACC), has now brought his twenty-third appeal in this court in just over a year. The one characteristic that all of these appeals have in common is that we have consistently, and summarily, affirmed the district court's dismissals.

The district court has warned Foley on more than one occasion that he would be subject to sanctions if he continued to harass correctional officers by filing frivolous claims that those officers have taken his personal property without due process of law. Notwithstanding this warning, Foley has again brought suit claiming, that Sgt. Santiago took his personal property without due process of law.

Foley's most recurrent allegation is that prison officials have taken his property. He has claimed that officials have stolen items such as earplugs, bubble gum, mayonnaise packets, and cheese spread.

Because Foley continued to bring claims for property deprivation, the district court notified Foley "that he may be sanctioned for filing frivolous pleadings if he continued to bring property deprivation claims" in the district court.

Undeterred, Foley brought a wrongful conviction claim because the reporting officer said that the strips of cloth which gave rise to Foley's destruction of state property charge came from a pillow, when Foley had instead (as evidenced by Foley's own complaint) cut them from a mattress. The district court dismissed this claim as frivolous.

It also denied as "utterly frivolous" Foley's request for a temporary restraining order against a correctional officer who allegedly "rakes through Foley's bag of Rolaids and his legal papers, looking for contraband." The district court noted that the request had "the ring of a kindergartner tattling to his teacher."

Similarly, Foley brought a claim alleging that the broken light over the sink in his cell gave him insufficient light to floss his teeth and shave.

**Before this Court:** Foley's frivolous appeals of other claims bolster our conclusion that sanctions are not only appropriate, but also necessary to stem his activities. It is obvious that the mere threat of sanctions has not caused Foley to restrain himself.

When he claimed that correctional officers retaliated against him for his previously filed lawsuits by requiring him to stand next to his bed for "count" (a procedure in which prison officials count the inmates), Foley had to admit that he stayed up nights writing new petitions and therefore was too tired to get up in the morning for "count." This prompted the district court to quip, "Although the court recognizes Foley's heavy caseload, no constitutional rights are implicated by requiring Foley to stand next to his bed in the morning."

**Verdict:** Having reviewed Foley's response to our order, we now conclude that the appeal was indeed "frivolous," and therefore impose the following sanctions: In lieu of particularized fees and costs, we AWARD the amount of $500 to the appellees and ordering that Foley be barred from filing any further appeals in this court until (1) the sanctions awarded by this court and the district court are fully paid; and (2) a district court certifies his appeal as having some arguable merit.

## 6-Hallucinating Mind

**Court:** U.S. District Court for the Eastern District of Pennsylvania

**Date:** 1992 OCT 26

**Report:** Nos. 92-5825, 92-5885 to 92-5887, 92-5889, 92-5890, 92-5982, 92-5891 to 92-5893 and 92-5981

**Case number:** 806 F. Supp. 1186

**Link:** https://merillionpress.com/cases/VI-006.pdf

**Plaintiff (Appellant):** Joseph MALLON

**Defendant (Appellee):** John R. PADOVA

**Opinion By:** Eduardo C. ROBRENO, District Judge

**Prior History:** Joseph Mallon, who purports to be God and the President of the United States ("Mallon"), has filed fourteen lawsuits in this Court, eleven of which are still pending. In all cases, Mallon has sought to proceed in *forma pauperis.*

The cases were transferred to my docket by Order of Chief Judge Louis C. Bechtle dated October 23, 1992. Among the individuals and entities named by Mallon as defendants in the various lawsuits are the United States, the U.S. Attorney's Office, Philadelphia, Harvard Law School, the People of England and the rock group the Pretenders.

I have reviewed the filing of papers in each case and find each action to be frivolous in that each lacks any arguable basis in law or in fact. Regardless of whether the filings are malicious or simply the result of a hallucinating mind, the cumulative effect of their frequency in number and proximity in time is to force the court to spend valuable resources in time and personnel disposing of them.

Based on this recent experience, there is no reason to believe this pattern of filing will not continue in the future.

**Before this Court:** No legally cognizable thread or grievance appears to run through this body of multiple filings. Because I find that Mallon is intentionally abusing the judicial system and will continue to do so unless restrained, I have entered on this date a temporary restraining order enjoining the filing of any paper purporting to start a new action unless each such paper receives prior approval by this Court.

Such approval shall be predicated upon Mallon filing a certification or attestation stating:

(1) That the claims he wishes to present are new claims never before raised and disposed of on the merits by any federal courts,

(2) That he believes the facts alleged in his complaint to be true, and

(3) That he knows of no reason to believe his claims are foreclosed by controlling law.

Failure to certify or in case of a false certification, Mallon may punished by contempt.

**Verdict:** The Clerk is directed to mark any papers submitted by Mallon as "Received," and shall direct same to my attention. It is so ORDERED.

## 7-Weary of Mr. Franklin

**Court:** United States Court of Appeals for the Ninth Circuit

**Date:** 1984 OCT 23

**Report:** Nos. 83-3939 to 83-3978

**Case number:** 745 F. 2d 1221

**Link:** https://merillionpress.com/cases/VI-007.pdf

**Plaintiff (Appellant):** Harry FRANKLIN

**Defendants (Appellees):** Ms. MURPHY and Hoyt CUPP, et al.

**Opinion By:** Arthur L. ALARCON, Circuit Judge

**Prior History:** Harry Franklin is a prisoner in the Oregon State Penitentiary. By 1980, he had filed and paid fees in 37 cases concerning his treatment in prison. On May 29, 1980, the district court dismissed 33 of these cases. By his own count, he has filed over 100 separate actions in the District Court of Oregon.

Franklin's filings have been extraordinary. A large portion of his filings have been undeniably frivolous, such as claims that his civil rights were violated by: a television announcer calling an 18-wheel truck a 14-wheeler; a prison officer over-watering the lawn; the prison's use of aluminum pans for baking desserts; and a federal regulation requiring seat-belts for automobiles but not for horses. The district court is understandably weary of Mr. Franklin.

Franklin sued the prison psychiatrist and the security sergeant for denying him exercise, while he was in the Psychiatric Security Unit. He sued an employee of the County Clerk's Office, the prison librarian, for allegedly preventing him from timely filing a civil rights complaint.

Franklin sued Yamhill County and a jail employee, for violating his civil rights by allegedly removing and copying his personal papers. The court dismissed the suit because they removed Franklin's papers at his request and did not copy them.

**Before this Court:** This appeal involves a district court's dismissal of 41 actions filed by Harry Franklin and attempting to put an end to his abuse of the court's IFP (*in forma pauperis* = court fees waived) procedure. The district court entered an order limiting Franklin to six in IFP filings per year. The court's order is an extraordinary sanction as are Franklin's filings.

We recognize that Franklin may not have served the correct defendants in this action because he was confused by the large number of lawsuits he had pending. However, even a pro se litigant must take some responsibility in the pursuit of his legal actions. Franklin may not rely solely on the allegations in his pleadings; he must present some "significant probative evidence tending to support the complaint."

**Verdict:** Dismissal is a harsh penalty and should be imposed only in extreme circumstances. An order limiting a prisoner's access to the courts must be designed to preserve his right to adequate, effective and meaningful access, while protecting the court from abuse. We agree with the district court that six free filings per year should be adequate access, but we cannot be certain that it will.

AFFIRMED in part, REVERSED in part.

## 8-Defective Ribbons

**Court:** Circuit Court for Washington County, Maryland - Civil System

**Date:** 2010 MAR 24

**Report:** None in original

**Case number:** 21C00010199

**Link:** https://merillionpress.com/cases/VI-008.pdf

**Plaintiff (Respondent):** Kelvin J. MILES

**Defendant (Appellant):** BROTHER International Corp.

**Opinion By:** M. Kenneth LONG Jr., Judge

**Prior History:** Kelvin J. Miles, an inmate serving a 45-year sentence for kidnapping and assault at Maryland Correctional Institution in Hagerstown MD, filed suit against Brother International Corp. of Bartlett, Tenn., a typewriter manufacturer.

Miles claims he would have won his parole hearing, if the typewriter ribbon hadn't broken each time while typing his parole papers. Miles said he purchased the typewriter on Jan. 18, 1999 and several ribbons for it on different dates, but he found each ribbon defective, as soon as he inserted it and began typing.

Miles is suing for $29,000 for damages, which includes $8,000 of his attorney's fees.

**Before this Court:** In light of Mile's pattern of repeatedly filing frivolous post-judgment motions and doing so despite that his case was dismissed with prejudice (cannot be filed again) several years ago and the undue burden, attorney's fees, and expense that this has caused Brother, his current filing is denied.

**Verdict:** ORDERED that Mile's Motion (for Reconsideration, etc.) it is hereby ORDERED that Brother shall not be expected or required to file any response or opposition to any future motion filed by Miles in this case unless otherwise directed by the Court, and ORDERED that Brother's many earlier filings in response or opposition to Miles' previous motions shall be treated as Brother's response or opposition to any future motion filed by Miles in this case.

## 9-Obduracy

**Court:** United States Court of Appeals for the Seventh Circuit

**Date:** 1995 JAN 11

**Report:** Nos. 94-3287, 94-3435

**Case number:** 45 F. 3d 185

**Link:** https://merillionpress.com/cases/VI-009.pdf

**Plaintiff (Appellee):** SUPPORT SYSTEMS INTERNATIONAL Inc.

**Defendant (Appellant):** Richard MACK

**Opinion By:** PER CURIAM

**Prior History:** Richard Mack was sued in a Wisconsin state court by SSI Inc. over a piece of machinery. He was fined $100 by the court for his legal tactics right at the get go, payable to his adversary SSI. Mack did not pay but instead created a Wisconsin corporation having the same name as his adversary and advised the district court that he had paid the sanction, as ordered, to SSI–but he meant his own corporation, though he did not tell the court this.

When the district court learned of his fraud, it increased the sanction to $500, and Mack, again without complying, appealed to this court and asked us to strike the appearance of the law firm that represents his adversary, on the ground that SSI had fired the firm.

But Mack was referring to his SSI, whereas the law firm represents the SSI that had sued him in state court.

This move didn't work, but Mack renewed his filings again and we directed him to show cause why we should not summarily affirm the district court's sanctions order and impose additional sanctions. Mack did not respond and on July 21, 1994, we summarily affirmed the district court's order and imposed an additional sanction on Mack (again payable to his adversary) of $5,000.

He has also taken to sending abusive letters to judges of this court. And he has yet to pay a cent of the sanctions imposed on him.

**Before this Court:** Many pleadings and other papers filed in this court as in other courts have no legal merit whatsoever; they are frivolous, sometimes vicious, not infrequently demented. Most of these frivolous filings are by people who are not assisted by counsel or knowledgeable in the law. Some of these people find it very difficult to understand or, if they understand, accept the orders that this court issues terminating their frivolous litigation. They keep on filing.

When monetary sanctions are levied on them for their obduracy, they refuse to pay. Their repetitive filings have no greater merit than their original filings, but the cumulative effect in clogging the processes of the court and in burdening judges and staff to the detriment of litigants having meritorious cases is significant. This case illustrates the problem and challenges us to be imaginative in its solution.

That is, we will not impede him from making any filings necessary to protect him from imprisonment or other confinement, but we will not let him file any paper in any other suit in the federal courts of this circuit until he pays the money he owes.

**Verdict:** The clerks of the federal courts of this circuit are hereby ORDERED to return unfiled any papers submitted to these courts either directly or indirectly (as by mail to individual judges) by or on behalf of Richard Mack, with the exceptions noted in the opinion. The injunction issued by the district court, though of limited significance in light of our order, is AFFIRMED.

# CHAPTER VII

# LUNACY

*"Perhaps a lunatic was simply a minority of one. At one time it had been a sign of madness to believe that the Earth goes round the Sun; today, to believe the past is inalterable. He might be alone in holding that belief, and if alone, then a lunatic. But the thought of being a lunatic did not greatly trouble him; the horror was that he might also be wrong." George Orwell (1903-1950) was an English novelist*

This family of entanglements is a rich source of the inanities of modern society of flawed men and laws. Intermittent insanity once believed to be related to phases of the moon, the litigation environment gives credence to unlimited hypothesis, at times taking on a Jerry Springer vibe. Exceedingly weak arguments and spurious correlations coupled with vivid hallucinations are the hallmarks. At times reasoning might sound strictly from outer space, aside from speculation (which is all it is).

## 1-Cause of Misery: Satan & His Staff

**Court:** United States District Court, W. D. Pennsylvania

**Date:** 1971 DEC 03

**Report:** Misc. No. 5357

**Case number:** 54 F.R.D. 282 (W.D. Pa. 1971)

**Link:** https://merillionpress.com/cases/VII-001.pdf

**Plaintiff (Respondent):** United States ex rel. Gerald MAYO

**Defendant (Appellant):** SATAN and his Staff

**Opinion by:** Gerald J. WEBER, District Judge

**Prior History:** Gerald Mayo, a 22 year old inmate at Western Penitentiary in Pittsburgh, filed this claim in which Mayo alleged that "Satan has on numerous occasions caused him misery and unwarranted threats against his will, that Satan has placed deliberate obstacles in his path and has caused his downfall and had therefore "deprived him of his constitutional rights," allegedly prohibited under several sections of the United States Code. Mayo filed *in forma pauperis* - that is, he would not be able to afford the costs associated with his lawsuit and that these costs should be waived.

**Before this Court:** We feel that the application to file and proceed *in forma pauperis* must be denied. Even if Mayo's complaint reveals a prima facie recital of the infringement of the civil rights of a citizen of the United States, the Court has serious doubts that the complaint reveals a cause of action upon which relief can be granted by the court. We question whether he may obtain personal jurisdiction over Satan and his Staff in this judicial district. The complaint contains no allegation of residence in this district.

We note that Mayo has failed to include with his complaint the required form of instructions for the United States Marshal for directions as to service of process (Contacting Satan and his Staff).

**Verdict:** For the foregoing reasons we must exercise our discretion to refuse the prayer of plaintiff to proceed. It is ordered that the complaint be given a miscellaneous docket number and leave to proceed *in forma pauperis* be DENIED.

## 2-Eye Injected With Radium Electric Beam

**Court:** United States District Court, D. New Jersey

**Date:** 1976 MAY 06

**Report:** Civil No. 76-262

**Case number:** 412 F. Supp. 413

**Link:** https://merillionpress.com/cases/VII-002.pdf

**Plaintiff (Respondent):** Ned SEARIGHT

**Defendant (Appellant):** State of New Jersey

**Opinion by:** Vincent P. BIUNNO, District Judge

**Prior History:** The complaint says that in October, 1962, Searight was taken to the Eye, Ear and Speech Clinic in Newark, while in custody, and that the State of New Jersey there unlawfully injected him in the left eye with a radium electric beam. As a result, he claims that someone now talks to him on the inside of his brain. He asks money damages of $12 million.

**Before this Court:** The State has moved to dismiss for failure to state a claim on the ground, if otherwise valid, is barred by the statute of limitations. The incident is said to have happened in October, 1962, and the complaint was filed in February, 1976. Absent an Act of Congress (there is none), the *Lex loci* (law of the locality) governs. The applicable New Jersey statute allows 2 years after the cause of action accrues to file suit. Thus, suit was filed here more than 13 years after the statute had run out.

The court observes that for other considerations, equally obvious, it lacks jurisdiction to entertain the claim, and so may also dismiss for that reason. Ordinary tort claims, though cast in terms of civil rights claims, but which do not rise to constitutional levels, are not within the jurisdiction of the district courts.

The allegations, of course, are of facts which, if they exist, are not yet known to man. Just as Mr. Houdini has so far failed to establish communication from the spirit world (See E. L. Doctorow, 'Ragtime', pp. 166-169, Random House, 1974), so the decades of scientific experiments and statistical analysis have failed to establish the existence of 'extrasensory perception' (ESP).

But, taking the facts as pleaded, and assuming them to be true, they show a case of presumably unlicensed radio communication, a matter which comes within the sole jurisdiction of the Federal Communications Commission.

And even aside from that, Searight could have blocked the broadcast to the antenna in his brain simply by grounding it. See, for example, *Ghirardi, 'Modern Radio Servicing', First Edition, p. 572, ff. (Radio & Technical Publishing Co., New York, 1935).* Just as delivery trucks for oil and gasoline are 'grounded' against the accumulation of charges of static electricity, so on the same principle Searight might have pinned to the back of a trouser leg a short chain of paper clips, so that the end would touch the ground and prevent anyone from talking to him inside his brain.

But these interesting aspects need not be decided here. It is enough that the bar of the statute of limitations clearly appears from the face of the complaint and, independently follows, that the court lacks jurisdiction.

**Verdict:** The complaint will be DISMISSED with prejudice.

## 3- Kent © Norman

**Court:** U.S. District Court D. Oregon

**Date:** 1982 JUN 09

**Report:** Civ. No: 81-1054

**Case number:** 95 F.R.D. 476

**Link:** https://merillionpress.com/cases/VII-003.pdf

**Plaintiff (Respondent):** Kent © NORMAN

**Defendant (Appellant):** Ronald REAGAN

**Opinion By:** James A. REDDEN, District Judge

**Prior History:** In this action, Kent © Norman seeks redress of grievances. I previously dismissed the action as frivolous. A panel of the Ninth Circuit disagreed and reversed. A brief summary of the contents of this file may be helpful in understanding my present decision to dismiss this case for lack of prosecution.

There are numerous defendants and claims. The first defendant appears to be Ronald Reagan, who, in terms of Norman's "amendment complaint," has caused him great vexation:

Norman alleges that defendant Reagan has acted with deliberate, reckless and nefarious disregard of his constitutional rights, in this, to Wit:

1) Defendant caused "civil death" without legislation.

2) Defendant allowed plaintiff to suffer irrepairable [sic] harm and neglect.

3) Defendant has acted with redundance [sic] and malicious conduct in neglecting plaintiff.

4) Defendant allowed numerous abuses of plaintiff's person, property, and liberty while governor of California and president.

5) Defendant Reagan has deprived of his right to vote and caused, either directly or indirectly, arrests upon false, incorrect, or misleading information.

6) Plaintiff has no adequate remedy at law to redress these wrongs without due course of process.

Norman's name apparently includes the copyright sign.

There are also a number of parking tickets in the file. The plaintiff apparently demands a jury trial in federal court for the parking fines assessed by Multnomah County. Norman also seeks an order requiring the Interstate Commerce Commission to investigate White Line Fevers From Mars, which is succinctly referred to elsewhere in the file as "W.L.F.F.M."

This defendant is not, despite the name, of genuine extraterrestrial origin, but is apparently a fruit company which shipped marijuana and cocaine in "fruit boxes" for Mother's Day. Norman's trucking license was suspended by the Interstate Commerce Commission as a result of some incident, and punitive damages against Reagan and the Secretary of the Treasury for withholding of the SSI payments.

There are also certain other claims which the court is at a loss to characterize, and can only describe. There is included in the file a process receipt which bears the "Received" stamp of the Supreme Court of the United States. On this form are the notations, apparently written by Norman; "Taxes due" and "D.C. Circuit was green" as well as "Rule 8...why did you return my appeal form? Why isn't the '1840' W 7th mailbox still next to the i830 one?" and "something suspicious about that mailbox."

**Before this Court:** Following the Ninth Circuit's remand the marshals attempted to serve the President and the other defendants. Norman, however, seems to have lost touch with the court, or lost interest, or both. Mail addressed to him is returned the discovery deadline and re-trial Order deadline have passed, without any response. Perhaps he has elected to pursue his remedies in some more convenient forum.

**Verdict:** I therefore DISMISS this action for want of prosecution.

## 4-Sorely Lacking "Wisdom"

**Court:** Superior Court of New Jersey, Appellate Division

**Date:** 1959 JAN 19

**Report:** None in original

**Case number:** 53 N.J. Super.574; 148 A. 2d 63

**Link:** https://merillionpress.com/cases/VII-004.pdf

**Plaintiffs (Respondents):** The TRUSTEES of Columbia University in the City of New York

**Defendant (Appellant):** Roy G. JACOBSEN

**Opinion By:** Sidney GOLDMANN, S.J.A.D.

**Prior History:** Columbia brought suit in the district court against Jacobsen and his parents on two notes made by him and co-signed by them, representing the balance of tuition he owed the University. The principal due was $1,049.50, but Columbia sued for only $1,000, the jurisdictional limit of the court.

Jacobsen then sought to file an answer and counterclaim demanding, among other things, $7,016 in damages. The counterclaim was in 50 counts alleging that Columbia had represented that it would teach Jacobsen wisdom, truth, character, enlightenment, understanding, justice, liberty, honesty, courage, beauty and similar virtues and qualities; that it would develop the whole man, maturity, well-roundedness, objective thinking and the like; and that because it had failed to do so it was guilty of misrepresentation.

While the case was bouncing around in the lower courts, Jacobsen's mother paid the amount claimed by Columbia, at which point it withdrew its action. Jacobsen then regrouped, transferred his misrepresentation claim to the Superior Court and asked Columbia to return the sum paid by his mother. In addition, he made an attempt at disqualifying the sitting Superior Court judge. It failed and the judge dismissed his claims and this is his appeal.

**Before this Court:** Following a successful freshman year at Dartmouth Jacobsen entered Columbia University in the fall of 1951. He continued there until the end of his senior year in the spring of 1954, but was not graduated because of poor scholastic standing. He admits the many quotations from college catalogues and brochures, inscriptions over University buildings and addresses by University officers cited in the schedules annexed to the counterclaim. The sole question is whether these statements constitute a basis for misrepresentations.

We are in complete agreement with the trial court that the counterclaim fails to establish the very first element, false representation, basic to any action in deceit. Columbia stands by every quotation relied on by Jacobsen. Only by reading into them the imagined meanings he attributes to them can one conclude – and the conclusion would be a most tenuous, insubstantial one – that Columbia University represented it could teach wisdom, truth, justice, beauty, spirituality and all the other qualities set out in the 50 counts of the counterclaim.

At the heart of it all is a single complaint. He concedes that "I have really only one charge against Columbia: that it does not teach Wisdom as it claims to do. From this charge ensues an endless number of charges, of which I have selected fifty at random."

We have thoroughly combed all the statements upon which he relies in his counterclaim, as well as the exhibits he handed up to the trial judge, including one of 59 pages setting out his account of the circumstances leading to the present action. They add up to nothing more than a fairly complete exposition of Columbia's objectives, desires and hopes, together with factual statements as to the nature of some of the courses included in its curricula.

In short, he chose to judge Columbia's educational system by the shifting standards of his own fancy, and now seeks to place his failure at Columbia's door on the theory that it had deliberately misrepresented that it taught wisdom.

As for the other reasons advanced by Jacobsen, we find nothing in the record which lends them even the shadow of support.

**Verdict:** The trial judge's decision is AFFIRMED.

## 5-Aspiring Opera Singer

**Court:** Appellate Division of the Supreme Court of the State of New York, First Department

**Date:** 1959 MAR 31

**Report:** None in original

**Case number:** 7 A.D. 2d 436

**Link:** https://merillionpress.com/cases/VII-005.pdf

**Plaintiff (Respondent):** Gloria B. GRAYSON

**Defendants (Appellants):** IRVMAR Realty Corp., et al

**Opinion By:** Charles D. BREITEL, Judge

**Prior History:** Ms. Grayson, a 21-year old woman who is engaged seriously in the study of music with an eye on an operatic career, sustained a fractured leg and an alleged impairment of her hearing as a result of a fall on the sidewalk in front of a building owned by Irvmar. The act of negligence charged was the failure to light properly a construction sidewalk bridge, as required by the Administrative Code of the City of New York. The jury awarded damages in the amount of $50,000.

The unusual issue tendered in this case is the probability of future earnings, which is not based on any prior actual engagement in the vocational earning of income. From an early age she had studied music and singing. This included five years of instrumental instruction; she had a professional teacher of voice and studied under an opera coach.

When she left school she participated successively in operatic workshops. As part of her operatic studies it was necessary to learn the various foreign languages closely associated with classic opera. While engaged in her studies she made a large number of appearances, all without income, on radio, in benefit performances, and in workshop-productions of opera. Her voice teacher and opera coach testified that she had a superior voice and, as a consequence, had a bright future, in their opinion, in the opera. There was testimony that she was preparing for a European debut.

She sustained her injuries when she fell, fracturing a leg, her head struck the surface, and as a result she sustained an impairment of hearing. The alleged hearing impairment has largely cleared up, leaving, however, a secondary result of an impairment of pitch.

Although she has continued to study singing and made a number of appearances it is claimed that the impairment of pitch has limited her performance and that this is likely to be permanent. However, there was highly credible proof from an eminent physician selected from the court-designated medical panel, stating that she had had ear trouble prior to the accident.

**Before this Court:** The jury in this case was very properly permitted to assess the damages with respect to Ms. Grayson's inchoate operatic career. But the award it made was highly excessive. The would-be operatic singer, or the would-be violin virtuoso, or the would-be actor, is not assured of achieving their objectives merely because they have some gifts and complete the customary periods of training. Their future is a highly speculative one, namely, whether they will ever receive recognition or the financial perquisites that result from such recognition.

**Verdict:** Based on the preceding discussion and allowing for the injury sustained by Ms. Grayson to her leg, any verdict in excess of $20,000 is excessive. Judgment REVERSED, and a new trial granted, unless Ms. Grayson accepts a judgment in the reduced amount of $20,000 ($175,000 today).

## 6-Financial Symphony

**Court:** United States Court of Appeals for the Eight Circuit

**Date:** 2002 AUG 01

**Report:** No. 00-3715

**Case number**: Non citable

**Link:** https://merillionpress.com/cases/VII-006.pdf

**Plaintiff (Appellant):** Kristin MADDOX

**Defendant (Appellee):** AMERICAN AIRLINES, Inc.

**Opinion By:** David R. HANSEN, Circuit Judge

**Prior History:** Kristin Maddox, a resident of Oklahoma, was a passenger on American Airlines Flight 1420 when it crashed after running out of runway while landing at Little Rock, Arkansas, on June 1, 1999. Eleven people died as a result of the crash and many, like Ms. Maddox, were severely injured. Prior to the crash, she had been a music major with an emphasis in vocal operatic performance and a minor in piano performance at Ouachita Baptist University. On the night of the crash, she was returning from Europe where she had been touring and performing with her college choir. She suffered severe smoke and toxic fume inhalation that damaged her lungs and vocal chords, destroying her ability to sing. She also suffered severe burns to her hands and arms, impairing her ability to play a keyboard instrument of any kind.

A federal jury awarded Kristin Maddox over $11,000,000 in damages for personal injuries she suffered. She now appeals, challenging the district court's rulings regarding prejudgment and post judgment interest rates.

American Airlines conceded liability, leaving the amount of damages due as the only issue for trial, and it does not cross appeal the jury's damage award. The district court granted in part and denied in part the motions to amend the judgment and she appeals.

**Before this Court:** The district court entered judgment in favor of Maddox and ordered that the judgment bear post judgment interest at the rate of 6.375% pursuant to federal statute. Maddox moved to amend the judgment, requesting prejudgment interest in accordance with Oklahoma law and requesting interest at Oklahoma's rate of 8.73% as opposed to the federal rate of 6.375%. Also, both parties agreed that the judgment should be amended to deduct from the total damage award the pretrial SDR (Special Drawing Rights) payments made by American Airlines to Maddox in the amount of $134,453.

We find no error in the district court's application of Arkansas's choice of law principles. Both parties agree that the district court should not have deducted from the verdict an amount representing interest on the pretrial SDR payments in light of the court's refusal to add prejudgment interest on the judgment. We agree, and accordingly, we reverse the portion of the district court's judgment that reduces the verdict by an amount representing interest on the SDR payments ($4,051.93). The verdict should have been reduced only by the actual amount of payments made as SDRs.

**Verdict:** Accordingly, we reverse the district court's decision to deduct from the verdict interest on the SDR payments, and we remand for entry of an amended judgment that reduces the verdict only by the actual amount of the SDR payments ($134,453). The amount of the judgment will be reduced to $10,876,495.07, in all other respects; we AFFIRM the judgment of the district court.

## 7-Powerful Inebriants

**Court:** In the Circuit Court of Cabell County, West Virginia

**Date:** 2012 JAN 23

**Report:** Non in original

**Case number:** 12-C-57

**Link:** https://merillionpress.com/cases/VII-007.pdf

**Plaintiff:** Louis HELMBURG, III

**Defendants:** THE ALPHA TAU OMEGA FRATERNITY Inc., of Huntington, West Virginia, a Fraternal Organization, and Travis HUGHES

**Assigned to:** Paul T. FARRELL Sr., Circuit Judge

**Prior History:** On May 1, 2011, at approximately 1:30 a.m., there were several persons present on the outside deck of the ATO fraternity house located on 5th Avenue in Huntington. The ATO had a "house party," and various persons, including Hughes and Helmburg with his girlfriend, congregated at the ATO house. Several of the people at the party were under the legal drinking age and most of them in attendance were also consuming alcohol with the full knowledge and consent of the ATO fraternity.

Hughes was highly intoxicated, and decided in his drunken stupor that it would be a good idea to shoot bottle rockets out of his anus on the ATO deck, located on the back of the ATO house. He placed a bottle rocket in his anus, ignited the fuse, but instead of launching, the bottle rocket blew up in his rectum, and this startled Helmburg to jump back, at which time he fell off of the ATO deck, and he became lodged between the deck and an air conditioner unit adjacent to the deck.

There was no railing on the deck at the time of the incident. The lack of a railing had existed for at least several months, if not years, before the incident and was approximately 3-4 feet high.

The lack of a railing constituted negligence per se, in that the ATO violated the applicable building codes when it failed to construct and/or maintain a railing on its deck.

Helmburg asserts that the lack of a railing was a direct and proximate cause of his injuries, which include pain and suffering, lost time from baseball with the Marshall University Baseball team, lost earning capacity, medical expenses, and other damages.

In addition, he claims Hughes also owed a duty of care not to drink under age, or to fire bottle rockets out of his anus. Hughes breached this duty when he both drank under age, which violated the law, and attempted to fire a bottle rocket out of his anus while under the influence. The act of firing a bottle rocket, within Huntington City Limits, was also a crime.

Louis Helmburg, III requests the Court to address his complaints against each defendant individually, seeking compensatory damages, as well as costs, attorney fees, pre-judgment and post-judgment interest.

**Before this Court:** The parties had come to a mutually agreeable settlement striking the action from the court's docket.

**Verdict:** On Nov 4, 2012 a DISMISSAL order was filed in Cabell County Circuit Court.

## 8-Not an Easy Rider

**Court:** Court of Appeal of the State of California First Appellate District Division Two

**Date:** 2015 NOV 24

**Report:** No. A141814 (San Francisco City and County Super. Ct. No. CGC12520316)

**Case number:** Non citable

**Link:** https://merillionpress.com/cases/VII-008.pdf

**Plaintiff (Appellant):** Henry WOLF

**Defendants (Appellees):** BMW North America, LLC. And Corbin-Pacific Inc.

**Opinion By:** J. Anthony KLINE, Presiding Judge

**Prior History:** On April 26, 2012, Wolf filed a form complaint against BMW and Corbin-Pacific for negligence, negligent infliction of emotional distress, and product liability after he suffered "a severe case of priapism (a persistent lasting erection)" after riding for two hours on his 1993 BMW motorcycle equipped with a Corbin-Pacific seat. He alleged that he was no longer able to engage in sexual activity. He asserted that his condition "was caused by the ridge-like seat on his motorcycle, negligently designed, manufactured and/or installed" by BMW and Corbin-Pacific.

Trial began on March 7, 2014. Wolf testified that he bought the 1993 BMW on September 5, 2009, from Edward Austin. The 1993 BMW was equipped with a custom seat manufactured by Corbin-Pacific. When he bought the BMW, Austin gave him the original BMW stock seat but Wolf never removed the Corbin-Pacific seat.

Wolf testified that he rode the BMW motorcycle at least twice a month between September 2009 and May 2010. His rides generally lasted "an hour or so." Until his two hour ride that caused his injury, he had not experienced any "erection problems" after riding the motorcycle.

He testified that he had owned about 20 or 25 different motorcycles and had been riding motorcycles for about 35 years. He described the overall vibration of this motorcycle in comparison to the others that he had ridden as being "a very buzzy bike. It makes a lot of high frequency vibrations."

Notwithstanding Wolf's medical and engineering experts' testimony and after the jury heard all the evidence, on April 3, 2014, the trial court entered judgment in favor of BMW and Corbin-Pacific against Wolf. Wolf filed a timely notice of appeal.

**Before this Court:** BMW and Corbin-Pacific contend that we should dismiss Wolf's appeal because his opening appellate brief fails to comply with the rules of appellate procedure. Most significantly, it contains no intelligible argument. It does not set forth the elements of his causes of action, fails to cite any legal authorities, and omits any legal analysis and is completely inadequate.

An appellate court cannot assume the task of discovering the error in a ruling and it is the duty of counsel by argument and the citation of authority to show the reasons why the rulings complained of are erroneous. Contentions supported neither by argument nor by citation of authority are deemed to be without foundation and to have been abandoned. One cannot simply say the trial court erred, and leave it up to the appellate court to figure out why.

Wolf failed to present any admissible evidence that his motorcycle ride or the vibrations from the motorcycle seat caused him to suffer a priapism. Accordingly, the trial court correctly dismissed his negligence and product liability claims.

**Verdict:** The judgment is AFFIRMED. Wolf is to pay the costs of appeal.

## 9-Word from Outer Space

**Court:** Human Rights Tribunal of Ontario, Toronto

**Date:** 2013 JUL 19

**Report:** No. 2013-14611-I

**Case number:** 2013 HRTO 1259

**Link:** https://merillionpress.com/cases/VII-009.pdf

**Applicant:** John DOE

**Respondent:** A & W Canada

**Opinion By:** David A. WRIGHT, Adjudicator

**Prior History:** This Application was filed on June 2, 2013, by e-mail under the name "Gloria Dawn Ironbox." It was sent from an e-mail account identified with that name. Gloria Ironbox is the name of a parody "feminist" cartoon character in an episode of the American TV series, Family Guy. The Application describes the applicant's identity as "womyn, expressing myself as a whole, empowered person free of the shekels [*sic*] of gender"; "lesbianism and radical feminism; complete separation from forced association with men"; and "living in a lesbian commune."

The narrative describes the allegations and their effect as follows:

On May 31, 2013, I attended the Cornwall Square Mall and ordered a hamburger meal from the A&W in the food court. It was my first time ordering from a fast food establishment of that sort. I noticed that the hamburger meals were given names of various family members (e.g. "Mama Burger", "Teen Burger", "Grampa Burger", etc.) The sizes of the hamburgers increased with maleness and seniority in the heteronormative family (i.e. Papa Burger bigger than Mama or Teen burger... etc.). I wanted a light burger so I ordered the "Mama Burger" meal.

As a lesbian feminist, the whole notion of labelling a burger patron as a "Mama" or "Papa" or "Teen" based solely on the choice of meal is highly degrading and an attack on my womyn identity. The level of humiliation and degradation I felt exceeded that which I felt when I was raped. The whole heteronormative, phallocentric marketing scheme of A&W is highly degrading to non-traditional families, especially members of the LGBTQ2S community. Since that visit, I have found myself isolating and I have started doubting my own self-worth.

The Application seeks $50,000 for loss of dignity and self-respect and the following order:

A&W should be required to develop and implement a modern burger family which is more inclusive and empowers members of the LGBTQ2S community. Science has shown that up to 5 adults can take part in the procreation process. Therefore, the notions of motherhood, and more importantly, fatherhood, should be completely abolished. Fatherhood is a concept which perpetuates the oppression of womyn and serves to legitimize our patriarchal, misogynistic society. Any references to males should be omitted, as at present, all forms of relationships between womyn and men are basic forms of institutional rape.

**Before this Tribunal:** On June 19, 2013, I issued a Case Assessment Direction, which was sent to the "Gloria Ironbox" e-mail address and by courier to the address provided in the Application. It did not take long for the applicant to respond.

On June 20, 2013 - among other documents - the applicant also filed a Request to Amend the Application, on the basis that the grounds for the original Application were poorly articulated and needed clarification. The Request adds further allegations, similar to those in the original Application.

The proposed amendments include that a "lesbian feminist" need not necessary be a biological female or identify as female, and a specific objection to the absence of the "Unappreciated Custodial Parent Burger", "That Aunt that No One Talks About Wrap", and "Morgentaler Combo"* from A & W's menu. The proposed revisions add various remedial requests, including proposed new products that, it is suggested, would better reflect the feminist views the applicant seeks to parody.

The applicant acknowledges, in the materials filed, that the Application is "outrageous", "ridiculous" and "abusive." The applicant states in his subsequent submissions (assuming this part is in fact true) that he is in fact a man bringing the Application in the name of a woman. In essence, I understand his argument to be that the Tribunal should process the Application so that he can demonstrate what he sees as flaws in human rights systems in Canada. I disagree that he is entitled to do so.

**Verdict:** the Application is DISMISSED, on the basis that it is outside the Tribunal's jurisdiction, the applicant has failed to provide identification as directed, and it is also an abuse of process.

* Morgentaler performed abortions in his private clinic.

## 10-Pants-on-Head Retarded

**Court:** Superior Court of the District of Columbia, Civil Division

**Date:** 2007 JUN 25

**Report**: No. 05 CA 4302 B

**Case number:** None in original

**Link:** https://merillionpress.com/cases/VII-010.pdf

**Plaintiff:** Roy L. PEARSON, JR.

**Defendants:** Soo CHUNG, et al.

**Opinion By:** Judith BARTNOFF, Judge

**Prior History:** This case has its origin in a dispute between Roy Pearson and Soo Chung, Jin Nam Chung and Ki Y. Chung over a pair of allegedly missing pants. The defendants own Custom Cleaners, a dry cleaning store on Bladensburg Road, NE, within walking distance of Pearson's home. He claims that he took his pants to Custom Cleaners for alterations in May 2005, which they lost, and that they then attempted to substitute another pair of pants for his. The Chungs deny his allegations, and they insist that the pants they attempted to return to him – which he has refused to accept – are the pants that he brought in to be altered.

Pearson also claims that a "Satisfaction Guaranteed" sign that, until recently, was displayed in Custom Cleaners was an unconditional warranty that required the defendants to honor any claim by any customer, without limitation, based on the customer's determination of whatever would make that customer "satisfied." According to the plaintiff, the defendants did not honor and had no intention of honoring that purported unconditional guarantee of satisfaction to their customers, which he contends is an unfair trade practice under the Consumer Protection Procedures Act, D.C. Code § 28-3901 et seq. ("CPPA"), on several grounds.

Pearson is seeking statutory, compensatory and punitive damages. He also is seeking attorney's fees, to which he claims to be entitled under the CPPA because he is an attorney who is representing himself in this action. He has presented various calculations of damages that go as high as $67 million. The defendants strongly dispute his claims regarding the reasonable interpretation of the "Satisfaction Guaranteed" sign, both as a legal and factual matter.

**Before this Court:** Pearson's claims regarding the "Satisfaction Guaranteed" sign are premised on his interpretation that the sign is an unconditional and unlimited warranty of satisfaction to the customer, as determined solely by the customer, without regard to the facts or to any notion of reasonableness. The plaintiff confirmed at trial that in his view, if a customer brings in an item of clothing, and the dry cleaner remembers the item, and the customer then claims that the item is not his, the cleaner must pay the customer whatever the customer claims the item is worth if there is a "Satisfaction Guaranteed" sign in the store, even if the dry cleaner knows the customer is mistaken or lying.

Nothing in the law supports that position.

The Court does not find that the evidence presented by Pearson in any way establishes that the defendants had no intention of honoring that guarantee. To the contrary, the evidence presented by him regarding his experience in 2002 demonstrates that they did. When a pair of his pants could not be located at that time, Custom Cleaners compensated Pearson fully for the value of the pants, based on his representations regarding value, without even requiring any further documentation.

**Verdict:** Judgment therefore will be AWARDED to the defendants, as well as their costs.

# CHAPTER VIII

# ALL RILED UP

*"If there is a hell to which disputatious, uncivil, vituperative lawyers go, let it be one in which the damned are eternally locked in discovery disputes with other lawyers of equally repugnant attributes." Wayne E. Alley is a retired American Judge*

Keeping lawyers above the poverty line and intense tit for tat squabbles can lead to strange glitches in logic as the following pages demonstrate. A creative legal hook coupled with a subsurface lode of hostility is all it needs and an otherwise ordinary divorce case can be turned into a constitutional challenge. Or, a confused blend of legality and sentiment can lead to interminable legal proceedings, running for 117 years, until the legal fees had exhausted the estate funds (See Charles Dickens: The Bleak House). As in this latter case, it can energize and fuel careers for generations of attorneys.

## 1-Stud Fee

**Court:** US District Court for the Southern District of West Virginia

**Date:** 1985 APR 09

**Report:** Civ. A. No. 2:85-0088

**Case number:** 608 F. Supp. 274

**Link:** https://merillionpress.com/cases/VIII-001.pdf

**Plaintiff (Respondent):** Ida Jane STEELE

**Defendant (Appellant):** Ricky Dewayne MORRIS

**Opinion By:** Charles H. HADEN, Chief Judge

**Prior History:** This action started out in the Circuit Court of Clay County, WV, where Steele brought a civil paternity suit against Morris. That lawsuit was followed by a countersuit brought by Morris against Steele, where Morris alleged Steele had contracted with him to pay for "stud fees" and that she had breached the agreement, for which Morris claimed compensatory and punitive damages.

Morris' breach of contract suit was voluntarily withdrawn by him on December 21, 1984, ostensibly with a view on Rule 11 (district court may sanction attorneys or parties who submit pleadings for an improper purpose, or contain frivolous arguments, unnecessary delays, and additional costs).

**Before this Court:** Steele's complaint alleges that as a result of Morris' actions she lost her job as a teacher, incurred expenses for attorney's fees, travel and moving, loss of benefits and has suffered emotional distress, embarrassment, mental anguish and damage to her reputation. Significantly, she has also claimed entitlement to punitive damages for Morris' willful, deliberate and outrageous conduct.

In her filing she states: It has cost her four and one-half (4½) hours of attorney's time at Seventy Five Dollars ($75.00) per hour. This is precisely the type of unnecessary expense Rule 11 is designed to avoid. These amounts appear to be reasonable to the Court both as to the time expended and the hourly rate.

Considering the grounds raised by Morris in support of his motion to dismiss the Court cannot help but conclude that, had he made a reasonable inquiry into "both the facts and the law" he would have been quickly dissuaded from filing that motion.

Having done so, the Defendant has seriously delayed the prosecution of this action; it has been over two months since the filing of the complaint.

**Verdict:** The Court grants Steele's motion for attorney's fees pursuant to Rule 11 and awards her $337.50. Morris is ORDERED to tender the amount to Plaintiff's counsel forthwith, but in any event, within ten days of the date this Order is entered.

The pleadings in this case do not reveal the disposition or status of Steele's paternity suit.

# 2-REDNECKED M*TH*R-F*CK*R

**Court:** Supreme Court of Iowa

**Date:** 1989 OCT 18

**Report:** No. 88-1613

**Case number:** 446 N.W. 2d 781

**Link:** https://merillionpress.com/cases/VIII-002.pdf

**Plaintiff (Appellee):** State of Iowa

**Defendant (Appellant):** William James FRATZKE

**Opinion By:** Linda K. NEUMAN, Justice

**Prior History:** Following his conviction for speeding 68 miles per hour in a 55 mile per hour speed zone, William Fratzke mailed his fine and court costs to the Fayette County Clerk of Court. He accompanied his payment with a nine-paragraph letter addressed to the clerk and the state trooper who had arrested him, Tom Keenan. The contents of the letter are at the center of this controversy.

Fratzke's letter began by characterizing his speeding arrest as a case of "legalized highway robbery." He claimed the trooper's conduct resulted in an unfair trial that was the product of highway safety priorities gone askew. Because Trooper Keenan had refused to show Fratzke his radar equipment at the scene, Fratzke accused him of being a liar as well as a "thief disguised as a protector."

Fratzke's contempt for the trooper and "others of his ilk" was revealed by his claim that Trooper Keenan "just enjoys stealing people's money so he can show everyone what a red-necked m*th*r-f*ck*r he is." (Asterisks in the original.) In closing, Fratzke expressed the wish "not to be interpreted as anything whatsoever in the way of a threat "that Trooper Keenan "have an early and particularly painful death hopefully at the side of a road somewhere where he's robbing someone else."

This correspondence reached the trooper by way of his supervisor, Lt. Noble. Lt. Noble, after determining that Trooper Keenan was annoyed by the letter, swore a complaint charging Fratzke with the crime of harassment.

Fratzke pleaded not guilty and the case went to trial before a Fayette County magistrate. Trooper Keenan testified that he was greatly annoyed by Fratzke's letter because it contained misstatements of fact which impugned his professional reputation and personal integrity. While conceding that "a person has a right to complain," he charged that the letter was no more than a vicious personal attack. In the trooper's words, "this is just a cheap shot, behind-your-back type thing, and I don't believe anybody in this line of work needs to put up with this kind of ___ from anybody."

Fratzke defended his letter as the "right... and duty of every American" to alert government officials "that there's something wrong." He testified that he thought the letter contained at least eighteen valid points of criticism concerning alleged unfair trial procedure and the conduct of the trooper at the scene of the citation. He asserted that the sole purpose and intent of the letter was to protest "injustices in the system." Because the letter had such a legitimate purpose, Fratzke argued, the State's evidence was insufficient to prove he committed the crime of harassment.

The magistrate found that the letter annoyed Trooper Keenan and was written without legitimate purpose because Fratzke's manner of complaint "would more quickly result in a fist fight" than bring about social change. He found Fratzke guilty as charged and sentenced him to two days in jail.

On appeal, the district court rejected all of Fratzke's contentions, concluding that protesting a speeding ticket was a "legitimate and constitutionally protected" activity, but that "there was no legitimate purpose for the language and terms used by the defendant in his letter." The court upheld the sentence imposed by the magistrate.

On appeal, Fratzke seeks reversal of his conviction.

**Before this Court:** At trial, Fratzke disclaimed any intent to annoy Trooper Keenan with the letter. We find substantial evidence to support the trial court's conclusion that Fratzke's intent to annoy Trooper Keenan could be inferred from his choice of disparaging, and occasionally profane, remarks concerning Keenan's performance.

The distinction drawn by the trial court between the words used and the communication itself raises the decisive question on this appeal: Can the use of offensive language negate (and thereby criminalize) the otherwise legitimate purpose of protesting governmental action? We think not. Such restraint on free speech can only be justified in the case of "fighting words," a narrowly defined exception to the first amendment that has been erroneously applied by the trial court in this case.

"Fighting words" are those personally abusive epithets which "by their very utterance inflict injury or tend to incite an immediate breach of the peace." The Constitution does not permit the states, however, to assume that every expression of a provocative idea will incite violence.

The First Amendment protects a significant amount of verbal criticism and challenge directed at police officers.... The freedom of individuals verbally to oppose or challenge police action without risking arrest is one of the principal characteristics by which we distinguish a free nation from a police state.

Not only were Fratzke's words contained in a letter a mode of expression far removed from a heated, face-to-face exchange the letter was mailed not to the trooper's home but to the clerk of court, a neutral intermediary in the Fratzke-Keenan dispute.

**Verdict:** In summary, Fratzke has been prosecuted and convicted because he wrote a letter; a letter critical of speed laws, critical of law enforcement priorities, and harshly critical of one state trooper. His conviction cannot stand because the finding that such criticism is "without legitimate purpose" would be equivalent to finding that the first amendment's promises are not worth the paper they are written on. The judgment of the district court must be REVERSED.

## 3-Discount for the Physically Handicapped, not for the Mentally Handicapped

**Court:** United States Court of Appeals for the Second Circuit

**Date:** 1990 DEC 26

**Report:** No. 98, Docket 90-6113

**Case number:** 922 F. 2d 112

**Link:** https://merillionpress.com/cases/VIII-003.pdf

**Plaintiff (Appellant):** Jonathan MARSH

**Defendants (Appellees):** Samuel K. SKINNER, individually and in his capacity as Secretary of the United States Department of Transportation, et al.

**Opinion By:** Frank X. ALTIMARI, Circuit Judge

**Prior History:** Marsh is a forty-six year old resident of Queens, New York, who suffers from an undisclosed mental disability. He is trained as a lawyer and has represented himself admirably in this litigation.

In 1985, Marsh orally applied for, and was denied, the benefit of discount transit fares provided to eligible persons under the New York City Department of Transportation's ("NYCDOT") Half-Fare Program. According to Marsh, the stated reason for this denial was that he did not meet the applicable statutory definition of a "handicapped person" entitled to Program benefits.

On September 9, 1988, Marsh submitted a written application for Half-Fare Program benefits, attaching a certification from the Social Security Administration that he is a recipient of Supplemental Security Income ("SSI"). Marsh's application was returned to him by the Program's director because it did not contain evidence that he was disabled within the terms of the Program's eligibility requirements.

Marsh's complaint alleged that a long list of defendants-appellees wrongfully excluded him from the discount fare benefits and violated several laws, including his constitutional rights. Marsh sought actual damages of approximately $400, as well as $10,000,000 in consequential damages, $10,000,000 in punitive damages, and injunctive relief. The district court, adopting a magistrate's recommendation, dismissed Marsh's complaint and he appeals.

**Before this Court:** The Urban Mass Transportation Act expressly defines "handicapped person" as: any individual who by reason of illness, injury, age, congenital malfunction, or other permanent or temporary incapacity or disability, including any person who is wheelchair bound or has semi-ambulatory capabilities, is unable without special facilities or special planning or design to utilize public transportation facilities and services effectively.

Marsh concedes that he is not a handicapped person as that term is defined by the UMT Act. He does not require "special facilities or special planning or design to utilize public transportation facilities and services effectively." The statutory limitation of benefits to "elderly and handicapped persons" is plain and unambiguous. So too, is the UMT Act's definition of "handicapped person." Under these circumstances, we may not construe the UMT Act to require that defendants-appellees extend discount fare benefits to a person who admits that he is not a handicapped person within the terms of the statute.

Under the express terms of the UMT Act, discount fare benefits are secured for only a limited category of persons defined as "handicapped persons," and Marsh does not fall within that group. Simply stated, Marsh was denied the contested benefits because he does not suffer from the type of handicap that the Half-Fare Program addresses.

**Verdict:** We have examined each of Marsh's remaining arguments and find them to be without merit. In light of the foregoing, we AFFIRM the judgment of the district court.

## 4-My Space

**Court:** United States Court of Appeals for the Seventh Circuit

**Date:** 1996 JUN 17

**Report:** No. 95-2932

**Case number:** 87 F. 3d 190

**Link:** https://merillionpress.com/cases/VIII-004.pdf

**Plaintiff (Appellant):** Frank H. GLATT

**Defendants (Appellees):** CHICAGO Park District, Jim HALPERN and Robert NELSON

**Opinion By:** Richard A. POSNER, Chief Judge

**Prior History**: Frank Glatt, the owner of a 40-foot yacht, was distressed when the Chicago Park District, the owner of Diversey Harbor in Chicago, reassigned him from slip D19 in the harbor to slip D5. So, since this is America, he brought suit against the Park District and two of its employees, claiming that the defendants had violated his constitutional rights.

The district judge dismissed this claim on the pleadings because he thought that the Chicago Park District Code makes clear that the holder of a harbor permit, even though it is called a "permanent" permit, as was Glatt's, does not have an entitlement to a specific slip.

**Before this Court:** The conditions that the Chicago Park District Code placed on Glatt's retention of slip D19 were too many and vague to allow him to have a secure expectation of continued use. The Marine Director is given discretion to change a permit holder's harbor or slip whenever the director thinks that the change is necessary because of "efficiency," whatever that means in this context.

If Diversey Harbor operates a bar for yachtsmen, we do not think that Glatt could claim a property right in a particular stool even if the manager of the bar promised him that it was his forever and had apparent or even actual authority to bind his employer by such a promise. The Constitution is trivialized, the majesty of constitutional law degraded, when the concept of property is allowed to expand to a point at which irascible rich men can use it to lever petty disputes with local officials (Glatt is worried lest underwater weeds at D5 foul the propellers of his yacht) into federal cases.

To deem such a transfer a deprivation of property under the due process clause is constitutional hyperbole.

The Marine Director did not kick Glatt's yacht out of Chicago, to make it The Flying Dutchman of Lake Michigan, or even out of Diversey Harbor, but merely transferred it from one boat slip to another nearby.

**Verdict:** We note in particular his contention that the Park District decided to abandon the investigation of his complaint because he had sued is based wholly on the principle of post hoc ergo propter hoc: the abandonment followed the suit, therefore must have been caused by it.

Enough said.

AFFIRMED.

## 5-One Size Fits All. Or Not

**Court:** United States District Court Southern District of New York

**Date:** 2011 SEP 07

**Report:** None in original

**Case number:** 11 CIV 6242

**Link:** https://merillionpress.com/cases/VIII-005.pdf

**Plaintiff:** Martin KESSMAN

**Defendant:** WHITE CASTLE MANAGEMENT Co. d/b/a White Castle System, Inc.

**Opinion By:** Vincent L. BRICCETTI, District Judge

**Prior History:** Kessman has been a patron of White Castle restaurants in the New York and New Jersey area since September 1959, having attended Junior High School around the comer from one of its outlets in the Bronx, New York. Now, in his sixties, he and his wife find the restaurants to be a convenient, quick venue to eat dinner or take out dinner before heading out for the evening.

On April 20, 2009, he went to the White Castle in Nanuet, New York to have a meal before he was scheduled to meet with a client. After paying for his meal, he decided to sit down to eat his meal at the restaurant. However, to his chagrin, he was unable to fit into the booth-style seating, which was extremely embarrassing for Kessman in front of a restaurant full of customers.

Looking around the restaurant for another location to sit, he quickly realized that there was no seating that would be able to accommodate his six (6) foot, two hundred ninety (290) pound frame.

After this incident on April 20, 2009, he immediately mailed a letter to corporate head-quarters expressing his frustration and concern with restaurant's lack of seating to accommodate individuals of his size.

Kessman received three patronizing boilerplate letters about thanking him for his "positive feedback" and "interest in White Castle." And a promise that seating arrangements will be addressed in the near future. He also received discount coupons he could use at the restaurants.

At this point, he was very disappointed with the lack of attention to his problem with the seating arrangements, and subsequent trips to the store were made by his wife.

In December 2009, he was attending a lodge meeting in an adjoining town to Nanuet, and his friends decided that they wanted to stop into the Nanuet White Castle for a quick bite before the meeting began. Rather than explain his embarrassing experience, which occurred eight (8) months prior, to his friends, joined his friends to the Nanuet White

Castle. When entering the store, he noticed that absolutely no improvements or upgrades were made to the premises.

When his friends suggested sitting at one of the larger tables, he tried to squeeze himself into the booth, but unavoidably slammed his knee into one of the metal posts under the table, causing great pain to himself and adding insult to injury.

Kessman was so embarrassed that he has not returned to the Nanuet White Castle since that incident.

Based upon the foregoing facts, White Castle has violated and interfered with the Kessman's rights under the laws of the United States, specifically under the Americans with Disabilities Act of 1990.

**Before this Court:** The parties had come to a mutually agreeable settlement striking the action from the court's docket in December, 2011.

**Verdict:** White Castle installed a table with movable chairs and in return Kessman dropped his suit.

## 6-Much Vile Talk

**Court:** Kansas Supreme Court

**Date:** 1905

**Report:** No number in original

**Case number:** 70 Kan. 634

**Link:** https://merillionpress.com/cases/VIII-006.pdf

**Plaintiff (Appellant):** MCNEIL

**Defendant (Appellee):** MULLIN

**Opinion By:** Sam KIMBLE, Judge

**Prior History:** McNeil sued Mullin for damages resulting from injuries inflicted in a fight. The petition was in the ordinary form for an assault and battery involving a mayhem. The evidence given at the trial indicated that insulting words were followed by a mutual stripping of hats and coats, a movement of Mullin toward McNeil in an angry manner, mutual challenges of each to whip the other, a statement by the defendant that it would not cost the plaintiff a penny to whip him, a reply by the defendant that he was no more afraid of a dollar than the plaintiff, much vile talk, and then a voluntary separation.

Immediately afterward, as the parties were going in the same direction along a public street, the quarrel was renewed. Mullin stopped, alighted from his buggy, tied his horse by the roadside, and removed his hat and coat. McNeil stopped his team, left his buggy, and removed his hat and coat.

McNeil said Mullin approached him in a threatening attitude and that as soon as they were near enough they clinched and fell. Other testimony was to the effect that they clinched before any blow was struck. Mullin said that McNeil struck him as soon as he could be reached; thereby delivering the technical "first blow" of the altercation, and his testimony was corroborated in this respect.

The succeeding conduct of the parties was characterized by perfect freedom from all hampering conventionalities.

McNeil sued in district court and the jury dismissed his claims. He complains that jury instructions were in error and he appeals.

**Before this Court:** Under the evidence the jury had the right to believe that each party voluntarily undertook to subdue the other by violence, taking the chances of receiving punishment himself; that they mutually consented to a physical combat with the mutual purpose of doing each other hurt, and the mutual expectation of encountering force in return; and that all injuries inflicted in the course of the contest were the product of this vicious animus of each participant toward his adversary. Such being the nature of the proof, it was consistent with the allegations of the McNeil's petition in every particular. There were an assault, a beating, a wounding and maiming, unlawful, malicious, and without just cause or provocation, precisely as alleged.

If the parties fought by mutual consent the circumstance of who committed the first act of violence was immaterial; and so long as each combatant persisted in his original determination to vanquish his antagonist the aggressions were mutual.

A resistance which has for its real object the securing of an opportunity to mangle the assailant is not legal self-defense ; and while it seems to be the law that, in a proper case, the jury may be required to follow the kaleidoscopic fortunes of a rough-and-tumble fight and determine whether, at a given moment of time, a finger was bitten off, or an eye was gouged, as a matter of self-protection rather than of, they are not obliged to take the striking of the first blow as the point of departure in a case of mutual combat.

If the encounter was the result of reciprocal desires to fight the conduct of each party was criminal. Each one was punishable at least for a breach of the peace, and for an assault and battery.

There is some natural repugnancy to allowing damages to be recovered by a bullying blackguard who has courted a fight and has been soundly thrashed, but the law can indulge in no sentiment regarding the matter. It can concede no legal effect to his vicious purpose. His consent to fight must be treated as utterly void, and each party must be left to suffer all consequences, civil and criminal, of his reprehensible conduct.

Although the evidence fully warranted that it should be done, the jury was not allowed to apply the foregoing principles to the case under consideration.

**Verdict:** The judgment of the district court is REVERSED, and the cause is remanded for a new trial.

## 7-Bad Marriage Violates Constitution

**Court:** Court of Appeals of Iowa

**Date:** 2013 JUN 12

**Report:** No 3-434/12-0504

**Case number**: None in original

**Link**: https://merillionpress.com/cases/VIII-007.pdf

**Petitioner (Appellee):** Annie LE

**Respondent (Appellant):** Tim D. LE

**Opinion By:** Michael R. MULLINS, Judge

**Prior History:** Tim and Annie met in Vietnam in 2004 and married that same year. They have two children together, A.L. (born 2007) and A.L. (born 2008). At the time of their subsequent divorce, both Tim and Annie were in good health. Tim earned approximately $31,200 per year while working at Wells Fargo and Annie earned approximately $19,000 per year as a nail technician—though Tim adamantly disputes the amount of Annie's annual income.

In October 2010, Annie filed for divorce. The parties stipulated to joint legal custody with Annie having physical care of the children. They also agreed to sell the marital home and share the proceeds, but disagreed about the proper proportion of those proceeds. The parties also disagreed about the value of the family's two vehicles and the value of the personal property in the marital home.

The district court's order contained several provisions dividing the marital estate. It awarded child support in accordance with Iowa's child support guidelines and then allocated one-third of the marital debt to Annie and two-thirds to Tim in rough proportion to their income.

Unpersuaded by the district court's property division, Tim appeals.

**Before this Court:** Tim argues, "Annie is trying to make my life miserable, taking away my rights of enjoying and defending life and liberty, acquiring, possessing and protecting property, and pursuing and obtaining safety and happiness. She's basically violating the Iowa Constitution."

He further argues, that he was denied effective assistance of counsel in violation of the United States Constitution and the Iowa Constitution because his attorney failed to verify Annie's annual income. He asserts that Annie's annual income is $46,800, that her employer paid half of her salary by check and half in cash. He further contends that Annie hid large sums of cash in a safety deposit box. The only evidence Tim offered in support of these allegations was a photograph of a box alleged to contain cash.

Finally, Tim asserts the district court erred in dividing certain personal property within the marital home. He contends that the resale value of this property is worth approximately $5000 and the court should have awarded him half of that value.

Iowa adheres to the principle of equitable division in marital dissolutions. *Equitable division does not necessarily mean equal division.* The key factor governing property division is what is fair and equitable under the circumstances.

Tim's random mention of issues, without analysis, argument or supporting authority is insufficient to prompt an appellate court's consideration.

**Verdict:** In light of all the facts and circumstances of this case, we find the district court's property division fair and equitable. Accordingly, we AFFIRM.

# 8-The First Lady*

**Court:** High Court of Justice, London, England

**Date:** 1970 FEB 02

**Report:** None in original

**Case number:** [1970] 2 All ER 33

**Link:** https://merillionpress.com/cases/VIII-008.pdf

**Petitioner:** Arthur Cameron CORBETT

**Respondent:** April CORBETT (neeé April Ashley, born George Jamieson)

**Opinion By:** Sir Roger F. G. ORMROD, Judge

**Prior History:** In September 1963 the parties went through a ceremony of marriage. At that time the husband knew that the wife had been registered at birth as of the male sex and had in 1960 undergone a sex-change operation consisting in removal of the testicles and most of the scrotum and the formation of an artificial vagina in front of the anus, and had since then lived as a woman.

In December 1963 (the parties having been together for no more than 14 days since the ceremony of marriage), the husband filed a petition for a declaration that the marriage was null and void because the wife was a person of the male sex, or alternatively for a decree of nullity on the ground of non-consummation.

The wife, by her answer, asked for a decree of nullity on the ground of either the husband's incapacity or his wilful refusal to consummate the marriage and she is demanding maintenance payments.

**Before this Court:** I think, obvious that both of them had considerable doubts about whether they could marry, or whether they could find anyone to marry them. In fact, the lawyer in Gibraltar succeeded in getting a special licence for them. They neither asked for, nor received, any legal advice as to the validity of such a marriage. The ceremony was fixed provisionally for 10 September when she suddenly agreed to go through with it and they rushed off to Gibraltar. I think that there can be little doubt that the husband was still in the grip of his fantasies and that the wife had much more sense of reality.

This case then, resolves itself into the primary issue of the validity of the marriage, which depends on the true sex of the respondent; and the secondary issue of the incapacity of the parties, or their respective willingness or unwillingness, to consummate the marriage, if there was a marriage to consummate.

On the primary issue, the basic facts are not in dispute; the problem has been to discover them. On the secondary issue, there is a direct conflict of evidence between them, but it lies within a narrow compass. An unusually large number of doctors gave evidence in the case, amounting to no less than nine in all, including two medical inspectors to the court.

On the medical criteria for assessing the sexual condition of an individual, I find that the wife had been shown to be of male chromosomal sex, of male gonadal sex, of male genital sex and psychologically to be a transsexual. My conclusion therefore is that the wife is not a woman for the purposes of marriage, but is a biological male and has been so since birth.

**Verdict:** It follows that the husband, is therefore, entitled, in my judgment, to a decree of nullity declaring that the so-called marriage of 10 September 1963 in fact is VOID.

* S/he subsequently published a book by that title

## 9-Deviations of Equilibrium

**Court:** Superior Court of New Jersey, Appellate Division

**Date:** 1951 JUL 06

**Report:** None in original

**Case number:** 82 A. 2d 210; 14 N.J. Super. 420 (1951)

**Link:** https://merillionpress.com/cases/VIII-009.pdf

**Plaintiff (Respondent):** John REILLY

**Defendant (Appellant):** 180 CLUB Inc.

**Opinion By:** Wilfred H. JAYNE, Judge

**Prior History:** On the evening of Memorial Day in the year 1949 the plaintiff John Reilly resolved to visit a nearby tavern known as the "180 Club" on Wilkinson Avenue in the City of Jersey City. Among its accommodations it contained a semicircular bar which we are informed is not by reason of its spherical form productive of any special hazards in its appropriate use. Wooden stools were advantageously stationed around its contour for the comfort of the patrons.

While the safe use of a stool probably depends particularly upon the capacity of the occupant to respond with alacrity to the deviations of equilibrium, yet our attention has not been invited to any authority holding that stools in a barroom are *per se* dangerous instrumentalities.

Upon entering at about 10:30 P.M. Reilly recognized among those present his acquaintances Messrs. Moriarity, McGee, and McKitrick in front of the bar with McDermott officiating behind it. Reilly forthwith mounted a vacant stool at the bar, "wrapped his feet around the rungs," and began to achieve the object of his visit. Presently Gillespie, O'Neill, and Gilligan dropped in.

The contingency which immediately attracted attention was that Moriarity was "needling" McGee with unprecedented continuity and persistence. Moriarity's inaugural comments ungraciously pertained to McGee's necktie, then to the latter's "sharp pants," then followed a dissertation concerning McGee's parsimony in which Moriarity proclaimed that "McGee was too cheap to buy a drink and he never did buy a drink and he wouldn't buy a drink for his own brother."

Gilligan supplied the following description of the march of affairs: "It would go on and on. Then it would seem Moriarity would get friendly with McGee; you would think everything was settled and, bingo, he would get sore at him again, and start, 'Ah, you never were any good.' McGee told me, 'I can only take so much.'"

And so Moriarity's "needling," McGee's exasperation, and the chosen beverages all continued to flow until about 1:30 A.M. when Moriarity uttered the remark that McGee had married a "Polack." Physical combat between the two immediately ensued, each made "one swipe" at the other went into a clinch and while thus struggling, they collided with Reilly, capsizing both him and the stool with which he had been theretofore peacefully and placidly intertwined.

Those who observed the affray experienced some embarrassment at the trial by reason of the following sequence.

Reilly sustained a fractured leg, and an ambulance was summoned, which emergency gave rise to the apprehension that the police might initiate an investigation. McDermott, the bartender, profoundly interested in avoiding any impairment of the reputation of the tavern, induced the others to explain, if officially interrogated, that no strife had occurred, but that Reilly had fallen off the stool. When subsequently summoned to testify at the trial of the present action, they were confronted with their fables. It suffices to state that we are not requested to evaluate the weight and credibility of the evidence.

Reilly sued and has a judgment against the defendant for $7,500 damages and this appeal ensues.

**Before this Court:** We are only required by the present appeal to review the propriety of the action of the trial judge in refusing at the conclusion of the entire case to direct the entry of a judgment in favor of the defendant.

The reasons asserted for a reversal of the judgment are: (a) "there was no proof adduced by plaintiff that defendant (through its agent in charge) ought reasonably to have anticipated the occurrence," and (b) "plaintiff was chargeable with contributory negligence or assumption of risk as a matter of law."

Reilly prosecuted his cause of action in pursuance of the allegation that the defendant's servant who was present and in charge of the premises throughout the period to which reference has been made, was negligent.

Negligence as a basis of civil liability was unknown to medieval law. 8 *Holdsworth, History of English Law,* 449. It emerged from the legal soil as a variant of trespass and was accorded the form of action known as trespass on the case. The word "negligence" is one of broad significance, and in the popular sense it connotes the failure to exercise reasonable care.

Actionable negligence from which liability arises consists of various essential elements including the disregard or violation of a legal duty. And so, actionable negligence is sometimes said to be the failure to exercise the care which an ordinarily prudent person would employ under the existing and surrounding circumstances in the discharge of the duty.

While the standard of care is that of an ordinarily prudent person, yet it must be realized that reasonable care is a relative term in that the degree of care must be commensurate with the risks and dangers attending the activity being pursued. It is a subject of common knowledge that the consumption of a procession of drinks of intoxicating liquors produces a variety of reactions in the deportment of human beings, the development of which emotions the tavern-keeper should be reasonably alert to detect.

In the present case it is conceivable that the ordinarily circumspect and precautious person would have contemplated the likelihood that the course of continuous bantering would eventually culminate in a fight or some similar exhibition of resentment. Human conduct may sensibly be anticipated to follow those propensities which proceed from the natural emotions of the individual aroused by the influences of the situation or environment in which he is placed.

We conclude that it was the function of the jury to determine the actual occurrences, to analyze the character and import of the remarks, their cumulative tendency to arouse resentment and ultimately to incite disorder, and having resolved those features of the evidence, to decide whether the defendant's bartender, amid such conditions and circumstances, exercised or failed to exercise that degree of care and forethought which an ordinarily prudent person would have exercised in the fulfillment of the duty reasonably to protect the plaintiff from injury.

Similarly it was for the jury to appraise the prudence of the conduct of the plaintiff in the circumstances in its relation to the preservation of his own safety. Upon consideration of the principles of law and the permissible deductions from the evidence, the jury rendered a verdict in favor of the plaintiff.

**Verdict:** AFFIRMED.

# CHAPTER IX

# WHILE COOLING YOUR HEELS

*"No one is entirely useless. Even the worst of us can serve as horrible examples." Anonymous prisoner*

The accounts of incidents in this portion are about lots of idle time spent in detention. With mailing privileges, typewriters, free paper, computers, law libraries and "jailhouse lawyers" on hand the temptation is almost irresistible. In addition, unlike normal litigants, indigents are immune from costs. Motivation is high, even though the chances of winning are less than 1%. As the late Mr. Justice Rehnquist noted: "Though he may be denied legal relief, he will nonetheless have obtained a short sabbatical in the nearest federal courthouse."

Such actions by the thousands - from a total prison population of over 2 million - are too frequently of revenge, personal satisfaction gained by harassing prison officials, or mere outlets for general discontent.

## 1-Privacy Expectation in a Swamp

**Court:** Court of Appeals of Georgia

**Date:** 1984 JUN 20

**Report:** Docket Numbers 67798, 67808 and 67809

**Case number:** 319 S.E. 2d 484; 171 Ga. App. 242

**Link:** https://merillionpress.com/cases/IX-001.pdf

**Plaintiff (Appellants):** GRAHAM, WOOD and JORDAN

**Defendant (Appellee):** State of Georgia

**Opinion By:** Robert BENHAM, Judge

**Prior History:** After the September 1981 escape from Cherokee County Jail in Center, Alabama using a homemade key by James Jordan, a lengthy crime spree ensued by the trio.

It included two kidnappings, two pursuing police officers being shot while giving chase, a high speed chase that ended when the escapees abandoned their vehicle and fled into the sparsely populated, swampy, wooded area in Cobb County, Georgia.

Three hundred law enforcement personnel, bloodhounds, and helicopters took part in the manhunt which followed. The three-some were tracked down by a bloodhound the next morning. When they abandoned their car, they took the shotgun (the weapon used for the kidnappings and shootings at the officers). However, none of them had it in his possession when captured.

Graham, whose father was the registered owner of the weapon, told a police officer that the gun had been thrown in the swamp near the place of capture. He went with law enforcement officers to the area and pointed out several places where he believed the gun to be. However, none proved correct and some days later it was found by a wading police officer armed with a magnet.

The conspirators were charged with kidnapping, aggravated assault and attempted armed robbery. A jury trial found all three guilty of all the crimes charged and Cobb County Superior Court Judge Brantley handed all three stiff sentences.

**Before this Court:** On appeal they all contend, that there was no conspiracy and that separate trials might have resulted in a different outcome. Each of the three contends that his defence was antagonistic to those of his co-defendants. Also the search of the swamp and seizure of the gun was illegal.

**Verdict:** There is sufficient evidence to show that if they didn't have a conspiracy, nevertheless they acted in concert with each other in an effort to affect an unlawful escape, kidnapping 2 people, shooting two police officers. All this accomplished in perfect harmony. As for illegal search and seizure only violates the rights of those who have a legitimate expectation of privacy in the invaded place. Since they threw the shotgun in the water they cannot have legitimate expectation of privacy in the swamp and have no standing to challenge its seizure.

Judgments AFFIRMED.

# 2-"I No Get My Canteen"

**Court:** United States Court of Appeals for the Eleventh Circuit

**Date:** 1994 FEB 10

**Report:** No. 92-3288

**Case number:** 13 F. 3d 1487

**Link:** https://merillionpress.com/cases/IX-002.pdf

**Petitioner (Appellant):** Marco GARCIA

**Respondents (Appellees):** Harry K. SINGLETARY and Robert BUTTERWORTH

**Opinion By:** Joseph W. HATCHETT, Circuit Judge

**Prior History:** On October 14, 1986, Deputy Robert Gardner, a corrections officer at the Hillsborough County Jail, Florida, observed smoke and flames coming from Marco Garcia's cell. Gardner approached the cell and, peering through a small glass window of the cell door, observed a figure moving about the cell. Upon entering the cell, Gardner saw a pink sheet draped over the sink in flames, and Garcia, the only person in the cell, placing stuffing from his mattress onto the fire. After directing Garcia to leave the cell, Deputy Gardner moved the sheet to the floor and extinguished the fire.

After extinguishing the fire, Gardner asked Garcia "why he set the fire." According to Gardner, Garcia responded to his question, stating, "I no get my canteen. I no get my canteen.... I got my rights." (At the time of this incident, Garcia, a recent immigrant from Cuba, spoke little English.) To this response, Deputy Gardner exclaimed, "Hey, everybody has got rights. These guys have a right to breath." Deputy Gardner, however, never informed Garcia of his Miranda rights.

The state prosecuted and convicted Garcia for first-degree arson. Following his trial, Garcia unsuccessfully appealed his conviction and subsequently exhausted all state remedies and hence his appeal.

**Before this Court:** The sole issue in this appeal is whether it is required that Deputy Gardner inform Garcia of his constitutional rights before asking why he started the fire.

Miranda warnings must precede any "custodial interrogation," whenever law enforcement officers question a person after taking that person into custody or otherwise significantly deprive a person of freedom of action.

Garcia contends that Gardner's inquiry was not merely "on-the-scene questioning," but constituted accusations. He argues that the deputy's question amounted to an interrogation because he was the only suspect, and Gardner was not "investigating a crime."

As a jail guard, charged with the care and safety of all of the inmates, Deputy Gardner acted within the scope of his authority to ensure the safety of Garcia and the other inmates. Therefore, his question was entirely appropriate, given the circumstances. Although accusatorial in tone, his question was not an interrogation within the meaning of Miranda his question was a spontaneous reaction to a startling event.

**Verdict:** We hold that under the facts of this case, Deputy Gardner's question to Garcia did not constitute a custodial interrogation within in the meaning of Miranda and AFFIRM the district court's decision.

## 3-Typewriter Memory Capability

**Court:** United States Court of Appeals for the Ninth Circuit

**Date:** 1989 SEP 29

**Report:** 87-2629

**Case number:** 886 F. 2d 1166

**Link:** https://merillionpress.com/cases/IX-003.pdf

**Petitioner (Appellant):** Royce Calvin SANDS, II

**Respondents (Appellees):** Sam LEWIS, Director, ADOC et al.

**Opinion By:** John C. WALLACE, Circuit Judge

**Prior History:** Sands, an incarcerated state prisoner filed a complaint against Lewis and other prison officials alleging that his constitutional rights to free speech and due process (right of access to courts) were violated when prison officials (1) refused to allow him to take possession of a new typewriter with a certain correction memory capability that had been mailed to him by his mother, and (2) prohibited him from purchasing, or possessing in his cell, carbon paper because it was a fire hazard. Sands attributed the denial of his typewriter to a prison policy prohibiting prisoners from possessing typewriters with memory capability of over 28 characters; Sands' typewriter had a capability of 40 characters.

**Before this Court:** Sands appeals from the district court's dismissal. At the outset we observe that Sands does not allege that he is being denied either an adequate law library or adequate assistance from persons with legal training. Instead, he challenges the deprivation of carbon paper and the prison's refusal to allow him to keep his memory typewriter in his cell. He fails to point to any specific instance in which he was actually denied access to the courts.

The prison's rule which Sands challenges merely limits his ability to keep an electronic typewriter above a certain memory capability in his cell. The challenged prison regulation in no way "impinges" upon inmates' constitutional rights. His free speech rights were not impinged at all.

**Verdict:** We AFFIRM the district court's dismissal of his first amendment claim. We REVERSE the dismissal of Sands' right of access claim and remand so that the district court may allow Sands the opportunity to amend this claim.

## 4-"This Subject"

**Court:** United States Court of Appeals for the Fifth Circuit

**Date:** 1987 FEB 05

**Report:** No. 86-3033

**Case number:** 808 F. 2d 1143

**Link:** https://merillionpress.com/cases/IX-004.pdf

**Petitioner (Appellant):** Patrick J. MULLEN

**Respondents (Appellees):** Frank BLACKBURN, Warden, Louisiana State Penitentiary et al.

**Opinion By:** PER CURIAM

**Prior History:** Patrick Mullen concedes that he was apprehended while committing armed robbery in a drugstore in Covington, Louisiana, as a result of which he was convicted by a jury of armed robbery and sentenced to 99 years imprisonment. His direct appeal was unsuccessful, and he filed two unsuccessful state petitions raising the same grounds asserted in his federal petition. The state concedes exhaustion.

Mullen advanced a host of claims in his original petition, most of which he pursues on appeal. He asserts that his constitutional rights were violated by eyewitness identification testimony at trial, by two state court evidentiary rulings, by references to him as "this subject" at trial and by the fact that the record furnished him for his appeal did not include a transcript of preliminary examination proceedings at his trial. He also alleges ineffective assistance of his lawyer and objects to purported errors in his presentence investigation report. Finally, he asserts that all of his claims, taken together, provide evidence of a due process violation even if none of the claims individually could be the basis for relief.

**Before this Court:** Unfortunately for Mullen, all of his claims are meritless. One example his prejudicial comments claim: He objects to the fact that a witness, the prosecutor, and his own attorney referred to him in the presence of the jury as "this subject." He asserts that this term indicated that he had been the subject of a police investigation and that knowledge of this fact might have prejudiced the jury.

Even the least perceptive juror can scarcely fail to infer that the defendant in a criminal trial must have been the subject of a police investigation at some time. Thus, Mullen was not prejudiced by being referred to as a "subject." Moreover, Mullen does not explain how the Constitution protects a criminal defendant from being referred to as a "subject."

Or, his sum total of all claims: He cites no authority in support of his assertion, which, if adopted, would encourage petitioners to multiply claims endlessly in the hope that, by advancing a sufficient number of claims, they could obtain relief even if none of these had any merit. We receive enough meritless claims as it is; we decline to adopt a rule that would have the effect of soliciting more and has nothing else to recommend it.

Twenty times zero equals zero.

**Verdict:** AFFIRMED.

# 5-Bad Dreams Resulting from Attempted Escape

**Court:** US Court of Appeals for the Fifth Circuit

**Date:** 1990 MAY 29

**Report:** None in original

**Case number:** 901 F. 2d 1276

**Link:** https://merillionpress.com/cases/IX-005.pdf

**Plaintiff (Respondent):** Michael F. WISNIEWSKI

**Defendant (Appellant):** Johnny KENNARD, et al.

**Opinion By:** PER CURIAM

**Prior History:** The State of Texas indicted Wisniewski. On July 29, 1988, the Sheriff's Office dispatched Kennard to Fort Lauderdale, Florida to escort Wisniewski, under warrant, to stand trial in Dallas. Wisniewski escaped from Kennard in Ft. Lauderdale International Airport. Kennard found Wisniewski in the parking lot hiding under a truck. Kennard alleged that he acted within his discretion in apprehending Wisniewski.

Wisniewski alleged that Kennard handcuffed him, pressed his service revolver against his mouth, and told Wisniewski to open his teeth or Kennard would blow them out. Kennard had the hammer on his service revolver pulled back. Kennard continued to threaten Wisniewski, screaming, along with other threats, that he could blow Wisniewski's brains out.

**Before this Court:** This is an appeal from a grant of summary judgment in a damages suit filed by a state prisoner against a deputy sheriff and the Dallas County Sheriff's Office. Wisniewski claims that upon his apprehension following an escape, the deputy sheriff handcuffed him, then placed his revolver in Wisniewski's mouth, threatened to blow his head off. When Kennard noticed a security guard watching, he threw him by his hair into a truck. When Wisniewski asked the security guard his name, Kennard punched him in the stomach three times.

Wisniewski argues that as a result he was frightened and has suffered bad dreams; he also claimed that he suffered excessive fear, mental anguish and duress, and nightmares as a result of the incident.

By referring to minor harms and transient distress, both physical and psychological, the district court dismissed the case against the deputy and the Sheriff's Office. An arrest is inevitably an unpleasant experience. An officer's use of excessive force does not give constitutional import to injuries that would have occurred absent the excessiveness of the force, or to minor harms. Nor can transient distress constitute a significant injury.

**Verdict:** The record is plain that Wisniewski's injuries are not significant; the lower court's decision is AFFIRMED with one dissent.

## 6-Fire Extinguisher

**Court:** United States Court of Appeals for the Fifth Circuit

**Date:** 1993 MAR 04

**Report:** No. 91-4897 Summary Calendar

**Case number:** 984 F. 2d 699

**Link:** https://merillionpress.com/cases/IX-006.pdf

**Plaintiff (Appellant):** Harry L. JACKSON

**Defendants (Appellees):** R. E. CULBERTSON, Sheriff, et al.

**Opinion By:** PER CURIAM

**Prior History:** Jackson, previously a prisoner confined in the Jefferson County Jail, based his excessive use of force claim on the following facts. While in prison, Jackson started a fire with a match and the core of a roll of toilet paper. The fire alarm went off, prompting prison officials to take action. One official arrived with a fire extinguisher. The fire had already gone out by the time he arrived; nonetheless, the official sprayed the remaining ashes, as well as Jackson and two other inmates.

At hearing Jackson testified that he did not receive any injuries.

He launched his action and the magistrate found this claim to be frivolous. The district court adopted the report and recommendation of the magistrate judge dismissing his complaint. He appeals that decision.

**Before this Court:** Because our precedent at the time of the magistrate's decision required a "significant injury" the magistrate found this claim to be frivolous. However, after the magistrate's decision, the Supreme

Court held that a significant injury is not required for an excessive force claim under the Eighth Amendment.

Although, Jackson need not show a significant injury, he must have suffered at least some injury.

Because he suffered no injury, we find that the spraying of Jackson with the fire extinguisher was a *de minimis* use of physical force and was not repugnant to the conscience of mankind.

**Verdict:** The dismissal of Jackson's case is therefore AFFIRMED.

## 7-Nazism Tactics

**Court:** United States Court of Appeals for the Seventh Circuit

**Date:** 1983 JAN 18

**Report:** 82-1071

**Case number:** 697 F.2d 801

**Link:** https://merillionpress.com/cases/IX-007.pdf

**Plaintiffs (Appellees):** LaCarttle JONES, Fred LAURIANO, Paul W. TEDDER, Alvin F. TONEY-EL

**Defendants (Appellants):** Gayle M. FRANZEN, James W. FAIRMAN and Captain HOSIE

**Opinion by:** Richard A. POSNER, Circuit Judge

**Prior History:** This is an appeal from the grant of a preliminary injunction in favor of inmates at the state prison in Pontiac, Illinois. The issue is the right of prisoners to copy documents for use in litigation.

In September 1979 LaCarttle Jones filed a pro se suit alleging that the conditions of his imprisonment constituted cruel and unusual punishment. The controversy arose over copying, for Jones charges, that prison officials had refused to let him have copies made of documents, which he planned to send to court.

Countering Jones' charges the prison librarian submitted an affidavit stating he had already copied some 800 pages of documents for Jones, that on one occasion Jones wouldn't let the papers he wanted copied out of his sight but asked that he be allowed to accompany them to the library where the copying machine was located, that this was against regulations since Jones was in disciplinary segregation. But, "As I recall, Jones was escorted to the library the following week."

Jones replied to the librarian's affidavit by charging that it "grossly falsified the number of copies requested by plaintiff." The defendants' riposte was to file an affidavit of Jones himself stating that "as of this date, April 18, 1980, I do not have any documents to be photocopied."

It would hardly be surprising if there had initially been some difficulty in satisfying Jones' requests for copying. Although Jones denied that the prison library had copied 800 pages of documents for him, it seems likely that his demands simply overwhelmed the library staff, for he is a most persistent litigant.

The allegations that he made in the district court that are unrelated to copying concern his assignment to a double cell, his being placed in disciplinary segregation for refusing to accept a cellmate, and the "Nazism tactics" used by the prison authorities to get him to accept one; their refusing to transfer him to a minimum security prison so that he could continue his education; their confiscation of his false teeth and interference with his shaving; their failure to treat his peptic ulcers, nervous conditions, paranoid tendencies, and "depress tendencies"; their refusal to let him buy "head cleaners" for his 8-track tape player and to supply him with a laundry bucket and with cable television; their forcing him to undergo a psychiatric examination; their confiscation of his "engineer's ruler" and his "audio and visual equipment," and storage of that equipment in a place where it might rust.

**Before this court:** Without meaning to disparage or prejudice these claims, which are not before us on this appeal, we think his complaint about copying is more likely to have reflected some transient misunderstanding with prison officials than a deliberate and actionable denial by them of access to the courts. He seems to have very free access to the federal district court and to be exploiting it to the hilt, but he cannot prevail without showing that the state has deprived him of life, liberty, or property without due process of law; and broad as the constitutional concept of liberty is, it does not include the right to xerox.

**Verdict:** District Court's decision REVERSED.

# 8-Morbidly Obese Prisoner's Rights

**Court:** United States Court of Appeals for the Fourth Circuit

**Date:** 1995 JUN 29

**Report:** No. 94-7206

**Case number:** 57 F. 3d 1340

**Link:** https://merillionpress.com/cases/IX-008.pdf

**Plaintiff (Appellee):** Anthony TORCASIO

**Defendants (Appellants):** Edward W. MURRAY, Director et al.

**Opinion By:** J. Michael LUTTIG, Circuit Judge

**Prior History:** Anthony Torcasio suffers from what he describes as "morbid obesity." He stands five feet, seven inches tall, weighs 460 pounds, and has a girth of 78 inches. His obesity, he claims, causes him a variety of physical discomforts, including back pain and sleep apnea. He is unable to walk long distances, incapable of standing or lying down for prolonged periods of time, and susceptible to losing his balance. In a memorandum he filed with the district court, Torcasio characterized his day-to-day existence as "a life of misery and heartache."

The present claim relates principally to his time at VDOC's Keen Mountain facility, where he was housed from April 22, 1993, until he was paroled in the spring of 1994. During his incarceration, Torcasio presented VDOC officials with a lengthy and ever-increasing list of modifications which he insisted were necessary to accommodate his obese condition.

VDOC officials took significant steps to address his obesity related grievances. Upon his arrival at Keen Mountain, prison officials first placed him in the prison infirmary, which was equipped with most of the disability accommodations he demanded, including side railings and wide bathroom access. Because inmates housed in the infirmary receive less freedom and fewer privileges than other inmates, he requested a transfer into the general population, which was granted.

Prison officials further accommodated his weight and mobility limitations by (1) providing him with a private cell originally designed to house two inmates, (2) removing the existing beds from that cell and installing a full-size hospital bed equipped with railings, (3) providing reinforced chairs for use in both his cell and the dining hall, and (4) installing mats and handrails in the shower area.

These attempts to accommodate Torcasio's condition at Keen Mountain were in keeping with the prior practice of VDOC officials, who, in response to his complaints during his confinement at other VDOC facilities, had granted him a step into the shower, a handrail in the shower, a freestanding locker as opposed to a footlocker, and a CPAP device (equipped with a backup power system to allow the machine to continue functioning if the electricity went out) to assist his breathing while he slept.

When the VDOC officials failed to grant him all of his demands Torcasio launched his suit in the district court claiming that prison official violated the Rehabilitation Act of 1973 and the Americans With Disabilities Act (ADA), and that as a state prisoner, he was entitled to the protections of these acts. His efforts to remedy his situation, as well as obtaining monetary damages were rejected by the district court and he appeals.

**Before this Court:** A prisoner is not normally thought of as one who would have occasion to "meet the essential eligibility requirements" for receipt of or participation in the services, programs, or activities of a public entity.

The terms "eligible" and "participate" imply voluntariness on the part of an applicant who seeks a benefit from the state; they do not bring to mind prisoners who are being held against their will. Prison authorities are entitled to adopt and execute policies and practices that in their judgment are needed to preserve institutional security, even if it requires treating disabled inmates somewhat differently.

The question before us, of course, is not whether Torcasio's obesity in fact constitutes a disability, but whether it was clearly established that his obesity amounts to a disability.

We find that neither the statutes, nor the applicable regulations clearly establish that the ADA or the Rehabilitation Act apply to the obese. A panel of this court earlier described Torcasio's complaints as "inconveniences," and ruled that they "do not, objectively, amount to a serious deprivation of a basic human need."

**Verdict:** We AFFIRM the judgment of the district court to the extent that it found the prison officials immune, and reverse to the extent that it did not.

# 9-Calling Him Derogatory Names

**Court:** United States Court of Appeals for the Sixth Circuit

**Date:** 1995 MAR 03

**Report:** No. 94-1422

**Case number:** 48 F. 3d 944

**Link:** https://merillionpress.com/cases/IX-009.pdf

**Plaintiff (Appellee):** Jack MCLAURIN

**Defendants (Appellees):** Keith MORTON and Roger MARRIOTT

**Opinion By:** Cornelia G. KENNEDY, Circuit Judge

**Prior History:** On August 9, 1991, while confined to administrative segregation, McLaurin intentionally broke a water sprinkler in his cell, causing his cell to flood. He was placed in a quiet cell for two hours for breaking the sprinkler and then was returned to his cell. When he returned he discovered that the mattress in his cell was soaked and he complained to employees of the Department of Corrections.

Later that day, McLaurin was allowed to go to an exercise cage in the segregation exercise yard. While he was in the yard, he continued to complain about his wet mattress. He alleged that Marriott made statements to the effect that he did not care about his complaint. McLaurin then climbed up on top of the basketball goal and started protesting.

He alleges that Marriott and Morton called him derogatory names and told him he better come down. One of the prison staff called the duty deputy to obtain approval to use mace if necessary to remove McLaurin from the goal. The officer-in-charge was informed that a psychologist had been ordered to go to the exercise yard to talk McLaurin into coming down voluntarily.

Before the psychologist arrived, he was gassed on Marriott's order. He then climbed from the basketball goal to a chain link fence with razor ribbon. The psychologist asked him what was going on. At the same time, correctional officers were yelling at him to get down and calling him an "asshole." McLaurin alleges that, without any warning whatsoever, Marriott said, "All right, gas him again and charge him." He was again gassed. It was too windy for the gas to be effective, so he had to be physically removed from the fence. He was taken to the emergency room, where a cut on his foot was treated.

Prison officials investigated the incident and disciplined Marriott, finding that he had acted capriciously in administering the gas and that he had failed to consult first with medical personnel.

McLaurin sued Morton and Marriott, alleging among other things that the use of the mace constituted excessive force. Morton and Marriott sought dismissal, contending that they were entitled to qualified immunity. The magistrate judge concluded, in a report adopted by the District Court, that Morton was entitled to qualified immunity but that Marriott was not. Marriott appeals the decision.

**Before this Court:** We find that the District Court improperly denied summary judgment because the policy directive creates no liberty interest. The policy directive creates a liberty interest if it constitutes more than a simple procedural guideline and uses "language of an unmistakably mandatory character, requiring that certain procedures 'shall,' 'will,' or 'must' be employed . . . and that the use of chemical agents will not occur absent specified substantive predicates – viz., 'the need for control' or 'the threat of a serious disturbance.'"

However, even if Marriott had followed the policy guidelines he still had discretion to determine whether chemical agents were necessary to prevent harm to McLaurin and to the other officers who were trying to get him to come down.

For instance, although it prohibits the use of chemical agents in a "capricious" manner, what is capricious must be determined by the officials. Furthermore, the officials have to make their own decision concerning when a prisoner is "resisting" or what is considered "self-mutilation or self-destructive acts."

Simply because prison inmates retain certain constitutional rights does not mean that these rights are not subject to restrictions and limitations.

**Verdict:** For the foregoing reasons, we REVERSE the District Court with respect to plaintiff's state-created liberty interest claim and remand for further proceedings consistent with this opinion.

# 10-Hosed Down

**Court:** United States Court of Appeals for the Seventh Circuit

**Date:** 1995 APR 11

**Report:** 93-4032

**Case number:** 52 F. 3d 634

**Link:** https://merillionpress.com/cases/IX-010.pdf

**Plaintiff (Appellee):** Francis MILLER, Special Administrator for the Unopened Estate of Melvin L. MILLER

**Defendants (Appellants):** Norman NEATHERY and Terrence TERRELL

**Opinion By:** Kenneth F. RIPPLE, Circuit Judge

**Prior History:** Melvin Miller was an inmate assigned to cell 3H09 of the segregation unit at Stateville Correctional Center, Illinois. At approximately 2:00 p.m. on March 31, 1990, Miller was sitting in his cell. Correctional officer Norman Neathery was on duty in the control room. Officer Neathery allowed inmate William Adkins, who had been assigned to clean the showers, to leave the 3H wing and to return with cleaning supplies. Officer Neathery observed Adkins hook a hose up to a faucet in the day room and attach a bottle of cleanser to the hose.

Officer Neathery then opened the door to the 3H wing and allowed Adkins to enter with the hose and cleanser. Adkins ambled down the corridor past the showers until he reached Miller's cell. He then began to douse Miller with the spray from the hose. Apparently, Adkins was retaliating because Miller had spat upon him earlier that week. Adkins continued to spray Miller until Terrence Terrell, a gallery officer assigned to the 3H wing, ordered him to stop. Miller complained that his eyes burned. He was taken to the prison infirmary for treatment. Miller subsequently filed a suit against Officers Neathery and Terrell. Upon his subsequent death, from causes not related to the incident before us, his mother continued the litigation as administrator of her son's estate.

At trial, Miller's theory of the case was that Officers Neathery and Terrell stood idly by and watched as inmate Adkins sprayed Miller with chemicals for several minutes. With respect to Officer Terrell, the jury heard conflicting testimony concerning whether he had been present when Adkins initially arrived with the hose. With respect to Officer Neathery, there was conflicting testimony concerning whether he should have evaluated Adkins' behavior in arriving to clean the showers as out-of-the-ordinary.

The jury returned a verdict against the defendants for $10,000 in compensatory damages, and assessed an additional $6,000 in punitive damages against Neathery and $14,000 against Terrell. Following the verdict, the officers filed for a new trial, which was denied, and they filed this appeal.

**Before this Court:** The officers' principal contention on appeal is that the district court erred in instructing the jury on deliberate indifference. The instruction did not, the officers argue, adequately explain the standard of recklessness necessary for the jury to find the officers liable.

When reviewing jury instructions, our task is to determine "if the instructions as a whole were sufficient to inform the jury correctly of the applicable law. We initially note that the district court's instruction did avoid many of the common pitfalls in this area. It did not explicitly instruct the jury that it could consider what the officers "should have known" in determining whether they were deliberately indifferent. The conflicting testimony at trial was susceptible to various interpretations on crucial issues of location and timing. Under these circumstances, it would be imprudent for us to determine that the lack of sufficient guidance in the instructions did not contribute significantly to the jury's conclusion.

**Verdict:** Accordingly, we REVERSE the judgment of the district court and remand the case for a new trial.

## 11-Poorly Prepared Beans

**Court:** United States Court of Appeals for the Seventh Circuit

**Date:** 1994 MAR 16

**Report:** 93-1763

**Case number:** 17 F. 3d 1574

**Link:** https://merillionpress.com/cases/IX-011.pdf

**Plaintiffs (Appellants):** Ronald D. LUNSFORD, Jr., Hazen E. UPHAM, and David GARY

**Defendants (Appellees):** Timothy BENNETT, Donald JARRETT, Laura PERRY, et al.

**Opinion By:** Harlington WOOD Jr., Circuit Judge

**Prior History:** Lunsford, Upham and Gary were convicted prisoners being held in Ward 9, a ward used for disciplinary segregation, of the Elkhart County Security Center, Indiana. The events that form the basis of their complaint occurred over a three day period in late December, 1989. During this three day period they were deprived of basic hygiene items, subjected to loud noises over the intercom, served poorly-prepared food, and verbally and physically abused by prison officials.

At lunch on December 26, they were served as part of their meal cold, poorly-prepared beans. Upset with this course of treatment, the prisoners (including plaintiffs) threw their trays, dishes, and eating utensils to the floor of the catwalk outside of their cells.

Several officers then did a "shakedown" search in Ward 9 to determine if any items had been kept by the prisoners. During the search the guards and prisoners were verbally abusive to one another, spitting at each other and some of the prisoners threatened to flood the ward. After dinner they did just that. The prisoners placed Styrofoam cups in their individual toilets and began flushing, subsequently causing the toilets to overflow and flood the ward with several inches of water.

Acting on Perry's instruction, jail officers removed the prisoners from their cells and shackled them to the bars of the flooded cells by their hands and feet, letting them stand ankle-deep in water while it was cleaned up. While the officers cleaned up the water, the inmates (including plaintiffs) and officers talked "trash" to one another, and splashed water on one another using their feet.

Officers Truex and Bennett responded by picking up a bucket of water and pouring it over Upham. Upham claims that when the water was poured on him he was hit in the head twice by the bucket, once as the water was dumped on his head and once as the bucket was removed. Since being hit in the head with the bucket, Upham claims that he gets daily headaches though he is still able to work.

The prisoners complain that this series of abuses, when viewed in their totality, constitute cruel and unusual punishment in violation of the Eighth Amendment. They also argue that by inflicting punishment without any form of notice or hearing, the officers violated their Fifth

Amendment Due Process rights. They launched their suit in district court where all claims were dismissed and they appeal.

**Before this Court:** Here the cumulative effect of the prisoners' complaints do not add up to the deprivation of a single human need. They received food in accordance with prison and constitutional guidelines; hygiene items were provided within a constitutionally permissible time frame; and the loud noises did not deprive the prisoners of rest or other necessity.

We find no threat to human health or safety posed by any of their complaints about the conditions imposed during their stay at the Elkhart County Security Center. The Constitution does not require prison officials to provide the equivalent of hotel accommodations or even comfortable prisons. Occasional discomfort is "part of the penalty that criminal offenders pay for their offenses against society."

**Verdict:** We find these arguments to be without merit and the district court's decision is AFFIRMED.

## 12-New Year's Eve Squabble

**Court:** United States Court of Appeals for the Seventh Circuit

**Date:** 1996 JUL 01

**Report:** 95-3847

**Case number:** 87 F. 3d 913

**Link:** https://merillionpress.com/cases/IX-012.pdf

**Plaintiff (Appellee):** United States of America

**Defendant (Appellant):** Yaphet K. JAMAL

**Opinion By:** Terence T. EVANS, Circuit Judge

**Prior History:** A New Year's Eve squabble with one's girlfriend seldom leads to the sort of consequence visited on Yaphet Jamal. But for Jamal, the result of such a spat, indirectly at least, is 10 years in a federal correctional institution for robbing banks.

In December of 1994 Jamal was unemployed and living with his girlfriend, Marie Fullwiley, at her home on Pine Street in Waukegan, Illinois. The couple had a tiff on New Year's Eve, and either he left or she tossed him out. The relationship was kaput. But Jamal's stuff (clothing, etc.) was still in the house and understandably, he wanted it back.

Apparently sensing that returning to her house for his things on New Year's Day would be unwise, Jamal sought help (and protection) from the Waukegan police department. He walked to the police station where he explained he wanted his belongings, but feared a confrontation. At Jamal's request, Waukegan Police Officer Stephen Gonyo drove with him in a squad car to Fullwiley's house. During the drive, Jamal and Gonyo reached an understanding that it would be best to let the officer "do the talking" with her.

When they arrived at the house, the officer said he was there "to pick up Mr. Jamal's duffel bags." Fullwiley, apparently not conversant with Emily Post, said, "No way is that motherfucker going to cross my threshold...." A few minutes later, she played the queen of hearts, asking Jamal, in front of Gonyo, "Why don't you tell the officer about the robbery you committed, you son of a bitch?" She added, a moment later, that the robbery was committed in Waukegan a few weeks earlier, on December 16.

This information triggered a chain of events that resulted in Jamal going to trial on an indictment alleging three bank robberies. A jury found him guilty on all three charges, and he's now serving a 10-year sentence, which he appeals.

**Before this Court:** On this appeal Jamal raises three issues:

(1) The district court erred in not suppressing his identification as the robber of each of the banks

This issue brings us back to Ms. Fullwiley, Jamal, and Officer Gonyo, who were at the home on Pine Street.

(2) It was error to try the robberies together.

Because the three robbery charges in the indictment are identical the issue comes to a screeching halt.

(3) The evidence was insufficient to support the conviction

This is a peculiar argument considering the eyewitness testimony of seven bank employees, each of whom identified Jamal as the robber either in open court during the trial or from a photo spread shown to them prior to their trial testimony. It also ignores the testimony of Ms. Fullwiley, who drove several nails into Jamal's coffin when she told the jury that Jamal was the person depicted by bank video cameras in the first two robberies and that he told her about the third and even gave her a little of the loot to boot. The evidence of Jamal's guilt, we find, was overwhelming.

**Verdict:** Finding less than a scintilla of merit to these claims, we AFFIRM.

## 13-My Battle Is Over Now I Must Expire

**Court:** United States Court of Appeals for the Seventh Circuit

**Date:** 1997 FEB 04

**Report:** None in original

**Case number:** 105 F. 3d 1188 (7th Cir. 1997)

**Link:** https://merillionpress.com/cases/IX-013.pdf

**Plaintiff (Appellee):** United States of America

**Defendant (Appellant):** Frank Feichtinger

**Opinion By:** Terence T. EVANS, Circuit Judge

**Prior History:** Feichtinger and another man concocted a plan to break into and rob two banks in Belleville and Collinsville, Illinois. They intended to use liquid helium and an oxyacetylene torch to crack open the bank vaults. To carry out their plan they stole military equipment from an Illinois Army Reserve Center.

Among the items stolen were night vision goggles, hand-held radios, bolt cutters, 26 chemical protective masks, compasses, watches, sleeping bags, Kevlar helmets, a practice claymore mine, and – astonishingly – a two-and-one-half ton cargo truck. One vehicle apparently not being enough, they obtained another Army truck from the Jefferson Barracks in Missouri. They drove this truck to Illinois. In all, the military equipment they snatched was worth almost half a million dollars.

Not surprisingly, on January 31, 1994, they were charged in federal court with theft of, and concealing stolen military equipment. On May 3, 1994, a five-count superseding indictment was filed against Feichtinger. It repeated the original charges and added two more–conspiracy to commit bank robbery and the interstate transportation of stolen government property.

Feichtinger's trial was scheduled to begin on October 11, 1994.

To understate, Feichtinger failed to appear for trial. What he did instead was to flee in dramatic fashion. He faked his own suicide by leaving his abandoned car and a suicide note on a Mississippi River bridge. The suicide note was a doozy. It was handwritten, 15 pages long, quoted Mark Twain, lamented "My battle is over now I must expire," and repeated "I'm dead as a doornail" 28 times.

But surprise, surprise. Unlike Marley's ghost, Feichtinger was not "dead as a doornail" despite his repetitious assertions that he was. It turned out, he was alive and kicking in Arizona, where he was nabbed 10 months later in August of 1995. Upon his arrival back in Illinois, a second superseding indictment was returned, with a sixth count for failure to appear for trial added to the old charges.

On February 29, 1996, Feichtinger entered–what a temptation to say leaped (though that would not be accurate)–into a plea agreement, in which he waived his right to appeal. On May 21, 1996, Judge William L. Beatty sentenced him to 37 months imprisonment on counts 1 through 5 and a 6-month consecutive term on the failure-to-appear count, giving him a grand total sentence of 43 months.

**Before this Court**: Feichtinger filed an appeal, alleging that the sentence on count 6 was an improper application of United States Sentencing Guidelines, in other words, he thinks his sentence is too long. His problem is, however, that before he can convince us to listen to his beef, he must hurdle his plea agreement, in which he waived his right to appeal.

If Feichtinger is right, what, we wonder, does a waiver waive?

**Verdict:** In the circumstances of this case, there is no breach of the plea agreement which would invalidate it and release Feichtinger from the waiver of his right to appeal. This appeal is DISMISSED.

# CHAPTER X

# SENSITIVE

*"In the cosmology behind psychology, there is no reason for anyone to be here or to do anything... I'm an accident - a result - and therefore a victim... if I'm only a result of past causes, then I'm a victim of those past causes.... or, if you look at it from the sociological perspective, I'm the result of upbringing, class, race, gender, social prejudices, and economics. So I'm a victim again. A result." James Hillman (1926 – 2011) was an American psychologist*

This caste of altercations posits that there is nothing so simple or straight-forward that it cannot be mangled to force-fit the law evolution narrative. Facts are seldom important, what counts is the interpretation of facts.

Entrepreneurial as always, lawyers have turned this segment into a carefully cultivated cash cow. There can be no doubt, that some may be more allergic, fragile, easily hurt. Or, as this group shows: cunning, conniving cranks displaying neurotic overreaction to trivial hurts attended to by the remorselessly good, ready to administer the judiciary Botox. This way, the dough can be raked in while posing as "caring."

## 1-Witness to Accident, Like Holocaust

**Court:** United States Court of Appeals for the Fifth Circuit

**Date:** 1959 FEB 25

**Report:** 17313.

**Case number:** 264 F. 2d 152

**Link:** https://merillionpress.com/cases/X-001.pdf

**Plaintiff (Appellant):** Robert T. CLEGG

**Defendant (Appellee):** HARDWARE Mutual Casualty Co.

**Opinion by:** John R. BROWN, Circuit Judge

**Prior History:** A truck proceeding south on Airline Highway near Norco, Louisiana, suddenly swerved onto its right shoulder to avoid hitting school children alighting from a northbound school bus. The truck hit and smashed several cars and ran into gasoline pumps of a roadside filling station causing fire and widespread destruction. Clegg, of Baton Rouge, was standing nearby. He was not physically injured, not even touched in any way by anything.

What happened to him, he says, was that on seeing this holocaust and the need for someone to rush in to help rescue victims, he suddenly became overwhelmed by fear and realized for the first time in his life that he was not the omnipotent, fearless man his psyche had envisioned him to be. This event precipitated great emotional and psychic tensions manifesting themselves as psychosomatic headaches, pain in legs and neck, a loss of general interest, a disposition to withdraw from social and family contacts, and the like.

At jury trial Clegg's compensation claims ranged from some nineteen hundred dollars covering numerous small items of medical, psychiatric, hospital bills, and car rental to a demand for seventy-five thousand to two-hundred fifty thousand dollars for mental pain and anguish.

To the Insurer the claim was bizarre and the amount was zero and the jury agreed.

**Before this Court**: On appeal Clegg raises procedural issues (one concerning the Court's use of a specific form and not another, use of the term *damage* instead of *injury*) and others.

While his case was grinding through the jury trials his life – despite the immense suffering and pain - took some unexpected turns. Irrefutable earth-bound events that made it sound all the more stranger. At the time of the accident, Clegg was a TV advertising salesman. Within a short space of time, he had changed employment. He became president of a company, in which he was personally invested, at a salary over twice as high as he had previously earned. He bought and sold several pieces of real estate, had made $25,000 in one trade, and had purchased and moved into a new $40,000 home. Within nine months of the accident he had successfully undertaken a campaign to become elected a city Councilman of Baton Rouge.

The psychiatrists, acknowledging these external facts, then reasoned that this was a part of his struggle by which to recapture his lost self-esteem, and that while these things were most assuredly being accomplished, it was being done at further damage to Clegg.

**Verdict:** To resolve this elusive and abstruse medico-psychic debate was, as plaintiff's counsel put it, "the function of the jury." To this the District Court responded "Well, they functioned." And since no error is found and the verdict is binding on all, including this Court, we may conclude that the Court below had the prerogative to say that "They functioned right."

District Court decision AFFIRMED.

## 2-Spicy Food

**Court:** Supreme Court of Florida

**Date**: 1976 MAY 12

**Report:** No. 46,952

**Case number:** 336 So. 2d 545

**Link:** https://merillionpress.com/cases/X-002.pdf

**Petitioner:** NATIONAL AIRLINES Inc.

**Respondent**: Theodora EDWARDS, aka Teddy Edwards

**Opinion By**: Bonnie K. ROBERTS, Justice

**Prior History:** Teddy Edwards purchased a ticket from National Airlines at the Fort Lauderdale airport for a flight from Miami to Jacksonville on July 23, 1971. Next day the flight took off as scheduled with her onboard. En-route the airplane was hijacked by a Cuban born passenger and the flight diverted to Havana's Jose Marti Airport.

During the late 60s, early 70s it was fairly common for commercial planes to be hijacked to Cuba – frequently by Che Guevara or Bolshevik wannabes – occasionally meeting their hero, Fidel Castro, on the tarmac.

Standard procedure at the time was that passengers of the hijacked aircraft were asked to disembark, stay in facilities provided locally and consume spicy foods and spicy drinks (rum) offered by the authorities of the Cuban government.

In order to sustain herself Teddy Edwards claims she was "forced" to consume the aforementioned food and drinks, resulting in her becoming ill, for which she seeks monetary damages from National Airlines on the theory of negligence and breach of contract.

The essential parts of her complaint are:

1- National Airlines knew, or should have known that unless they exercised extreme care in screening and inspection of their passengers and baggage that their aircraft may again be hijacked (In 1969 alone, there were nine such occurrences) and that National Airlines failed to take precautions against the possibility of hijacking.

2-It is a well-known fact that the food provided on the island of Cuba, various South American and Caribbean countries often does cause serious gastrointestinal ailments to those not accustomed to it.

3-As a result of the hijacking, she was exposed to various foods and beverages in Cuba, which caused her to become sick and to suffer a long term illness, physical and/or mental disability and loss of earning capacity.

The Trial Court dismissed the original case; the District Court of Appeal reinstated it and National Airline appeals.

**Before this Court:** We find that the trial court properly dismissed the complaint and that the damages alleged by Edwards to be a result of National's negligence or contract of carriage were too remote as a matter of law to be recoverable. We hold National Airlines responsible for the hijacking and awarding nominal damages, but dismissing the gastrointestinal ailments allegations, as too remote to be compensable.

**Verdict**: For the foregoing reasons, the decision of the District Court of Appeal is quashed and the cause REMANDED with directions to reinstate the order of dismissal by the trial court, with three judges dissenting.

## 3-Fast Frank Feature

**Court:** Appellate Division of the Supreme Court of the State of New York, Second Department

**Date:** 1986 SEP 29

**Report:** None in original

**Case number:** 119 A.D. 2d 252

**Link:** https://merillionpress.com/cases/X-003.pdf

**Plaintiff (Respondent):** Maurice FRANK

**Defendants (Appellants):** National Broadcasting Company, Inc., et al.

**Opinion By:** Sybil H. KOOPER, Judge

**Prior History:** Maurice Frank, a resident of Westchester County, is described in his amended complaint as being "engaged in business as an accountant, tax consultant and financial planner." The defendants Richard Ebersol and Lorne Michaels are the producers of the late night television comedy program "Saturday Night Live." SNL is broadcast weekly throughout New York and the United States by the defendant National Broadcasting Company Inc.

Frank's complaint concerns an SNL broadcast initially aired nationwide on April 14, 1984, the day before the general deadline for the filing of 1983 income tax returns. The program that evening included a segment known as the "Saturday Night News," the name of which implies a parody of standard, televised news broadcasts. It is a skit contained within the "Saturday Night News" which is the subject of this defamation suit.

Maurice Frank refers to the objectionable skit as the "Fast Frank Feature." In the skit a performer was introduced to the audience as a tax consultant with the same name as himself, Maurice Frank. The performer allegedly bore a "noticeable physical resemblance" to himself. This character then gave purported tax advice, which the real Frank described in his complaint as "ludicrously inappropriate."

Specifically, the complaint recites the following monologue as defamatory:

"Thank you. Hello. Look at your calendar. It's April 14th. Your taxes are due tomorrow. You could wind up with your assets in a sling. So listen closely. Here are some write-offs you probably aren't familiar with — courtesy of 'Fast Frank's. Got a houseplant? A Ficus, a Coleus, a Boston Fern — doesn't matter. If you love it and take care of it — claim it as a dependent. Got a horrible acne? . . . use a lotta Clearasil . . . that's an Oil-Depletion Allowance. You say your wife won't sleep with you?

You got withholding tax coming back. If she walks out on you — you lose a dependent. But . . . it's a home improvement — write it off. Should you happen, while filling out your tax form, to get a paper cut — thank your lucky stars — that's a medical expense and a disability. Got a rotten tomato in your fridge? Frost ruined your crops — that's a farm loss. Your tree gets Dutch Elm Disease . . . Sick leave — take a deduction. Did you take a trip to the bathroom tonight? If you took a trip . . . and you did business — you can write it off. Wait, there's more. Did you cry at 'Terms of Endearment'? That's a moving expense. A urologist who's married to another urologist can file a joint return. Got a piece of popcorn stuck between your teeth? . . . Or a sister who drools on her shoes? . . . You got money comin' back — and I can get it for you fast, because I'm Fast Frank. Call me. I have hundreds of trained relatives waiting to take your call. At Fast Frank's, we guarantee your refund will be greater than what you earned."

In June 1984, Frank's attorney wrote to Ebersol requesting both a public apology and compensation. It appears, that only a private, written apology was offered. In August 1984, the SNL program, including the "Fast Frank Feature," was rebroadcast nationwide.

**Before this Court:** Frank commenced this action in November 1984 and sought damages for defamation and because it was broadcast by television, it is also classified as a libel. Additionally, a third cause of action was directed solely against NBC, which he claims violated his Civil Rights.

The contested statements here were so extremely nonsensical and silly that there is no possibility that any person hearing them could take them seriously. Neither were the statements themselves so malicious or vituperative that they would cause a person hearing them to hold Frank in "public contempt, ridicule, aversion or disgrace." We believe that the lunacy of the statements themselves, presented as they were as a small comic part of a larger and obviously comic entertainment program, coupled with the fact that they were neither a malicious nor vicious personal attack, requires a finding that they were not defamatory as a matter of law. Rather, this case involves just that sort of humour which is "of a personal kind that begets laughter and leaves no sting," and it thus cannot form the basis of a lawsuit.

Frank is required to establish that the allegedly defamatory statements constituted libel per se, the words complained of are "reasonably susceptible of a defamatory connotation." He must prove that the statements tended to expose him "to public contempt, ridicule, aversion or disgrace, or induce an evil opinion of him in the minds of right-thinking persons."

He failed to provide evidence to any of these questions and it can also be asserted without hesitation that no person of any sense could take the so-called tax advice of 'Fast Frank' seriously. If anything, the statements here are even more plainly the obvious figments of a comic imagination.

**Verdict:** We find that the complaint must be DISMISSED in its entirety.

## 4-Howard for Governor

**Court:** Supreme Court, New York County

**Date:** 1995 APR 20

**Report:** None in original

**Case number:** 626 N.Y.S. 2d 694

**Link:** https://merillionpress.com/cases/X-004.pdf

**Plaintiff (Respondent):** Howard STERN

**Defendant (Appellant):** DELPHI Internet Services Corp.

**Opinion By:** Emily J. GOODMAN, Justice

**Prior History:** New York radio shock jock Howard Stern announced his candidacy for the office of Governor of the State of New York in the spring of 1994. Delphi is a subscription based Internet provider and for this occasion, it set up an on-line electronic bulletin board for its subscribers to debate the merits of Stern's candidacy.

In June 1994 Delphi took out full page advertisement in New York Magazine and the New York Post featuring Stern in leather pants which largely exposed his buttocks. The ad caption read: "Should this man be the next governor of New York? You've heard him. You've seen him. You've been exposed to his Private Parts. Now he's stumping to be governor. Maybe it's time to tell the world exactly what you think. The Internet's the one frontier even the King of (Almost) All Media hasn't conquered. And Delphi's where you get aboard. The online service that "leads the way in Internet access."

With Delphi, navigating the Net is as easy as falling down. Assistance is available at every turn. From help files, guides and books, to hundreds of online experts, including Wald Howe, Delphi's resident Internet guru and all around smart guy. So whether you think Howard-the-Aspiring-Governor should be crowned King of the Empire State, or just greased up and sent face-first down a water slide, don't put a cork in it. Sit down, jack in, and be heard."

**Before this Court:** In this action Stern alleges that Delphi's use of his name and photograph is unlawful and without his consent, seeking damages. He does not deny that it is his picture and buttocks that appear in the advertisement, nor does Delphi.

The latter asked the court to dismiss the action claiming that the "incidental use" exception to a state law should be applied. First Amendment protections should be extended to electronic news disseminators, the same way as enjoyed by traditional media, such as newspapers or television networks.

**Verdict:** The complaint is DISMISSED and perhaps indirectly so was his surreal candidacy.

## 5-Shoeless Passage

**Court:** United States Court of Appeals for the Ninth Circuit

**Date:** 1992 APR 20

**Report:** No. 89-56315

**Case number:** 962 F. 2d 866

**Link:** https://merillionpress.com/cases/X-005.pdf

**Plaintiff (Appellant):** S. Myron KLARFELD

**Defendants (Appellees):** United States of America; United States District Court; United States Marshal

**Opinion By:** PER CURIAM

**Prior History:** The United States courthouse in downtown Los Angeles, like all government buildings nowadays, is considered at risk of terrorist attack. To stem the flow of ordnance into the halls of justice, the United States Marshals Service operates a security checkpoint much like those seen at airports and other government buildings around the country: All visitors must pass through a metal detector and submit their belongings to an X-ray scan before they will be admitted into the building.

Klarfeld, a lawyer, walked through the metal detector twice, but the alarm sounded. The court security officer then asked him to remove his belt and shoes and walk through the detector a third time. Klarfeld objected and asked to be scanned with a hand-held magnetometer instead.

The officer declined, giving Klarfeld a perfectly plausible explanation: The shoes would have to be X-rayed because "you could have a gun there." Klarfeld grudgingly complied and walked through the metal detector in his stocking feet.

This time the alarm remained silent; the X-ray machine revealed that a metal shank in Klarfeld's Brooks Brothers loafers had triggered the alarm.

Klarfeld sued alleging that his constitutional rights had been violated because he was forced to walk through the metal detector in his socks. The district court did the only sensible thing it could under the circumstances: It dismissed the complaint and he appeals.

**Before this Court:** Klarfeld, does not challenge the need for security screening, or claim it is a subterfuge.

What then is the problem? Klarfeld complains that compelling him to take off his shoes (and/or belt) violates the Constitution because the guards could have used less intrusive methods to find out whether he had a gun hidden there. If courthouse visitors may be subjected to that ordeal as a condition for coming into the building, Klarfeld can have no legitimate complaint about being asked to walk 5 or 6 feet without his shoes.

Klarfeld's complaint, however, turns not on the objective intrusiveness of the screening, but on the guard's refusal to tailor it to comport with Klarfeld's personal preferences – "that he would rather be searched by the hand metal detector than to take off his shoes.

Klarfeld believed that walking through the magnetometer in his stocking feet was beneath his dignity and requested to be scanned with a hand-held metal detector. Are security officers required – as a matter of constitutional law – to weigh the preferences and sensibilities of every one of the billion-plus people screened every year?

Klarfeld's snobbish complaint is that he was constitutionally entitled to better treatment than everyone else, just because he is a lawyer. Or are lawyers constitutionally entitled to superior treatment because they come from the same social stratum as judges?

What he is really after is to do it his way: But if Klarfeld is entitled to such individualized treatment, surely everyone else is also. The billion-plus security checks conducted in the United States every year will turn into potential dickering contests, as every airline passenger, every visitor to a government building, can hold up the line while he negotiates what procedures he personally finds least offensive, making the guards choose between letting someone who might be carrying a weapon board a plane and finding themselves on the business end of a lawsuit brought by the Mr. Klarfelds of the world.

Is it any wonder that our legal system continues to hurtle out of control if lawsuits like Klarfeld's are taken seriously—indeed, are celebrated as a vindication of important constitutional rights? It trivializes the important values of the Fourth Amendment and rewards effete prissiness. Although lawsuits asserting violations of civil liberties are to be commended when they challenge governmental tyranny, when a case rests on such a catchpenny constitutional foundation it undermines public confidence in the court and its officers

The opinion in this case gives everyone who passes through a security checkpoint the right to haggle about how the screening will be conducted—down to picayune details like whether his shoes will be X-rayed - and to sue in federal court if he doesn't like the bargain. This ruling conflicts with our precedents, not to mention simple common sense. It holds judges and lawyers up to public ridicule.

**Verdict:** A majority of the active judges have voted to DENY the bench review request.

## 6-Mummer's Costume

**Court:** United States District Court, E. D. Pennsylvania

**Date:** 1981 MAR 31

**Report:** Civ. A. No. 79-3940

**Case number:** 510 F. Supp. 255

**Link:** https://merillionpress.com/cases/X-006.pdf

**Plaintiffs:** Joseph MARTIN & Margaret MARTIN, husband & wife

**Defendant:** MUNICIPAL Publications t/a Philadelphia Magazine

**Opinion By:** Clifford S. GREEN, District Judge

**Prior History:** In its January 1, 1979 issue Philadelphia Magazine published a photograph of Joseph Martin wearing his Mummer's costume. The photograph bore the following caption:

"Dead animal of the month.

A New Year's tribute here to all the ostriches who gave their tails to make the world free for closet transvestites from South Philly to get themselves stinking drunk. Have a nice year."

Martin has brought this suit, alleging that this publication has libeled him, invaded his privacy by placing him in a false light and intentionally inflicted severe emotional distress. In addition, his wife Margaret Martin, sues for the loss of her husband's services, society and companionship, allegedly the result of the distress he suffered by the publication of his picture.

Philadelphia Magazine has requested dismissal of the case arguing: "it is abundantly clear that the publication was not intended to be understood in a literal sense" and "was plainly a spoof, satire, and nothing more."

Philadelphia Magazine further argues that even if the publication were capable of a defamatory meaning, it is shielded by the First Amendment in this case as Martin, in his capacity as a Mummer, is a "public figure."

**Before this Court:** The complaint alleges that the magazine has libeled Joseph Martin by publishing his photograph in the manner previously described. Such a description is clearly derogatory and would tend to lower the person described in the estimation of the community or deter others from associating with him. The merits of a defamation is the task of the jury to determine if recipients of the communication have understood it to be defamatory.

Since the picture and caption appeared in the "FLASH" section of the magazine, known to readers as potpourri of light humor, satire and parody, defendant urges that no reasonable person would interpret it to be a serious statement. The problem with this argument is that people who were not familiar with the magazine and the nature of the "FLASH" section may have seen Martin's photograph. Defendant may be able to convince a jury that the publication was so obviously humorous that no person seeing it would have taken it as defamatory, but I am not persuaded.

Contrary to the magazine's assertion Martin is not a "public figure." It is clear that he, as one of some 15,000 Mummers, does not possess the requisite fame and notoriety to qualify as a public figure. Also, there is no evidence that he has thrust himself to the forefront of any controversy which would justify treating him as a public figure for some limited purpose.

Given the facts of this case, however, I believe the issue of whether publication's conduct was sufficiently extreme and outrageous must be decided by the jury.

**Verdict:** The case is REMANDED for further processing consistent with this opinion.

## 7-Dust in the Eyes

**Court:** Superior Court of New Jersey

**Date:** 1906 JUN 11

**Report:** No number in original

**Case number:** 73 N.J.L. 405; 63 A. 860

**Link:** https://merillionpress.com/cases/X-007.pdf

**Plaintiff (Appellant):** Anna PORTER

**Defendant (Appellee):** DELAWARE, LACKAWANNA AND WESTERN RAILROAD Company

**Opinion By:** John F. FORT, Judge

**Prior History:** Porter was walking upon the public highway in the city of Newark and just as she was passing from under the overhead railway bridge of the defendant company, which spans the street, it fell, with an engine upon it, and she claims that something hit her upon the back of the neck and that the dust from the crash got into her eyes.

She also claims injuries resulting from the shock. The chief injuries are alleged to be to her eyes and nervous system. The contention of the defendant is that she received no physical injury whatever, but that the condition she alleges she is suffering from is due to fright alone. If that were true, of course, she could not recover. But if she received physical injuries, all the resultant effects to her system, due to the accident, are recoverable.

Porter sued at the Passaic Circuit for negligence and received a favorable verdict and the railroad company appeals demanding a new trial.

**Before this Court:** Accepting the finding of the jury that she thus suffered physical injury, she was entitled to damages for the results flowing from it.

We do not think the weight of the evidence is so clearly against her having received the physical injuries she alleged as to justify us in disturbing the verdict on that ground.

Other reasons alleged as errors of the trial judge relate to the admission of evidence on the redirect examination of witnesses and to the refusal to strike out evidence.

These rulings do not seem to have been injurious to the defendant on the merits of the case, and were entirely within the discretion of the trial judge, and we can see no abuse of that discretion in the record.

But the granting of the new trial in this case could have been as well put upon the ground of excessive damages, owing to the consideration by the jury of this improper element of damages, and in other parts of the decision was practically so put.

**Verdict:** The only remaining ground is that the damages were excessive. The injuries to Porter were not severe. We think them greatly exaggerated. The verdict is clearly excessive. On this ground the ruling will be REVERSED, unless Porter will consent to the reduction of the verdict to $500 ($14,000 today).

## 8-Don't Panic

**Court:** Supreme Court of Missouri

**Date:** 1983 FEB 23

**Report:** No. 63926

**Case number:** 646 S.W. 2d 765

**Link:** https://merillionpress.com/cases/X-008.pdf

**Plaintiff (Appellant):** Collette BASS

**Defendants (Appellees):** NOONEY Company and Otis Elevator Company

**Opinion By:** Solbert M. WASSERSTROM, Judge

**Prior History:** Collette Bass was employed by General Dynamics Company which occupied several floors of the Pierre Laclede Center, a structure owned and operated by Nooney. Her duties in part consisted of serving as a relief receptionist so that the regular receptionists on various floors could take periodic rest breaks and lunch periods.

On April 6, 1976, Bass entered an elevator at the 20th floor about 11:15 a.m. in order to go to the 23rd floor to relieve the receptionist there. The elevator started in the usual manner, but then she heard a grinding noise and the elevator came to a stop. She waited a short while, hoping that the elevator would start up again, but when it did not she began punching the emergency button. She could hear the emergency bell ring, but no voice came through the intercom, nor did any help come from the outside.

After about 10 to 15 minutes, Bass began to pound on the door of the elevator and shout for help. Response came from a man in the corridor who announced himself simply as "Don." she asked him to summon someone who could get her out and also to notify her work supervisor. Don cautioned her "don't panic" and he said he would get help. Soon thereafter plaintiff's supervisor did call to her through the door and asked how she was.

She responded that she was beginning to feel dizzy. After about 15 minutes, she was getting warm and feeling strange. She went to a corner of the elevator and slid to the floor.

The maintenance people eventually arrived about thirty minutes after the elevator stalled, and they freed her at about 11:45 a.m. The elevator doors were opened, disclosing the elevator to have stopped about a foot above the floor.

She reported to work the next day and when she boarded an elevator, after ascending one floor she fell over, was caught by other passengers and eventually was taken to a hospital. The hospital record showed that she had experienced acute anxiety, slurred speech, her equilibrium was off, she felt lightheaded, cold and thoroughly frightened and too scared to sleep the night before.

This was confirmed by her attending psychiatrist stating that the elevator incident precipitated her condition. He agreed, however, that contributing factors to the situation were the facts that she was at that time in the process of obtaining a divorce and that she was taking care of her mother who had recently suffered a stroke.

The psychiatrist also reported to General Dynamics that she was able to return to work and she would not have any permanent disability from the emotional damage done to her.

Bass seeks damages for mental distress caused by the alleged negligence of defendants Nooney Company (owner of the building) and Otis Elevator Company.

The jury trial tossed out her case and her appeal to the Missouri Court of Appeals, Eastern District was also dismissed. She appeals that decision.

**Before this Court:** The entrenched rule presently in force in Missouri is that a defendant is not liable for negligence resulting in emotional distress unless the plaintiff suffered a contemporaneous traumatic physical injury. Under these rules, the trial court had no choice but to dismiss and the court of appeals had no choice but to affirm.

The question before this court is whether the long standing "impact rule" should be reconsidered and changed.

A painstaking review of this whole subject has convinced this court that the time has come for Missouri to join the mainstream of Anglo-American jurisprudence by abandoning the classic impact rule. We are further of the opinion that logic and practicality argue in favor of avoiding any requirement that "physical injury" result from the emotional distress.

**Verdict:** The judgment of dismissal is REVERSED and this cause is remanded for new trial.

## 9-Something Missing

**Court:** United States Court of Appeals for the Fifth Circuit

**Date:** 1992 OCT 08

**Report:** No. 92-4139

**Case number:** 974 F. 2d 598

**Link:** https://merillionpress.com/cases/X-009.pdf

**Plaintiff (Appellant):** Timothy C. COTITA

**Defendant (Appellee):** PHARMA-PLAST, USA Inc.

**Opinion By:** John M. DUHE, Circuit Judge

**Prior History:** Cotita is a registered nurse. While providing nursing services to an AIDS patient, he was stuck by a syringe manufactured by Pharma-Plast. The syringe, although still in its sterile packaging, was missing the protective cap that normally covers the tip of the needle. This improper packaging allowed the needle to pierce its sterile plastic covering and penetrate the protective gloves that he was wearing.

Because of the presence of the patient's blood on his gloves at the time of the needle stick, Cotita feared that he had been exposed to the HIV virus. Subsequent tests revealed that he was not HIV-positive; nevertheless, he sued Pharma-Plast seeking damages for mental anguish stemming from his fear of contracting AIDS.

Pharma-Plast admitted defective packaging and the damage issue was tried before a jury which returned a verdict for $150,000 in Cotita's favor. This amount was reduced by 30%; a figure which the jury found reflected Cotita's own negligence. He maintains that the issue of his negligence should not have been considered by the jury, nor used to reduce the amount of his award.

**Before this Court:** Pharma-Plast presented evidence that the procedures used by Cotita were in violation of the universal precautions and procedures which are standard in the health care field. Cotita's argument that a reduction in the manufacturer's liability will reduce its incentive to produce safer products could be made any time comparative fault principles are applied. Because we find no error in the district court's application of comparative fault, we defer to its judgment and affirm its holding on this point.

Cotita also contends that the district court also erred in refusing to let him present additional evidence regarding the fault of Pharma-Plast. We do not agree with his characterization of this decision. The damage phase of the proceeding was separate and apart from the previously decided liability phase. The actions of Cotita in his use of the defective syringe were properly considered in evaluating the damages awarded.

**Verdict:** Finding no error in the district court's handling of these issues, we AFFIRM its decision.

# 10-Mirth and Girth

**Court:** United States Court of Appeals for the Seventh Circuit

**Date:** 1994 FEB 01

**Report:** 92-2991, 92-3177

**Case number:** 16 F. 3d 145

**Link:** https://merillionpress.com/cases/X-010.pdf

**Plaintiff (Appellee):** David K. NELSON, Jr.

**Defendants (Appellants):** Allan STREETER, Dorothy TILLMAN and Bobby L. RUSH

**Opinion By:** Richard A. POSNER, Chief Judge

**Prior History:** Harold Washington, Chicago's first black mayor, died suddenly of a heart attack in November 1987, shortly after being re-elected. He had become a revered figure to the black community of Chicago – so much so that shortly after his death a poster went on sale in which a smiling Harold Washington is shown in the company of Jesus Christ floating above the Chicago skyline; the poster is captioned "Worry Ye Not."

David Nelson, a student at the School of the Art Institute of Chicago, did not think Washington deserving of deification, and so for his entry in the school's annual fellowship competition Nelson submitted a painting intended (he claims) to portray Washington in a more human light.

The painting, entitled "Mirth and Girth" and based on a rumour that doctors at the hospital to which Washington had been brought when he suffered his fatal heart attack had discovered that underneath his suit he was wearing female underwear, is a full-length frontal portrait of a portly grim-faced Harold Washington clad in a white bra and G-string, garter belt, and stockings.

Nelson's painting, together with the submissions of the other students, was placed on exhibition on May 11, 1988. The exhibition was opening to students, faculty, and invited guests, but not to the public at large. The students' works were to be judged by four experts. The winners would receive cash prizes, and their winning works would be exhibited at a public exhibition.

"Mirth and Girth," however, was destined not to be judged—not in the expected fashion, at any rate. As soon as the exhibition of student work opened and visitors saw Nelson's painting, it became the focus of outraged attention. A security guard was quickly posted in front of it to protect it from an angry crowd of students. The school began receiving enraged phone calls. School officials asked Nelson to remove the painting. He refused.

Word of the painting came to the Chicago City Council, which was in session. Alderman Bobby Rush prepared a resolution, which was signed by, among others, Alderman Allan Streeter and Dorothy Tillman, threatening to cut off the City's contribution to the Art Institute unless the Institute apologized for displaying "Mirth and Girth." The resolution passed, together with another resolution, which requested the Art Institute to remove the painting immediately.

Then, they proceeded to visit the exhibition, but they were not the first aldermen to arrive at the scene. Aldermen Henry and Jones arrived first. Henry brandished a gun, and Jones removed the painting from the wall and placed it on the floor, facing the wall.

They left, and a student re-hung the painting. Then the defendants arrived. They took the painting down and tried to carry it out of the school, but were stopped by a school official, then diverted (carrying the painting) to the office of the president of the School of the Art Institute, Anthony Jones. When the painting arrived in Jones's office, it had a one-foot gash, but it is not known precisely when, or by whom, the gash had been inflicted.

The aldermen told Jones that they were there to carry out the City Council's resolution to remove the painting from the Art Institute. The aldermen wrapped the painting in brown paper to prevent anyone from seeing it. According to one witness, Alderman Tillman threatened to burn the painting right there in President Jones's office but was dissuaded by a police lieutenant who was present, Raymond Patterson.

Another alderman (not one of the defendants) called Chicago Police Superintendent Leroy Martin. He telephoned Patterson in President Jones's office and ordered him to take the painting into police custody. A police sergeant, accompanied by the three defendant aldermen, carried the wrapped painting to a police car. The scene was televised, and broadcast widely, confirming, if confirmation was needed, that Chicago had replaced Boston as the censorship capital of the United States.

"Mirth and Girth" was kept in custody until the evening of the following day, when it was released (we assume on its own recognizance) to David Nelson. The painting has not been repaired, exhibited, or sold. It is an exhibit in this suit, and Nelson's lawyer has physical custody of it. In the president's office Jones had signed a statement promising that if the painting was returned it would not be "displayed or shown in any way without a meeting and resolution of the Board of Trustees and members of the City Council." Later the president of the Art Institute's board, Marshall Field, issued a public apology in which he promised that the painting would not be returned to public display.

**Before this Court:** The appeals are from the district judge's rejection of the defense of official immunity. Nelson filed this civil rights damages suit in 1988, shortly after the incident. The suit charges that the defendants deprived Nelson of rights secured to him by several statues. Although the bizarre facts and the prominence of the defendants have attracted public attention to the case, it is straightforward from a legal standpoint and we are distressed by its protraction. We are being asked to resolve the threshold issue of immunity in a case that is five years old.

A public official is not answerable in damages for a violation of the Constitution unless, at the time he acted, the law was clear that what he was doing really *did* violate the Constitution. In other words, he is not chargeable with predicting expansions in constitutional liability. So we must ask whether in 1988 the law was clear that local government officials may not go onto private property without invitation (the aldermen had not been invited to the exhibition of student work), seize a painting that they do not like because it vilifies a public official with whom they had been associated, and wrap it in brown paper and remove it so that no one can see it. To ask the question is pretty much to answer it. If the City owned the Art Institute, it would have some power – how much we need not decide –to regulate offensive displays.

**Verdict:** The district judge's rejection of the defense of official immunity is AFFIRMED.

## 11-Train Whistled at Him

**Court:** United States Court of Appeals for the Eighth Circuit

**Date:** 1996 FEB 16

**Report:** No 95-2488

**Case number:** 76 F. 3d 893

**Link:** https://merillionpress.com/cases/X-011.pdf

**Appellant:** Michael Wayne GADDIS

**Appellee:** Shirley S. CHATER, Commissioner of Social Security

**Opinion by:** John B. JONES, Senior District Judge

**Prior History:** Gaddis was a thirty-five-year-old man when he was injured on the job with Burlington Northern Railroad on March 15, 1987, when a train whistled at him, while he was standing at a crossing. As a result he suffers from tinnitus described as "constant high pitched ringing hiss in his ears." He cannot tolerate loud or sustained noise, but that he can hear and tolerate conversation. Gaddis testified he has difficulty concentrating and that he now suffers "mental pain" and he suffers from nervousness, anxiety and depression which preclude him from working. All on account of the tinnitus.

Inconsistencies in his testimony and the medical records indicate that his claimed disability is subjective. When he ran out of private/employer disability insurance benefits he managed to land a job as a liquor store salesclerk. It didn't last long, nevertheless, he confined to his treating psychiatrist that "he can go out and find a minimum wage job at any time, but he is more worried about the future."

In addition, while he testified to the effect, that he could not tolerate noise at the workplace, he was seen going on a motorcycle trip and shooting off fireworks on the Fourth of July.

Following the initial hearing, an administrative law judge (ALJ) denied Gaddis' application, a decision which was affirmed by the Appeals Council. He then sued in federal district court in Missouri, dismissed again and this is his 4th attempt to obtain favorable judgment in 9 years of litigation.

**Before this Court**: Our task on review is to determine whether the denial of benefits is supported by substantial evidence in the record as a whole. On appeal it is argued that the ALJ erred in evaluating the medical evidence by improperly disregarding the opinion of Gaddis' treating psychiatrist, Dr. Christy. Based on our review of the record we find no error in the evaluation of the medical evidence.

Regarding subjective complaints, Gaddis contends the ALJ erred when he found Gaddis' complaints of disabling "mental pain" associated with his tinnitus not credible. The record indicates that the ALJ found that Gaddis suffers from tinnitus (as well as depression and anxiety), but that the condition is not disabling as defined by the Act.

Further, we agree with the ALJ that inconsistencies exist in the record which could justify discounting Gaddis' testimony regarding the severity of his injury. Apparently after private disability insurance benefits and employer disability benefits ended, Gaddis filed a lawsuit against his former railroad employer. The record indicates his frustration at the time required to receive financial support through the litigation. At one point Gaddis was trying to decide to "work for a year and a half until a settlement comes through on his lawsuit."

We agree with the ALJ that there is a "strong element of secondary gain in this case" and that Gaddis' conduct belies his sincere belief that he is truly disabled and unable to perform any substantial gainful activity.

**Verdict:** Based on the record, we are convinced that the ALJ's decision is adequately supported by substantial evidence. Accordingly, we AFFIRM.

## 12-War Games

**Court:** United States Court of Appeals for the Second Circuit

**Date:** 1996 DEC 24

**Report:** Nos. 86, 87, Dockets 96-6046, 96-6048

**Case number:** 102 F. 3d 693

**Link:** https://merillionpress.com/cases/X-012.pdf

**Plaintiff (Appellants):** Bernard J. MORTISE and Cheryl L. MORTISE

**Defendant (Appellee):** United States of America

**Opinion By:** Joseph M. McLAUGHLIN, Circuit Judge

**Prior History:** On a Saturday night in early March, 1991, Bernard and Cheryl Mortise and their friends, the Wagners, were riding on All Terrain Vehicles (ATVs) in upstate New York on land owned by Oneida County (the "County"). ATVs are three or four wheel motorized recreational vehicles somewhat akin to motorcycles. The Mortises had their own ATVs, as did each of the Wagners.

They sported on logging roads near Route 49 close to the town of New London. The Mortises had made similar trips in the past; as before, they did not notice any signs or fences restricting the use of the land. On the fateful Saturday evening, unbeknownst to the Mortises, the County had given the 108th Infantry Regiment of the Army National Guard permission to use the same land for training exercises.

Three years earlier, in 1988, the County had entered into an agreement with the 108th Infantry Regiment regarding the use of the land near New London. Under the Agreement, the National Guard would "on occasion" use the land for overnight field training exercises. The National Guard advised the County that blank ammunition and smoke would be used during some training exercises. The National Guard, for its part, had agreed that the United States would be responsible for any damage, injury or death caused by the National Guard during these exercises.

Near dusk, the Mortises and the Wagners travelled into the woods on the logging road. They had been driving on this particular land for a number of years, and noticed only the occasional hiker or ATV. This Saturday evening, however, Cheryl Mortise spied shadows in the woods, but thought nothing of it. The four continued up the wooded trail.

The Mortises did not realize that those shadows were cast by members of the 108th Infantry Regiment. The Guardsmen were engaged in mock "war-games," setting up mortar placements, and roaming the woods, armed with M-16 assault rifles, 0.9 mm semi-automatic pistols, and 81 mm mortars. As is common in such exercises, Guardsmen had placed trip wires near mortar placements. When faux "enemies" approached mortar placements they would trigger the tripwires, setting off smoke flares, and revealing the "enemy" position.

Lieutenant Thomas Hanley, the mortar platoon leader, saw the four ATVs travel into the woods on the logging road. He did not, however, try to stop them, or inform his men to take precautions because he assumed that other Guardsmen saw the ATVs as well. The Mortises had passed within a few yards of a mortar position. After the group went up the trail, a Guardsman rigged a tripwire across the road behind the ATVs, and attached it to a flare.

Around 9:30 P.M., the Mortises and their friends were returning from the woods, driving back down the logging road, single file. Bernard

Mortise was in the lead; his wife was about 50 feet behind him, and the Wagners behind her. Bernard Mortise tripped the wire, igniting a flare that spewed debris over him and his vehicle. Instantly, Guardsmen in camouflage uniforms roared out of the woods. The Guardsmen pointed their rifles at his head, and "dry-fired" (i.e., no bullets) the triggers. He pleaded with them not to shoot. The Guardsmen told him to "shut up" and to shut off his ATV. One of the Guardsmen actually fired a blank round.

Cheryl Mortise saw the explosion, the Guardsmen raising their guns to her husband, and she heard the blank shot fired. She thought her husband had been shot and began to scream. A Guardsman told her to shut up. Moments later, Bernard Mortise approached her and told her to calm down. She wanted to run away, but the husband told her not to because there were "too many of them." The Guardsmen, convinced that the four ATV'ers were enemy decoys in the war game, treated the Mortises brusquely, cursing, and telling them that they were "prisoners."

Lt. Hanley soon arrived on the scene. He told the Mortises that they had stumbled into a National Guard training exercise, and that their capture had been a misunderstanding. He tried to explain the Guardsmen's confusion. After a brief conversation, the Mortises and their friends were allowed to leave, shaken by the outrageous conduct of the National Guard.

Cheryl Mortise subsequently entered the care of a psychologist. She has nightmares, and harbors fears of going out at night, of people in uniforms, and of shopping by herself.

In December 1993, the Mortises filed individual lawsuits against the United States in the United States District Court for the Northern District of New York. The Mortises alleged that the negligence of the National Guardsmen caused them "mental and emotional injuries." Their claim was dismissed and now they appeal.

**Before this Court:** The Mortises argue that there are jury questions whether the National Guardsmen's conduct constitutes assault or negligent infliction of emotional distress. We conclude that there is no legal basis either for a claim of assault or for a claim of negligent infliction of emotional distress.

Under the Federal Tort Claims Act, the government has waived its sovereign immunity for a number of torts. However, section 2680 of the Act, expressly refuses to waive sovereign immunity for any claims arising out of assault or battery. In short, any claim the Mortises have against the government for assault is barred for lack of jurisdiction.

The Mortises concentrate most of their effort regarding their claim for negligent infliction of emotional distress. Logically, Cheryl Mortise is the only one who could conceivably recover under a "bystander" theory, because she witnessed the bizarre attack on her husband. Her claim, however, is fatally deficient both because her own physical safety was never threatened and she did not see her husband suffer a serious physical injury.

**Verdict:** Although the conduct of the National Guard was outrageous, the law requires us to AFFIRM the district court's decision.

## 13-Polish Mug

**Court:** Court of Appeals of the State of New York

**Date:** 1980 DEC 22

**Report:** None in original

**Case number:** 52 N.Y. 2d 813

**Link:** https://merillionpress.com/cases/X-013.pdf

**Appellant:** State Division of Human Rights, on Complaint of Donald GLADWIN

**Respondent:** MCHARRIS Gift Center

**Opinion by:** Lawrence H. COOKE, Chief Judge

**Prior History:** This is a complaint charging discrimination through the display and sale of ethnic "joke" novelty items. Donald Gladwin, an individual of Polish heritage, charges the McHarris Gift Center with the unlawful discriminatory practice of denying him equal advantages, facilities, privileges and accommodations of a place of public accommodation (all enshrined in state and federal laws), because of his national origin.

The basis of the complaint was the sale and display by McHarris Gift Center of three novelty items that were demeaning to persons of Polish extraction. The three items were a cylinder marked "Polish bowling ball", a mug with the handle inside marked "Polish mug" and a pencil with an electric cord marked "Polish Calculator."

Gladwin commenced this action with the State Division of Human Rights charging the McHarris Gift Center with the unlawful discriminatory practice of denying him equal advantages, facilities, privileges and accommodations of a place of public accommodation because of his national origin. The case ended up at the Appellate Division which concluded that the items were "offensive and in poor taste," but they were not communications prohibited by any existing law and dismissed the complaint.

This appeal followed.

**Before this Court:** Presented here is only one question whether the State Division of Human Rights has jurisdiction to act on a complaint charging discrimination through the display and sale of ethnic "joke" novelty items. The majority holds that it does not.

This court is not called upon at this time to say that the display here necessarily evinces the prohibited conduct and constitutes an unlawful discriminatory practice. Indeed, the court is not asked to decide whether the complaint should be sustained on the merits. The only issue is whether the State division has jurisdiction over this complaint. At the very least, the possibility of a veiled discriminatory tactic can be discerned here. Not only does the majority ignore this, but in denying jurisdiction here, it effectively prohibits complaints of discrimination that take the form of exclusion by indirection.

**Verdict:** The court majority AFFIRMED the lower court's verdict in favor of McHarris Gift Center with three dissents.

## 14-Fly in the Bottle

**Court:** Supreme Court of Canada

**Date:** 2008 MAY 15

**Report:** [2008] 2 SCR 114

**Case number:** 31902

**Link:** https://merillionpress.com/cases/X-014.pdf

**Plaintiffs (Respondents)**: Waddah MUSTAPHA (aka Martin Mustapha) and Lynn MUSTAPHA

**Defendant (Appellant):** CULLIGAN of Canada Ltd.

**Opinion By:** Beverley M. MCLACHLIN, Chief Judge

**Prior History**: The Mustaphas of Windsor, ON maintain a spotless home. Cleanliness and hygiene are matters of utmost importance to them. On November 21, 2001, an incident occurred that offended their sense of purity of their home and shattered their life. Attempting to replace an empty bottle of Culligan water on the dispenser provided by Culligan, he and his wife saw a dead fly, and one half of another dead fly in the unopened replacement bottle.

Even though neither Mustapha, nor any member of his family drank from the bottle, he became obsessed with thoughts about the dead fly in the water and its "revolting implications" and about the potential implications for his family's health and the possibility of drinking unpurified water in the past.

He sued. The lower court trial judge accepted the medical evidence, that Mustapha suffers from a major depressive disorder, with associated phobia and anxiety – all triggered by the fly-in-the-bottle incident. As a result, Mustapha obtained judgment at trial in the amount of C$341,775

(US $300,000 today), plus pre-judgment interest for psychiatric injuries suffered because of the incident.

Culligan appeals the finding of its liability and, in the alternative, seeks to reduce the amount of damages awarded.

**Before this Court:** Psychological disturbance that rises to the level of personal injury must be distinguished from psychological upset. Personal injury connotes serious trauma or illness. The law does not recognize upset, disgust, anxiety, agitation or other mental states that fall short of injury. I would not purport to define compensable injury exhaustively, except to say that it must be serious and prolonged and rise above the ordinary annoyances, anxieties and fears that people living in society routinely, if sometimes reluctantly, accept.

Quite simply, minor and transient upsets do not constitute personal injury, and hence do not amount to damage.

One of the questions that arose in this case was, in judging whether the personal injury was foreseeable, one looks at a person of "ordinary fortitude" or at a particular plaintiff with his or her particular vulnerabilities. This question may be acute in claims for mental injury, since there is a wide variation in how particular people respond to particular stressors. The law has consistently held – albeit within the duty of care analysis – that the question is what a person of ordinary fortitude would suffer: "The law expects reasonable fortitude and robustness of its citizens and will not impose liability for the exceptional frailty of certain individuals."

In this case, however, there was no evidence to support a finding that Culligan knew of Mustapha's particular sensibilities. Having failed to establish that it was reasonably foreseeable that a person of ordinary fortitude would have suffered personal injury, it follows that his claim must fail.

**Verdict:** For the reasons discussed, I conclude that the loss suffered by the plaintiff was too remote to be reasonably foreseen and that consequently, he cannot recover damages from the defendant.

Appeal DISMISSED with costs.

## 15-Schooling Pigs

**Court:** United States District Court, W.D. Michigan, Southern Division

**Date:** 2012 OCT 10

**Report:** No. 1:12-CV-321

**Case number:** 902 F. Supp. 2d 1038

**Link:** https://merillionpress.com/cases/X-015.pdf

**Plaintiffs:** Kendra VELZEN and Fair Housing Center of West Michigan

**Defendants:** GRAND VALLEY STATE UNIVERSITY, et al.

**Opinion By:** Robert H. BELL, District Judge

**Prior History:** Kendra Velzen began treatment for depression in 2007 with therapist Merrill E. Graham, a licensed master social worker, clinical social worker, and registered physical therapist. To manage her depression, she has relied upon the attachment and emotional support she derives from animals. In 2009, Velzen was diagnosed with severe neurologically mediated cardiac arrhythmia and had a pacemaker implanted. In August 2011, before she moved on-campus at GVSU, where she was a student, Graham formally prescribed an emotional support animal for her.

Velzen moved into Calder Residence, an apartment-style building on campus, owned and operated by GVSU, on August 24, 2011, bringing with her a letter from Graham and her guinea pig, Blanca. The letter explained her conditions, and it concluded that "the use of a comfort object, such as Blanca, is a necessary means of controlling stress and managing symptoms." Graham added that "the presence of Blanca provides Velzen with continued emotional support and attachment (thereby reducing symptoms of depression), physiological benefits (such as decreased heart rate), and psychological benefits (such as increased Oxytocin levels, which directly impact the sense of life satisfaction)."

School officials granted her temporary permission to keep Blanca for the evening, but told her the next day that her request to live with the guinea pig was denied because it was not a trained service animal and she did not have a physical impairment.

On March 30, 2012, Velzen with the help of the Fair Housing Center of West Michigan brought a seven count suit against GVSU, Grand Valley State University Board of Regents and several of its employees alleging unlawful discrimination under the Fair Housing Act, Federal Rehabilitation Act, and Michigan Persons with Disabilities Civil Rights Act. Plaintiffs request changes to the current rules, as well as monetary compensation.

Three days later, GVSU gave Velzen permission to bring the guinea pig back into her residence. GVSU contends that it "approved" her accommodation request. Velzen asserts that GVSU stood by its policy and characterized it as an "interim exception" and "temporary." Since then, Velzen has moved out of Calder Residence and cancelled her application for on-campus housing for the Fall 2012/Winter 2013 school year.

**Before this Court:** GVSU argues that Velzen's claims should be dismissed because she has moved out of on-campus housing.

However, Velzen is still a student. She has "not ruled out" the possibility of living on-campus in a future year. Moreover, at least part of the reason she chose to not live on campus during the present school year was fear that GVSU would take away her temporary exception to live with her guinea pig.

**Verdict:** Five of the claims will be DISMISSED and two claims REMAIN.

Prior to further proceedings GVSU has reached a $40,000 settlement with Velzen in order to avoid litigation costs.

# 16-Setbacks and Courts

**Court:** The High Court of Justice, Queen's Bench Division, London, England

**Date:** 2010 APR 28

**Report:** No. [2010] EWHC 924 (QB)

**Case number:** HQ09X01648

**Link:** https://merillionpress.com/cases/X-016.pdf

**Claimant:** Robert DEE

**Defendant:** TELEGRAPH Media Group Ltd.

**Opinion By:** Victoria M. SHARP DBE, Justice

**Prior History:** Dee is a 23 year old tennis professional. He sues in respect of an article published on the bottom left hand corner of the front page of the *Daily Telegraph* on 23 April 2008 under the heading "World's worst tennis pro wins at last."

The front page article of which he complains said this: "A BRITON ranked as the worst professional tennis player in the world after 54 defeats in a row has won his first match. Robert Dee, 21, of Bexley, Kent, did not win a single match during his first three years on the circuit, touring at an estimated cost of £200,000. But his dismal run ended at the Reus tournament near Barcelona as he beat an unranked 17-year-old, Arzhang Derakshani, 6-4, 6-3."

Underneath the front page article, are the words in bold, "**Full story: S20"** and below those words is a photograph of Dee apparently playing tennis.

The "**Full story"** to which reference is made appears on the back page of the Sports supplement of the same edition, it says this: "A British tennis sensation – the world's worst British globetrotter Dee ends his losing streak at the 55th time of asking," writes Mark Hodgkinson. "In the history of British tennis failures, and it's been a long and rich history, no one had previously come close to the serial defeats that have flowed from his racket" the article continues. "Perhaps Dee has earned the right to be bracketed with such global sporting icons as jumping's Eddie the Eagle or swimming's Eric the Eel."

"When it comes to losing, he's absolutely world class. Dee equalled the world record for the longest run of consecutive defeats, and all of them in straight sets. That's 108 lost sets in succession. But he even failed in his efforts to make the record his own, after he last week won a first-round match in qualifying at a lowly Futures tournament in Spain. He soon returned to form, losing in the next round ... and in straight sets."

Dee and his father have taken very great offence at what the *Daily Telegraph* published and sue for libel claiming over £500,000 (US $750,000 today) in damages. Aside from the ridicule, the claim states the article made him look absurdly bad at his chosen profession, deterring people from using him as a coach in the future. The newspaper claims in its defense; the articles are not arguably defamatory, that no tribunal of fact could rationally conclude that Dee had been libelled.

The *Daily Telegraph* was one of a very large number of media outlets that covered the story. Settlements and apologies have been achieved by Dee from a very large number of them, including the BBC and Reuters.

**Before this Court:** I have no trouble in concluding that the words complained of when read in their context (as identified above) are capable of bearing a meaning defamatory of the Claimant: for example, that he lacks insight into his own lack of talent, and unreasonably persists in pursuing a career to which he is not suited; or that he unreasonably and unrealistically persists in a career as a professional tennis player which is an expensive waste of money and doomed to failure. That meaning says something about him and his character and people might think the less of him, if that is what the words complained of did mean. But this is not the meaning of which he complains.

The pleaded meaning strongly suggests this case has more in common with an action for malicious falsehood. Dee's lawyer said at one point for example, that he was made to look like the "Inspector Clouseau" of the tennis world.

An innate lack of talent – even for professional sportsmen – particularly where they play on their own, might be said to be a misfortune but no more. Whether the words are in fact defamatory of the Claimant is a matter which must be left therefore to the good sense of a jury properly directed.

**Verdict:** As it is however, there is no other compelling reason why the claim should be tried; and in my view for the reasons given, the Defendant is entitled to SUMMARY JUDGMENT against the Claimant.

# CHAPTER XI

# COMMON SENSE IMPAIRED

*"If you demand money from someone in exchange for your silence, it's called 'blackmail'. If your lawyer demands money from someone in exchange for your silence, it's called a settlement. If you do big things they print your face, and if you do little things they print only your thumbs." Arthur Baer (1886 – 1969) was an American journalist and humorist*

Highlights of this constituent part showcase the law's extortive potential. High Lamas of litigation in the business of selling solutions to problems they create, exaggerate, and exacerbate and have no desire to solve.

Doggedly searching for some kernel of genuine issue lurking in the background and road-testing new forms of a shakedown. It's no secret, all filings here point to "deep pocket" defendants with the unstated – but all too obvious – aim of extracting fees.

## 1-No Harm Trying

**Court:** United States District Court, S. D. New York.

**Date:** 1977 MAR 04

**Report:** 76 Civ. 3138

**Case number:** 427 F. Supp. 971 (S.D.N.Y. 1977)

**Link:** https://merillionpress.com/cases/XI-001.pdf

**Plaintiffs (Respondents):** George KARFUNKEL and Renee KARFUNKEL

**Defendant (Appellant):** Compagnie Nationale AIR FRANCE and Singapore Airlines, Ltd.

**Opinion By:** Inzer B. WYATT, District Judge

**Prior History:** On June 6, 1976, George and Renee bought from a Manhattan travel agency two tickets for a June 8 flight on TWA from New York to Milan, Italy. On the same day, they also bought two return tickets on TWA for a June 30 flight from Paris to New York. On June 7, 1976, they purchased from the same travel agent two tickets for a June 18 Swissair flight from Milan (through Zurich) to Tel Aviv, Israel.

On June 23, 1976, while in Israel, George purchased for him and Renee two tickets for an Air France flight from Tel Aviv to Paris for June 27. These tickets were sold to the Karfunkels by a Jerusalem travel agent at a special reduced fare known as the "student and youth" tariff.

On June 27, the Karfunkels departed Tel Aviv for Paris aboard the Air France flight. During a scheduled stopover at Athens, Greece airport, the airplane they were travelling on was boarded by four terrorists armed with guns and explosives.

Shortly after take-off from Athens, the terrorists seized control of the aircraft and directed that it be flown to Benghazi, Libya. The plane was then flown at the hijackers' direction to Entebbe Airport in Uganda. At Entebbe, crew and passengers were held hostage in the airport terminal building, while the hijackers made several demands upon the governments of various countries. On July 4, Israeli military troops staged a raid on Entebbe Airport, rescuing the hostages and transporting them to Israel aboard military aircraft.

**Before this Court:** The complaint pleads four claims, two against Air France and two against Singapore Airlines. Singapore Airlines is sought to be held liable for having brought the terrorists to Athens Airport.

In their two claims against Air France, the Karfunkels seek damages for bodily injuries and false imprisonment suffered by them at the hands of the hijackers. It is averred that Air France was negligent in failing to take adequate security precautions which would have prevented the hijackers from boarding the airplane with weapons.

In such cases The Warsaw Convention is the supreme law of the land. One of the important "conditions" of an "action for damages" is the *place* where it must be brought. It provides that such an action must be brought either before the court of the domicile of the carrier (this would be France in the case at bar), or of the principal place of business of the carrier (this would also be France), or where the carrier has a place of business through which the contract has been made (this would be Israel), or "before the court at the place of destination."

The only possible basis for jurisdiction here in New York is that New York was "the place of destination."

Not even plaintiffs seriously contend for this, nor could they.

**Verdict:** The destination of the Air France flight on which the Karfunkels were riding was Paris, not New York. The motion of defendant Air France is GRANTED and the motion of plaintiffs Karfunkels is DENIED as moot.

## 2-Too Short to Fly

**Court:** Canadian Human Rights Tribunal

**Date:** 1987 OCT 23

**Report:** No. 9 C.H.R.R.

**Case number:** TD 12/87

**Link:** https://merillionpress.com/cases/XI-002.pdf

**Complainants:** Lucie CHAPDELAINE and France GRAVEL

**Respondent:** AIR CANADA

**Intervener:** Canadian Air Line Pilots Association

**Opinion By:** Daniel H. TINGLEY, Arbitrator

**Prior History:** The complainants are pilots and they both applied for employment with Air Canada as pilots. They were both refused employment for the stated reason that they did not meet Air Canada's minimum height requirements for pilots. The required minimum height is 5'-6" (167.6 cm). Chapdelaine is 5'-4" tall and Gravel is 5'-3" tall.

They both claim that the minimum height requirement policy amounted to a discriminatory practice on the ground of sex and that they have suffered damages as a result. They seek compensation from Air Canada for amounts representing the difference between what they might have earned as a pilot from the dates their application was turned down and what they actually earned, plus compensatory and moral damages.

Chapdelaine claims loss of earnings of $83,054 for the contested period and $10,000 for loss of opportunities, while Gravel claims $52,418 for the contested period and also $10,000 for loss of opportunities. According to the evidence, Chapdelaine earned marginally more in 1985 with a competing airline than she would have earned with Air Canada.

In the spring of 1982, about one year after learning of the complaints, Air Canada lowered its minimum height requirements for pilots from 5'-6" to 5'-2" (157.5) and invited both candidates to resubmit their applications, which they did. Air Canada followed up with interview requests to which Gravel did not respond, however, Chapdelaine was interviewed by a panel of three pilots. At the end of the interview she informed the panel that she was no longer interested in pursuing her application with Air Canada.

The Tribunal infers from this and from their testimony that the complainants are not prepared to accept employment with Air Canada unless hired with seniority retroactive to the dates they were first refused employment.

**Before this Tribunal:** 1-MONETARY CLAIMS: Considering all circumstances of this case including the possibility of layoffs between 1980 and 1984 and other unknowns, the Tribunal believes it is not unreasonable to assess Air Canada for 40% of the complainants' potential monetary claims. In Chapdelaine's case, this amounts to $24,480 and the amount for Gravel is $32,000 (US $40,000 and $55,000 respectively today).

2-SENIORITY CLAIMS: The Tribunal refuses the complainants' request to order their instatement in pilot positions with Air Canada with seniority backdated to the time when they were refused. Air Canada invited the complainants to employment interviews when positions were open in 1985 and the Tribunal declines to order Air Canada to repeat this process.

3-MORAL CLAIMS: Both complainants expressed feelings of humiliation upon being refused by the respondent. Yet, both must have known of the employer's height requirements before they submitted their application. Both therefore took a calculated risk in applying for a position, including stretching the truth about their respective height in their applications. The Tribunal awards each complainant an amount of $1,000 under this head of claim.

**Verdict:** The Tribunal declares that the complaints are substantiated, that Air Canada engaged in discriminatory practices, namely sex and orders the company to pay the amounts described above with interest to Chapdelaine and Gravel.

# 3-Composite Scooter

**Court:** Court of Appeal of Louisiana, First Circuit

**Date:** 1973 JUN 20

**Report:** 9402

**Case number:** 280 So. 2d 231 (1973)

**Link:** https://merillionpress.com/cases/XI-003.pdf

**Plaintiffs (Respondent):** R. L. LANDRY et al.

**Defendants (Appellants):** E. A. CALDWELL Inc., R. CROOMS, SEARS et al.

**Opinion By:** Paul B. LANDRY Jr., Judge

**Prior History:** Dean Landry, a minor, was riding his bike when he suffered an accident on January 10, 1970, when his "Allstate" motor scooter was struck by a truck belonging to Caldwell and driven by Crooms.

The scooter involved had a checkered past to put it mildly.

It was a hybrid vehicle composed of parts from two "Allstate" scooters, which for purposes of this litigation, were manufactured by Sears. One of the vehicles, a blue and red motor bike had numerous prior owners. It changed hands frequently, at times for money, at other times in exchange for cutting grass and at one time it was also repossessed. Throughout its existence it was neglected, left outside at the mercy of the elements.

The second scooter used in fabricating subject vehicle was a "white scooter," the same model Allstate as the red and blue one. In reality, it was merely a "frame" with attached handlebars and fenders. It had no seat, engine, wheels, gas tank, brakes, clutch or control cables or levers. The previous owners removed the engine, wheel, clutch and brake and throttle cables from the blue machine and installed them on the white frame which was in better condition than the frame of the blue scooter. The "new" vehicle could be started and the engine running by pouring gasoline directly into the carburetor, when it was traded to Landry for another type of vehicle.

At the time of the accident, Landry started the vehicle in gear in the yard of a friend he was visiting. All of a sudden, the bike threw him out on the road. As he stated: "I had the clutch in, and when I cranked it up, it was in gear; so I pulled on the clutch and I hit the pavement, and it threw me up in the air."

On April 6, 1971, the scooter was examined by Robert E. Williams, Mechanical Engineer, in charge of a Sears's testing laboratory. He found the scooter badly damaged and suffering the ill effects of abuse and neglect of proper maintenance and care.

Landry alleges the motor scooter malfunctioned at the time of the accident, and that Crooms, the truck driver was guilty of various acts of negligence causing the accident. The trial court dismissed the petition and they appeal.

**Before this Court:** The facts involved here are the alleged jamming of the throttle in an open position and failure of the clutch to disengage and causing the rider to lose control. The malfunctioning is attributed to the negligent manufacture of a scooter having a mechanically defective throttle and clutch.

Depositions of Sears clearly show that – among others - the throttle mechanism on the scooter at the time of the accident was not the one manufactured by Sears. It was a completely foreign device. Mere belief by a litigant is unlikely to prevail on the merits, unless genuine dispute exists between the parties as to issues of fact.

**Verdict:** The judgment of the trial court is AFFIRMED.

## 4-Robber's Premature Release

**Court:** District of Columbia Court of Appeals

**Date:** 1987 MAR 31

**Report:** No. 85-1456

**Case number:** 526 A. 2d 933

**Link:** https://merillionpress.com/cases/XI-004.pdf

**Plaintiff (Appellant):** Mark AKINS

**Defendant (Appellees):** District of Columbia, et al.

**Opinion By:** John M. STEADMAN, Associate Judge

**Prior History:** Mark Akins initiated this lawsuit after having been gravely wounded during an armed robbery on May 11, 1982. The perpetrator, Clifford Henry Williams, was out on $ 3,000 bond for two previous armed robberies at the time. The arraignment judges who had twice released Williams in the preceding three-month period had done so on the basis of information which failed to include the record of the disposition of Williams' prior juvenile offenses.

The Pretrial Services Agency (PSA) report did note, however, that Williams had a number of prior juvenile arrests. The disposition information was not included in the PSA report because the computer, installed and maintained by IBM, failed to operate and the PSA employees failed to manually retrieve the information.

Nonetheless, the PSA report recommended that a hearing be conducted to determine whether Williams would pose a threat to community safety.

Akins alleges the following facts to demonstrate liability for negligence:

(1) The PSA computer, installed and maintained by IBM, failed to operate on two important occasions;

(2) Each time, the PSA discovered that their computer was not working, and they could not obtain a full record of Williams' arrest and conviction record;

(3) Rather than searching for the information by hand, both times the PSA informed the arraignment court that the computer did not work and they could not provide all of the requested information; therefore;

(4) The arraignment judge released Williams, once on his own recognizance and then on a $ 3,000 bond, because he was unaware of the full scope of Williams' previous record.

After a hearing, the Superior Court of the District of Columbia dismissed Akins' complaints, and now he appeals.

**Before this Court:** This court has recognized that the District of Columbia and its law enforcement officials "generally may not be held liable for failure to protect individuals from harm caused by criminal conduct." We have allowed an exception to this rule only where a specific undertaking to protect a particular individual has occurred, and that individual has justifiably relied upon such an undertaking.

Nowhere in the record has Akins alleged any specific undertaking toward the PSA, much less a justifiable reliance on it. We conclude, then, that his suit against the District and the PSA employees is barred by this "public duty doctrine".

IBM's liability and negligence could be pursued only when IBM had actual knowledge of, or good reason to anticipate, Williams' assault.

**Verdict:** Lower court decision AFFIRMED.

## 5-Washed out of Camaro

**Court:** Court of Appeal of Louisiana, Fifth Circuit

**Date:** 1988 OCT 12

**Report:** 88-CA-222

**Case number:** 532 So. 2d 948

**Link:** https://merillionpress.com/cases/XI-005.pdf

**Plaintiffs (Appellants):** Tamara BOUBEL et al.

**Defendants (Appellees):** Joseph A. GILARDI et al.

**Opinion By:** Thomas C. WICKER Jr., Judge

**Prior History:** Boubel's daughter, Dorothy Benjamin, was driving her 1985 Camaro while drunk. She collided violently with another car, driven by Joseph Gilardi, which resulted in her car's flipping over and landing upside down in a drainage canal.

Although she was wearing her seat belt, the impact of the accident allegedly caused the driver's seat to break or bend backwards, loosening the seat belt. The swift current of the canal, due to heavy rainfall, swept Benjamin out of the seat in spite of the seat belt and out of the car itself. Her body was ultimately found wedged between the windshield and the sprung hood and the autopsy determined that she died of drowning and not from the collision itself.

Boubel initially sued the other driver, the cocktail lounge where her daughter had been drinking the night of the accident, the State Department of Transportation, Jefferson Parish, and the City of Kenner. She later modified her petition to include General Motors Corporation, the manufacturer of the Camaro. Her claim against GMC was that the driver's seat and/or the seat belt were defective in that they allowed Benjamin to be washed out of the automobile, making it impossible for rescuers to find her and resulting in her death by drowning.

In its defense GMC argued that;

(1) Boubel isn't entitled to damages for loss of love and affection of her daughter. According to Louisiana law, only Benjamin's surviving children were entitled to wrongful death damages.

(2) Boubel had not alleged any defect in the car which was a cause of the accident;

(3) The car was not in normal use at the time of the accident;

The trial judge granted a judgment dismissing GMC from the suit, stating that the defects complained of are the effects of the accident, not the cause of it.

**Before this Court:** No other parties but GMC and Boubel are involved in this appeal.

In our view, the trial judge erred in focusing his attention on whether the automobile was in normal use, whether the automobile was the cause of Benjamin's death, whether drunken driving was a foreseeable use of the automobile, and whether the automobile caused an enhancement of Benjamin's injuries.

The proper focus for these questions is the safety device, the combination of seat belt and seat, since this is what has been alleged by Boubel to be defective and the cause of the damages. While Benjamin's drinking may have been a factor of the initial collision with Gilardi's vehicle, a contention not yet proven, there is no allegation that her drinking caused the alleged failure of her seat belt and/or seat.

The obvious purpose of a seat belt is not to guard against the initial accident but to guard against the second collision - being thrown out of the car or smashing against the windshield. An automobile accident, whatever its cause, is the use and purpose for which the safety device was designed and installed. People who are never involved in accidents or sudden emergencies never need their seat belts. Violent automobile accidents, such as that alleged by Boubel, are a "normal" and foreseeable use of seat belts.

**Verdict:** We hold that Tamara Boubel has stated a cause of action in her pleadings; and we REVERSE the judgment of the trial court dismissing her claims against General Motors Corporation and remand for further proceedings. General Motors Corporation must pay the costs of this appeal.

## 6-Why Not Try This

**Court:** U.S. District Court for the District of New Mexico

**Date:** 1984 MAR 23

**Report:** No. Civ. 83-0514 BB

**Case number:** 581 F. Supp. 728

**Link:** https://merillionpress.com/cases/XI-006.pdf

**Plaintiff (Respondent):** Connie DANIELL

**Defendant (Appellant):** FORD Motor Co.

**Opinion By:** Bobby R. BALDOCK, Judge

**Prior History:** In 1980, Daniell locked herself inside the trunk of a 1973 Ford LTD automobile, where she remained for some nine days. She now seeks compensation for psychological and physical injuries arising from that occurrence.

She contends that the automobile had a design defect in that the trunk lock or latch did not have an internal release or opening mechanism. She also maintains that the manufacturer is liable based on a failure to warn of this condition.

Her claim advances several theories for recovery:

(1) Strict products liability, (2) Negligence, (3) Breach of express warranty and implied warranties of merchantability and fitness for a particular purpose.

**Before this Court:** Three uncontroverted facts defeat Daniell's search for justice under any of these theories. First, she ended up in the trunk compartment of the automobile because she felt "overburdened" and was attempting to commit suicide.

Second, the purposes of an automobile trunk are to transport, stow and protect items from elements of the weather.

Third, she never considered the possibility of exit from the inside of the trunk when the automobile was purchased.

The overriding factor barring her recovery is that she intentionally sought to end her life by crawling into an automobile trunk from which she could not escape. This is not a case where a person inadvertently became trapped inside an automobile trunk. She was aware of the natural and probable consequences of her perilous conduct. Daniell, at least initially, sought those dreadful consequences and she, not the manufacturer of the vehicle, is responsible for this unfortunate occurrence.

**Verdict:** Case DISMISSED.

## 7-Suing Everybody in Sight

**Court:** Supreme Court of Michigan

**Date:** 1987 AUG 04

**Report:** Nos. 77914, 77926

**Case number:** 428 Mich. 439; 410 N.W. 2d 706

**Link:** https://merillionpress.com/cases/XI-007.pdf

**Plaintiff (Appellee):** Ethel LOWE, by her Conservator, Frank F. GAZLEY

**Defendants (Appellants):** ESTATE MOTORS Ltd. et al.

**Opinion By:** Dorothy C. RILEY, Chief Judge (In Part), Charles L. LEVIN Judge (In Part)

**Prior History:** On April 18, 1979, Ethel Lowe was a passenger in the rear seat of a 1979 Mercedes 300D owned and driven by her son. While traveling southbound on I-75 near Lima, Ohio, he lost control of the vehicle when approaching a construction zone. The Mercedes sideswiped a construction truck parked in the right lane, traversed the southbound lanes, and struck a concrete dividing barrier. At some point after the initial impact, the right rear door opened, and she was ejected from the vehicle, sustaining multiple injuries.

Lowe commenced this action asserting negligent design and breach of implied warranty. She alleged that the cause of the accident was attributable to a defectively designed floor mat which had wedged under the brake pedal, contributing to her son's loss of control of the car. She also contends that her injuries were also caused by a defectively designed door and door-locking mechanism which rendered the automobile un-crashworthy.

She is suing Mercedes-Benz of North America (MBNA), Estate Motors Limited, a local distributor from which the automobile was purchased, and Newark Auto Products, manufacturer of the floor mat.

In her suit she argues, that her failure to wear a seat belt did not constitute negligence because she "owed no duty" to the manufacturer to wear a seat belt, that her failure to buckle up did not contribute to the cause of the accident.

In its defense MBNA pleaded the following: The injuries suffered by Lowe in the accident were the results of her own negligence, including, but not limited to her failure to wear the 3-point seat belt or other safety restraint available to rear seat passengers in the car.

**Before this Court:** In this automobile products liability action, we review the Court of Appeals reversal of the trial court's decision.

The seat-restraint system goes to the heart of the issue in similar cases in which injuries are sustained after being ejected from the vehicle. Seat belts are specifically designed and installed to prevent such occurrences.

In crashworthiness cases, the vehicle is to be considered as an integrated whole. Accordingly, seat belt evidence is admissible for that purpose. In the event that this cause proceeds to trial, the jury should be permitted to consider evidence concerning the seat-restraint system, along with all other relevant factors, in determining whether the vehicle was defective in design.

Whether Lowe presents her case through a negligence theory – attempting to establish that the design of the vehicle created an unreasonable risk of injury – or through a breach of implied warranty theory – that the vehicle was not reasonably fit for its intended and foreseeable uses – the overriding issue of liability concerns whether the vehicle was unreasonably unsafe because of its design.

**Verdict:** Court of Appeals decision is REVERSED and further proceedings ordered.

# 8-Belligerent Pelican

**Court:** Superior Court of New Jersey, Appellate Division

**Date:** 1976 AUG 10

**Report**: 143 N.J. Super. 474

**Case number**: 363 A. 2d 908

**Link:** https://merillionpress.com/cases/XI-008.pdf

**Petitioner (Respondent):** David YORKIN

**Respondent (Appellant)**: VOLVO Distributing Co.

**Opinion By:** PER CURIAM

**Prior History:** Yorkin from New Jersey, an employee of Volvo Distributing Co. had been attending a convention in Miami Beach, Florida. Following thc convention he did not return home, but stayed with relatives in Florida for the rest of the week, at his expense and as per the mutual agreement with his employer.

While enjoying himself at the ocean beach on a Saturday, he was attacked by a belligerent pelican and sustained injuries to his head.

Upon returning to New Jersey he filed a claim for Worker's Compensation, alleging a workplace accident. The judge of compensation found, that although the employee at the time of his injury was engaged solely in rest and recreation activities in Miami, the accident arose incidentally to a business trip. The judge's verdict – citing the "mutual benefit doctrine"– effectively shifts the burden of compensation to the employer.

Volvo Distributing appeals the determination of compensability of the Division of Worker's Compensation.

**Before this Court:** In this case we think the compensation judge erred.

Nobody would suggest that an employee injured while on vacation would be entitled to a declaration of compensability simply because he was being refreshed to return more capably to his employment.

While an injury suffered during a period of relaxation at the convention, or during the travel to and from made necessary by the required attendance at the convention, would unquestionably ordinarily be compensable (the former activity justifying compensability on the basis of the mutual benefit doctrine), we are satisfied that a three-day personal vacation tacked on to the end of the convention removes any injury occurring during that period from the course of the employment.

**Verdict:** The judgment is REVERSED and judgment is entered in favor of Volvo Distributing. No costs.

## 9-Alimony....

**Court:** Appellate Court of Illinois

**Date:** 1953 DEC 15

**Report:** Gen. No. 46,022

**Case number:** 116 N.E.2d 182, 1 Ill. App. 2d 48

**Link:** https://merillionpress.com/cases/XI-009.pdf

**Plaintiff (Appellant):** Josephine M. LINNEMAN

**Defendant (Appellee):** Francis P. LINNEMAN

**Opinion By:** Edwin A. ROBSON, Justice

**Prior History:** Josephine Linneman and Francis Linneman were divorced by a decree of the superior court of Cook County, Illinois on July 2, 1947. By the terms of the decree she was given custody of their minor son and provision was made for his support by defendant. The decree also provided for alimony payments to be made monthly to her "until her death or remarriage, whichever event shall first occur."

On June 10, 1950, she married John Foster Corlett in Glencoe, Illinois. She had been and was then a resident of this State. On June 24, 1950, they left for San Francisco, California, where they made their residence.

Following her marriage to Corlett, Linneman ceased making alimony payments to her. There was no protest from her. Four months later the marriage soured and she filed a complaint for annulment of her marriage with Corlett in the superior court in San Francisco on the ground of impotency.

After the entry of the decree of annulment, while she was still in California, she made a demand on Linneman to resume his alimony payments. Her demand was again made in August of 1951 when she returned to live in Glencoe, Illinois. Linneman refused to pay.

This is an appeal by Josephine M. Linneman, from an order dismissing her petition why her first husband should not be held in contempt for failure to pay alimony. The plaintiff, who had divorced the defendant and remarried in Illinois, subsequently had her second marriage annulled in California. She predicated her petition for renewal of her alimony payments on the ground that the annulment of her second marriage revived her first husband's responsibility to support her.

**Before this Court:** On these facts alone, based on the decisions discussed, we are of the opinion that unless the California decree of annulment was granted on grounds that were recognized in Illinois, where she had been a resident and where the marriage was performed, it would not be binding on Francis P. Linneman.

Is impotency a ground for annulment of a marriage in Illinois? In this State there are no statutory provisions for annulment of marriage. We, therefore, hold that impotency is not ground for annulment in Illinois. It follows that the decree of the California court granting plaintiff an annulment from her second husband on this ground is of no force or effect in this State and is not binding on the defendant.

**Verdict:** The judgment of the trial court is AFFIRMED.

## 10-No Smoking Will Be Allowed

**Court:** Court of Appeals of Michigan

**Date:** 1996 JUN 11

**Report:** No. 172876

**Case number:** 550 N.W. 2d 846; 217 Mich. App. 163

**Link:** https://merillionpress.com/cases/XI-010.pdf

**Plaintiff (Appellant):** Jaci DILLON

**Defendants (Appellees):** DeNOOYER CHEVROLET GEO, d/b/a DeNooyer Chevrolet, and Air Borne Group, d/b/a WRKR

**Opinion By:** Richard A. GRIFFIN, Judge

**Prior History:** In 1992, during the height of the media attention for the Biosphere "experiment", defendant car dealer and defendant radio station organized a contest and publicity stunt termed the "Geo-sphere." The contest called for two men and two women to live in a Chevrolet Geo automobile as long as humanly possible. The person who, consistent with the contest rules, was able to reside in the Geo automobile the longest would win the vehicle in an "as is" condition.

The contest provided for ten minute breaks every four hours. Among other rules of conduct, the contest rules provided "no smoking will be allowed in the vehicle." Further, "any violation of the rules could result in immediate disqualification" and "contest officials have the ultimate say as to all rule violations and their decision is final."

On June 6, 1992, the Geo-sphere contest began with Dillon and three other contestants entering the vehicle. Within eighteen hours, one contestant dropped out; a second quit after a week and a half. Dillon and contestant Jeff Whaley continued to occupy the Geo automobile. It is undisputed that on June 19, 1992, Dillon got out of the vehicle during a scheduled break and began smoking a cigarette. At the conclusion of the break, she reentered the automobile with her lit cigarette in hand. She proceeded to close the door subjecting the atmosphere inside the "Geo-sphere" to her cigarette smoke. She extinguished her cigarette while inside the vehicle.

The organizers disqualified Dillon from the contest for violating the rule forbidding smoking in the vehicle and awarded the Geo automobile to the remaining contestant, Jeff Whaley.

She filed suit against defendants in the Kalamazoo Circuit Court, claiming that they breached the contest contract by disqualifying her. She argued that she was not smoking inside the vehicle because she did not inhale and exhale smoke from her lit cigarette.

The trial court dismissed Dillon's complaint as frivolous and she appeals.

**Before this Court:** On appeal, she contends that the term "smoking" is ambiguous and should have been determined by a jury. By every conceivable view of what happened in this case, this party was smoking a cigarette when they walked – or sat in that vehicle with a lighted device.

There can be no other possible interpretation of that.

She also contends that the trial court erred in finding that her suit was frivolous. For the reasons stated by the trial judge, we agree that plaintiff's claims were utterly without merit. Further, we conclude that the present appeal is vexatious because it was taken without any reasonable basis for belief that there was a meritorious issue to be determined on appeal.

**Verdict:** AFFIRMED. Remanded to the trial court for determination of an award of actual damages and expenses incurred on appeal.

## 11-Tastes Pure Wallpaper Paste

**Court:** Supreme Court of Kentucky

**Date:** 1978 MAR 14

**Report:** No number in original

**Case number:** 563 S.W. 2d 8

**Link:** https://merillionpress.com/cases/XI-011.pdf

**Plaintiff (Appellant):** Kentucky Fried Chicken of BOWLING GREEN Inc.

**Defendants (Appellees):** Harland SANDERS, Courier-Journal & Louisville Times, Inc., Dan KAUFFMAN and KFC Corporation

**Opinion by:** PER CURIAM

**Prior History:** Colonel Sanders was interviewed by staff writer Dan Kauffman on the subject: "Is a chicken wing white meat?" The portion of the article on which the suit is based is as follows:

And while he was on the subject of something Kentucky Fried Chicken should do differently, the Colonel thought of a few other things. The stuff on the mashed potatoes, for instance. 'My God, that gravy is horrible. They buy tap water for 15 to 20 cents a thousand gallons and then they mix it with flour and starch and end up with pure wallpaper paste.

And I know wallpaper paste, by God, because I've seen my mother make it.' To the 'wallpaper paste' they add some sludge and sell it for 65 or 75 cents a pint. There's no nutrition in it and they ought not to be allowed to sell it.' And another thing. That new 'crispy recipe is nothing in the world but a damn fried dough ball stuck on some chicken.'

Bowling Green local KFC franchisee sought damages for libel and defamation growing out of statements made by Colonel Harland Sanders and published in the Courier-Journal. The initial suit was dismissed for failure to state a claim. Bowling Green appeals.

**Before this Court:** Appellant contends it was error to dismiss the complaint because Colonel Sanders made a statement published in a local Bowling Green newspaper, the pertinent part of which was: "Sanders claims the new operators of Kentucky Fried Chicken Corp., a wholly-owned subsidiary of Heublin Inc., are serving chicken which is not prepared exactly according to his original recipe."

There was no direct reference to Kentucky Fried Chicken of Bowling Green, Inc. Moreover, the assertion that the chicken served by Kentucky Fried Chicken Corp. was not prepared exactly according to Sanders' original recipe was not defamatory. It is almost inevitable that at least slight deviations would occur. Indeed, prospective customers would expect that.

**Verdict:** The judgment of the lower court is AFFIRMED.

## 12-Fire Alarm Causing a Collapsed Lung

**Court:** United States Court of Appeals for the Fourth Circuit

**Date:** 1996 SEP 03

**Report:** No. 95-1315

**Case number:** 94 F. 3d 169

**Link:** https://merillionpress.com/cases/XI-012.pdf

**Plaintiffs (Appellants):** Corrine JUISTI and Samuel JUISTI

**Defendants (Appellees):** HYATT Hotel Corporation of Maryland et al.

**Opinion By:** Hiram E. WIDENER, Circuit Judge

**Prior History:** On May 5, 1991, at approximately 5:00 a.m., the fire alarm went off in the Hyatt Regency Hotel in Baltimore, Maryland. Mr. and Mrs. Juisti, who were staying on the fourteenth floor of the hotel that night, evacuated the building by taking the stairs.

Mrs. Juisti experienced shortness of breath upon reaching the ground floor and was given oxygen by the Baltimore City Fire Department. The hotel also gave her an oxygen tank to use in her room. The couple returned home to Pennsylvania that afternoon. The next day, Mrs. Juisti still experienced shortness of breath, and she also had chest pains. She went to the hospital where she was diagnosed as having a collapsed lung.

According to the hotel security report, the fire alarm apparently was set off by a cleaning crew that cleaned the oven hood in the kitchen without using the exhaust fans. The Juistis sued in the district court on February 3, 1994 seeking damages for negligence. The district court dismissed their case and they appeal.

The court's basis for this decision was that her "injury itself is of a completely different nature, outside the 'general danger area' or 'general class of harm,' from what reasonably could be expected to result from the Hyatt's negligence." The court determined that a collapsed lung is outside the field of danger one can expect from negligent oven cleaning and that "no reasonable jury could find . . . that the injury was a reasonably foreseeable result of negligent oven cleaning."

**Before this Court:** Under Maryland law, however, is not whether the hotel's negligence in setting off the alarm could reasonably be expected to cause the specific injury, but whether such negligence could reasonably be expected to cause any injury.

**Verdict:** The judgment of the district court must be VACATED and the case remanded for further proceedings, with Chief Judge Wilkinson strongly dissenting.

## 13-Battery Fumes Causing Vocal Cord Dysfunction

**Court:** United States Court of Appeals for the Fourth Circuit

**Date:** 1996 MAR 05

**Report:** No. 95-1086

**Case number:** 77 F. 3d 736

**Link:** https://merillionpress.com/cases/XI-013.pdf

**Plaintiff (Appellant):** Donna VAUGHN

**Defendant (Appellee):** NISSAN Motor Corporation of U.S.A. Inc.

**Opinion By:** Kenneth K. HALL, Circuit Judge

**Prior History:** On May 5, 1991, Donna Vaughn was driving her 1989 Nissan Pulsar on Interstate 95 in Colleton County, South Carolina. The voltage regulator failed, which in turn caused excessive current, which in turn caused the battery fluid to boil.

According to Vaughn, toxic fumes (chiefly various compounds of sulfur) entered the passenger compartment through the car's ventilation system. She inhaled these fumes, and, as a result, now suffers from vocal cord dysfunction and reactive airway dysfunction syndrome (RADS), a severe form of asthma.

Two experts testified for Vaughn that the voltage regulator was of inferior design and contained construction defects that caused the malfunction. One concluded from his experiment that the fumes, though toxic at their point of release, did not enter the passenger compartment in harmful concentrations, and that the overheating occurred slowly enough to give the driver ample warning of a problem and hence ample opportunity to flee the vehicle.

On the other hand, the test driver's eyes became irritated, he coughed, and he smelled a "rotten egg" odor. Moreover, at the very same time the driver experienced this discomfort, Nissan's test meter detected no hydrogen sulfide.

The wrecker driver who came to the scene of Vaughn's mishap testified that a foul odor was obvious at a distance of five to ten feet from the car, and he held his breath while inside the car to release the brake for towing. Even the next day, when he was trying to start the car, the same witness found the fumes to be "extremely strong," causing his eyes to burn and water.

Four physicians, including Vaughn's treating physician, testified that she had developed RADS as a direct result of inhaling the sulfur laden fumes.

Nissan presented evidence that Vaughn suffers from somatization disorder, which dates from abuse she experienced as a very small child. Nissan's experts testified that Vaughn does not have RADS, but does have vocal cord dysfunction (which mimics and is often misdiagnosed as asthma).

She sued and after a jury trial the district court judge dismissed her case and now she appeals.

**Before this Court:** From the record we determine that erroneous instruction was given to the jury. It reads: If you find that she has asthma, then you must consider whether her asthma was caused by inhalation of toxic fumes from the battery of the Nissan Pulsar.

This faulty instruction requires reversal. It could very, very easily explain the verdict, because the evidence on this point was perhaps the most clear-cut in Nissan's favor of any issue that went to the jury. Vaughn concedes that she has a history of psychiatric illness from which she has never completely recovered.

**Verdict:** The judgment of the district court is VACATED, and the case is remanded for a new trial.

## 14-Fear of Possible Brain Damage

**Court:** United States District Court of Appeals, Fifth Circuit

**Date:** 1993 MAR 08

**Report:** No. 92-3461

**Case number:** 985 F. 2d 208

**Link:** https://merillionpress.com/cases/XI-014.pdf

**Plaintiff (Appellant):** Richard M. NESOM

**Defendants (Appellees):** TRI HAWK INTERNATIONAL; Kansa General Insurance Company, et al.

**Opinion By:** Edwin F. HUNTER Jr., Senior District Judge

**Prior History:** On April 8, 1987, Richard Nesom, underwent a craniotomy at Meadowcrest Hospital in Gretna, Louisiana. The operation was performed by Dr. Carl Culicchia, a neurosurgeon. Human dura was grafted to torn tissue in Nesom's brain.

B. Braun Melsungen A.G. ("BBM"), a German company, harvests dura from cadavers, prepares and packages it in sealed containers, and sells it internationally through a number of distributors under the trade name "Lyodura". BBM sold the Lyodura used on Nesom to Tri Hawk, a Canadian corporation. Tri Hawk sold the Lyodura to Meadowcrest in October of 1984.

Shortly after Nesom's operation, Meadowcrest Hospital received an FDA Safety Alert dated April 28, 1987, which stated that there was a risk of transmitting Creutzfeldt - Jakob disease ("CJD") to surgical patients through possibly contaminated batches of human dura. A case of CJD in Connecticut linked to the use of Lyodura prompted the Alert. The Alert stated that the material in question was prepared by BBM and distributed by Tri Hawk.

Following this Safety Alert, Dr. Culicchia informed Nesom that the dura used in his operation may have been contaminated with CJD-causing agents. At the outset, he told Nesom that they had currently calculated that the likelihood of a recipient of dura from lot 2105 developing CJD was one-in-one thousand. To date, Nesom has not suffered any symptoms of CJD, nor has any doctor diagnosed the presence of CJD during the almost six (6) years since the neurosurgery.

On March 16, 1988, Nesom filed this suit against Tri Hawk alleging that Tri Hawk is strictly liable for having distributed contaminated Lyodura in this country, and also that it is liable in negligence for failing to test the Lyodura and failing to verify that the processor of the Lyodura had followed stringent procedures. The district court dismissed his suit and he appeals.

**Before this Court:** At the core of this appeal is the question of whether Nesom can maintain a claim for emotional distress absent evidence that the Lyodura was actually contaminated and absent evidence of physical injury resulting from the Lyodura. This Court agrees that Nesom cannot maintain this claim under the facts of this case.

He cannot demonstrate that he has been exposed to the CJD agent. To allow someone to be compensated merely because he fears that he may have been exposed to a dangerous substance goes too far. To sanction the theory of monetary damages argued here, would open the door to thousands of litigants who claim that they have suffered damages caused by fear of possible exposure to some dangerous substance or another without even proof of actual exposure to that danger.

**Verdict:** We find no legal error and the judgment of the district court is AFFIRMED.

## 15-Jar of Peanuts

**Court:** United States Court of Appeals for the Seventh Circuit

**Date:** 1994 FEB 22

**Report:** No. 93-2080

**Case number:** 17 F. 3d 209

**Link:** https://merillionpress.com/cases/XI-015.pdf

**Plaintiff (Appellant):** Richard WELGE

**Defendants (Appellees):** PLANTERS LIFESAVERS Company, et al.

**Opinion By:** Richard A. POSNER, Chief Judge

**Prior History:** Richard Welge, forty-something but young in spirit, loves to sprinkle peanuts on his ice cream sundaes. On January 18, 1991, Karen Godfrey, with whom Welge boards, bought a 24-ounce vacuum-sealed plastic-capped jar of Planters peanuts for him at a K-Mart store in Chicago.

To obtain a $2 rebate that the maker of Alka-Seltzer was offering to anyone who bought a "party" item, such as peanuts, Godfrey needed proof of her purchase of the jar of peanuts; so, using an X-acto knife (basically a razor blade with a handle), she removed the part of the label that contained the bar code.

She then placed the jar on top of the refrigerator, where Welge could get at it without rooting about in her cupboards. About a week later, Welge removed the plastic seal from the jar, uncapped it, took some peanuts, replaced the cap, and returned the jar to the top of the refrigerator, all without incident. A week after that, on February 3, the accident occurred.

Welge took down the jar, removed the plastic cap, spilled some peanuts into his left hand to put on his sundae, and replaced the cap with his right hand–but as he pushed the cap down on the open jar the jar shattered. His hand, continuing in its downward motion, was severely cut, and is now, he claims, permanently impaired.

Welge brought this products liability suit in federal district court against K-Mart, which sold the jar of peanuts; Planters, which manufactured the product–that is to say, filled the glass jar with peanuts and sealed and capped it; and Brockway, which manufactured the glass jar itself and sold it to Planters.

The district judge dismissed the suit on the ground that Welge had failed to exclude possible causes of the accident other than a defect introduced during the manufacturing process. Welge appeals.

**Before this Court:** No doubt there are men strong enough to shatter a thick glass jar with one blow. But Welge's testimony stands uncontradicted that he used no more than the normal force that one exerts in snapping a plastic lid onto a jar. So the jar must have been defective. No expert testimony and no fancy doctrine are required for such a conclusion. A non-defective jar does not shatter when normal force is used to clamp its plastic lid on. The question is when the defect was introduced.

Testimony by Welge and Karen Godfrey, if believed – and at this stage in the proceedings we are required to believe it – excludes all reasonable possibility that the defect was introduced into the jar after Godfrey plucked it from a shelf in the K-Mart store. From the shelf she put it in her shopping cart. The checker at the check-out counter scanned the bar code without banging the jar.

After the bar-code portion of the label was removed, the jar sat on top of the refrigerator except for the two times Welge removed it to take peanuts out of it. Throughout this process it was not, so far as anyone knows, jostled, dropped, bumped, or otherwise subjected to stress beyond what is to be expected in the ordinary use of the product.

It is the kind of accident that would not have occurred but for a defect in the product, and if it is reasonably plain that the defect was not introduced after the product was sold, the accident is evidence that the product was defective when sold.

**Verdict:** The district court's decision REVERSED and remanded.

## 16-Attempted Suicide and Failed

**Court:** United States Court of Appeals for the Seventh Circuit

**Date:** 1994 AUG 10

**Report:** No. 93-2970

**Case number:** 32 F. 3d 1094

**Link:** https://merillionpress.com/cases/XI-016.pdf

**Plaintiff (Appellant):** Daniel T. CASEY

**Defendants (Appellees):** UDDEHOLM Corporation and Uddeholm Health Benefits Plan

**Opinion By:** Michael S. KANNE, Circuit Judge

**Prior History:** Daniel Casey attempted to commit suicide by throwing himself in front of an elevated train in Chicago on March 6, 1991. He survived, but he was severely and permanently injured. This case involves Casey's attempt to compel his health insurance carrier to pay his medical expenses.

Uddeholm Health Benefits Plan refused to pay Casey's medical bills because, it claimed, his injuries were not "sustained accidentally" as his policy required. Casey protested, and a hearing on his case was held before the plan's administrator. The administrator ruled against Casey.

He then brought a civil suit in federal district court to "enforce his right under the terms" of an insurance benefits plan. The district court ruled in favor of Uddeholm and against him. This appeal by Casey followed.

**Before this Court:** The Uddeholm Health Benefits plan provided medical benefits for non-occupational injury. It defined "injury" as "an injury to the body that is sustained accidentally." It did not define "accidentally." The plan has nineteen exclusions, but it does not explicitly exclude attempted suicide or intentionally inflicted injuries.

The plan administrator concluded that Casey's injuries were not accidental because they were the reasonably foreseeable consequence of his actions. Therefore Casey's claim was not covered. The administrator also rejected the argument that "accidentally" could mean "not intended."

However, the benefit plan does not grant discretion to the administrator to construe uncertain terms. The district court found that the plain language of the Uddeholm plan was ambiguous and did not mandate the result reached by the administrator. Specifically, (1) the word "accidentally" was not defined, (2) it is not explicit that "accidentally" may not be equated with "unintended" and, (3) the plan did not specifically exclude suicide attempts or self-inflicted injuries.

The district court determined that Casey would prevail if he could show that either (1) "he did not know or understand the nature or quality of his actions," or (2) that "he was overcome by an irresistible impulse that essentially forced him to jump in front of the train against his will."

The court employed the language used in the cited cases and characterized such a mental state as "insanity." The district court also emphasized that "a mere attempt to commit suicide, without more, does not evidence insanity."

The injury was self-inflicted, but not intended, hence accidental. In the case of a suicide attempt like Casey's, he claims he lacked intent because he had a mental incapacity which prevents the formation of intent, in which case his self-inflicted injury is an accident.

We agree with the district court's analysis, but not its decision. Given the lack of factual determination by the administrator, the district court applied the right standard of review – but in the wrong proceeding. The district court's decision, rejecting the administrator's interpretation of the language of the plan and "adopting an interpretation that would extend coverage for injury sustained as a result of a suicide attempted while insane" is correct.

However, there remains a genuine issue concerning Casey's mental state at the time he was injured and it was error for the district court to resolve that factual dispute through dismissal.

**Verdict:** Therefore the district court's decision is VACATED and the case is REMANDED for trial consistent with this opinion.

## 17-Daughter and Mother and a Lawyer

**Court:** United States Court of Appeals for the Seventh Circuit

**Date:** 1995 OCT 19

**Report:** No. 94-3943

**Case number:** 68 F. 3d 1010

**Link:** https://merillionpress.com/cases/XI-017.pdf

**Plaintiff (Appellant):** Heather WALLACE, a minor, by her mother and next friend, Phyllis WALLACE

**Defendants (Appellees):** THE BATAVIA SCHOOL DISTRICT 101, a municipal corporation, and James CLIFFE

**Opinion By:** Michael S. KANNE, Circuit Judge

**Prior History:** This case affords a view of an unfortunately common situation faced by teachers in many public schools today. The incident occurred in a suburban community west of Chicago in Kane County, Illinois.

The undisputed facts are as follows.

When business teacher James Cliffe returned to his Batavia High School classroom after a few minutes' absence, two sixteen-year-old female students, Heather Wallace and Kim Fairbanks, were facing each other screaming and calling each other "fucking bitches." Cliffe ordered both girls to take their seats and be quiet.

That tactic didn't work. Wallace sat down but stood up again when Fairbanks approached her yelling, "I'm going to kick your ass right here and now." Cliffe again told both students to sit down. Wallace did so, but Fairbanks attempted to take a swing at Wallace. Cliffe stepped between the two girls. While facing Fairbanks, he told Wallace to get her books and leave the classroom.

Wallace gathered up her books and began to walk out of the classroom–slowly. Cliffe reached over another student's desk and took Wallace by her left wrist to speed her exit. As he pulled Wallace, she bent over the desk. Cliffe told Wallace to hurry up and grasped her right elbow to move her out of the classroom. Wallace stopped her movement toward the door and told Cliffe to let go. When he released his hold on Wallace, she walked out of the classroom and slammed the door. A fight indeed did occur later in the day. Both girls were suspended from the school for three days.

Wallace claims the contact with Cliffe caused injury to her elbow. Through her mother, she sued Cliffe and the Batavia School Corporation alleging violations of her Fourth Amendment right against unreasonable seizures and her Fourteenth Amendment right to substantive due process. The district court dismissed her claims, and Wallace appeals that ruling.

**Before this Court:** We have concluded that public school students have protection of their liberty rights under the Fourth Amendment, but we ought not countenance the degradation of this historic shield into a device by which ill-informed or inventive litigants attempt to undermine the necessary authority that teachers and school administrators exert over students. Public school teachers and administrators must have considerable latitude in performing their educational responsibilities, including maintaining order and discipline by reasonably restraining the liberty of students.

Here, a teacher was confronted in his classroom with two teenage girls shouting obscenities and a fight about to break out; he separated the girls and ordered one out of the classroom – briefly seizing her in the process. This most emphatically is not a matter rising to the level of a constitutional violation. This type of litigation denigrates the Constitution and is a disservice to school systems, the federal courts, and the public they serve.

**Verdict:** The summary judgment entered by the district court is AFFIRMED.

## 18-It's in my Head

**Court:** United States Court of Appeals for the Seventh Circuit

**Date:** 1996 APR 16

**Report:** No. 95-2445

**Case number:** 81 F. 3d 714

**Link:** https://merillionpress.com/cases/XI-018.pdf

**Plaintiff (Appellant):** David L. MARSCHAND

**Defendant (Appellee):** NORFOLK AND WESTERN RAILWAY Company

**Opinion By:** William J. BAUER, Circuit Judge

**Prior History:** On May 12, 1991, Marschand was the engineer on a Norfolk train that struck a pickup truck at a grade crossing. He did not see the collision between the locomotive engine and the truck. However, he testified at trial that when he realized the collision was imminent, he instinctively slid back into the engineer's chair to brace himself.

Marschand also testified that he heard the collision and that he "could feel it through the floorboards of the train." A brakeman riding in the locomotive cab testified that he felt only a small bump at the time of the collision. Marschand learned after the accident that all three passengers in the pickup truck had died.

On the first anniversary of the accident, Marschand had flashbacks of the accident while at work. He began to cry uncontrollably. Shortly thereafter, he met with a psychologist, who diagnosed Marschand as suffering from post-traumatic stress disorder ("PTSD").

In May 1993, Marschand filed this negligent infliction of emotional distress claim against Norfolk. After a four day bench trial, the district court concluded that Marschand "was never in any true danger of physical impact or injury because at all times he rode safely in the locomotive cab," that Marschand never feared for his own safety, and that his emotional distress was not caused by fear for his own safety. The court therefore found that he had not satisfied the zone of danger test, and entered judgment in favor of Norfolk.

He appeals that decision.

**Before this Court:** Marschand consistently argued that he could recover for his emotional distress because he reasonably feared for his own safety at the time of the accident, and because his fear proximately caused his emotional distress. When he did mention "impact," it was in the context of asserting that he had been threatened imminently with physical impact, which is a far cry from the argument he makes now that he sustained a physical impact in the collision.

In fact, Marschand discussed the threat of imminent physical impact only to support his claim that he feared for his own safety at the time of the accident. The district court rejected his claims, and he does not challenge that determination. Instead, he now attempts to satisfy the zone of danger test by arguing that he sustained an impact in the accident.

Marschand's failure to appraise the district court of the "impact" issue at the pre-trial conference and to ensure that the pretrial order included that issue, despite reasonable opportunity to correct the order before the district court signed it, precludes him from raising it on appeal.

It is clear from the record that Marschand based his case on the threat of physical impact and fear for his own safety, and thus it is not surprising that the district court focused on these issues in entering judgment for Norfolk. Marschand presented to the district court one theory, and now attempts to advance a second theory. This he cannot do.

**Verdict:** For the foregoing reasons, we AFFIRM the judgment of the district court.

## 19-Switched at Birth for an Hour

**Court:** Appellate Division of the Supreme Court of New York, Second Department

**Date:** 2011 APR 12

**Report:** No. 2010-09480

**Case number:** 920 N.Y.S. 2d 415

**Link:** https://merillionpress.com/cases/XI-019.pdf

**Plaintiffs (Respondents):** Lynda WILLIAMS et al.

**Defendants (Appellants):** LONG ISLAND COLLEGE HOSPITAL et al.

**Opinion By:** PER CURIAM

**Prior History:** Lynda Williams and Martin Williams, are the parents of a daughter (the infant), who was born on May 21, 2008, at Long Island College Hospital (the hospital).

On the evening of May 21, 2008, the infant was placed overnight in the hospital's nursery. The following morning, the hospital's nursing staff allegedly inadvertently delivered the infant to the wrong mother, and delivered that mother's newborn to Mrs. Williams. The error was corrected that same morning, and the infants were returned to their respective mothers.

However, prior to being returned to Mrs. Williams, the infant allegedly was breast-fed by the other mother. Subsequently the couple commenced this action against the hospital, among others, alleging that for months they had suffered "extreme emotional pain, suffering, and anxiety." Their particular concern is the other mother, who might have been an alcoholic or a drug user. The gravamen of their claim is that the infant may have suffered injuries as a result of being breast-fed by a stranger and that, as a consequence, they suffered emotional distress.

As relevant here, the Supreme Court denied the hospital's request to dismiss the complaint and the hospital appeals.

**Before this Court:** Reviewing the records the Williams have failed to allege a cognizable cause of action to recover damages for emotional distress against the hospital. They may not recover damages from the hospital for any mental distress or emotional disturbances they may have suffered as a result of the alleged direct injury inflicted upon the infant by the hospital's breach of its duty of care to. In addition and contrary to their contention, with respect to the hospital's treatment and care of the infant, the hospital did not owe a specific duty directly to the parents.

**Verdict:** Accordingly, the Supreme Court should have granted the hospital's request and its decision is REVERSED with costs.

# CHAPTER XII

# SABBATICAL FROM REALITY

*"Making of unreality a possibility, then a probability, then an incontrovertible fact." William C. Faulkner (1897 – 1962) was an American writer*

In this category the reader is entering prime wishful-thinking territory. The struggle here is about what dismal foolishness is disguisable as a new legal definition, out of which new entitlements can be fashioned. Often skating on thin legal ice or suffering from a periodic lull in cases of merit there is no shortage of day dreaming. As the late Yale law professor Fred Rodell pointed out in 1939: "The legal trade, in short, is nothing but a high-class racket." As the following cases exemplify there is no shortage of inventive litigants.

## 1-Bud Light

**Court:** Michigan Court of Appeals

**Date:** 1994 MAY 16

**Report:** No. 145986

**Case number:** 517 N.W. 2d 308

**Link:** https://merillionpress.com/cases/XII-001.pdf

**Plaintiff (Respondent):** Richard OVERTON

**Defendant (Appellant):** ANHEUSER-BUSCH Co.

**Opinion by:** Clifford W. TAYLOR, Judge

**Prior History:** On June 6, 1991, Overton sued Anheuser-Busch Co. the maker of the popular Bud Light beer, claiming that the brewer had violated the provisions of the PAA (the state's Pricing and Advertising Act) by placing before the public advertisements for its products that contain "statements and/or representations which are untrue, deceptive and/or misleading."

As a result, Overton claimed, he and the general public had been led to consume A-B Co.'s products, which they knew were dangerous and likely to cause serious health problems, including addiction and death. In support of his claims, he pointed to the company's television advertisements featuring Bud Light as the source of fantasies coming to life. Fantasies involving tropical settings, and beautiful women and men engaged in unrestricted merriment. He sought monetary damages in excess of $10,000, alleging that the company's misleading advertisements had caused him physical and mental injury, emotional distress, and financial loss.

In its defense, Anheuser-Busch Co. argued among other things, that it had no duty to warn of commonly known dangers. The trial court agreed with the company's analysis and dismissed the suit.

**Before this Court:** Overton's appeal makes a two-pronged attack. First, he asserts that Bud Light advertising is deceptive and misleading; because it falsely suggests that the beer is the source of fantasies come to life. Such a grandiose suggestion constitutes puffing, which does not give rise to actionable fraud.

Second, he asserts that the advertising is deceptive and misleading because it portrays beer in a positive light only, without reference to the dangers inherent in the consumption of alcoholic beverages.

Because the dangers inherent in the consumption of beer are well known to the general public, nothing material was concealed. Anheuser-Busch Co. had no duty under the common law or the PAA to "disclose" in its advertisements damages that are already well known.

**Verdict:** Lower court's decision is proper and AFFIRMED.

## 2-Loss of Psychic Powers

**Court:** Court of Common Pleas of Pennsylvania, Philadelphia County

**Date:** 1986 AUG 07

**Report:** No. 4408

**Case number:** 39 Pa. D. & C. 3d 381

**Link:** https://merillionpress.com/cases/XII-002.pdf

**Plaintiff (Respondent):** Judith HAIMES

**Defendant (Appellant):** TEMPLE University Hospital

**Opinion By:** Leon KATZ, Judge

**Prior History:** Judith Richardson Haimes testified that she was born with psychic powers. A person endowed with psychic powers has the ability to use an extra sense, other than sight, smell, hearing and touch. Although she has had clairvoyant experiences, her forte was her ability to read auras. An aura is a light or glow that surrounds people and objects. By interpreting the shapes, colors, sizes and flecks of the aura, an aura reader can discover different things about the individual, including things about the subject's past and future.

In 1969, Haimes opened an office in New Castle, Delaware, out of which she read auras and provided psychic counselling. In addition, she devoted one day a week to assisting law enforcement agencies. She also lectured and appeared on radio and television.

On September 7, 1976, on her physician's recommendation, she went to the radiology department of Temple University Hospital to undergo a CT scan. Prior to performing the CT scan, contrast medium or dye had to be introduced into her bloodstream. Judith Hart, M.D., radiologist was to administer the test. Prior to the injection Haimes explained to Dr. Hart that she had previously undergone tests that utilized dye and had suffered reactions including nausea, vomiting, hives and difficulty breathing. As a result of these discussions, Dr. Hart set up an intravenous line so that if a problem arose, drugs could be administered quickly.

Almost immediately after the injection, she experienced difficulty breathing, tightness of the throat, pain, nausea, vomiting, hives and welts. For the next 15 or 20 minutes she remained in the radiology department under observation. At her own insistence, she then reported for a previously scheduled appointment with another physician at the same hospital. After her visit, she returned to the radiology department where Dr. Hart examined her and advised that she could leave the hospital.

Over the next 48 hours and beyond, she experienced vomiting, nausea and headaches. Her condition didn't improve and the Haimes brought this medical-malpractice action to recover damages suffered by her as a result of undergoing the CT scan.

Much of Haimes' testimony concerned her psychic activities and her inability to practice. To read an aura, according to her, it is necessary to go into an altered state, a state of deep concentration. Because she no longer could read auras, she closed her office in Delaware. She was also unable to continue reading the auras of her husband and children. As a result, she holds herself responsible for the death of her son in "an automobile accident that didn't have to take place."

Damages sought by her are related to chronic and disabling headaches which prevented her from practicing her occupation as a psychic. The case was tried over four days and the 8-member Common Pleas Court jury deliberated less than an hour before awarding damages.

$600,000 (which included her husband's claim for loss of consortium) plus $388,000 in interest against Judith Hart, M.D., the physician who administered the CT scan, and Temple University Hospital.

Dr. Hart and Temple University Hospital appeal.

**Before this Court**: In reviewing defendants' claim seeking a new trial based on the excessiveness of the verdict it is clear, that it is excessive. The Haimes did not prove that her loss of income from the psychic readings were the direct result of her allergic reaction to the treatment.

The amount awarded resulted from a misconception of law and we find the verdict grossly excessive.

First, plaintiff's compensable injuries consisted of nausea, vomiting, shortness of breath and the attendant pain and suffering. Although these injuries were such that she remained in bed until the symptoms subsided, they are no greater than the symptoms experienced by a person suffering from a flu or virus.

Secondly, only some of her symptoms, i.e., the welts, hives, nausea and vomiting, were demonstrated by physical evidence.

Third, the injuries were transient and did not affect Haimes permanently.

Fourth, her legally proven injuries did not affect her ability to work.

Lastly, she had no special damages and thus the disparity between her out-of-pocket expenses and the amount of the verdict is great. In light of the above, it is within our discretion to grant a new trial based on the excessiveness of the jury verdict.

**Verdict:** The case is REMANDED for a new trial. Three years later, in 1989 it was dismissed altogether.

# 3-They'll Never See You Coming

**Court:** United States Patent and Trademark Office

**Date:** 1989 SEP 27

**Serial Number:** 73827956

**Registration Number:** 1642870

**Link:** https://merillionpress.com/cases/XII-003.pdf

**Plaintiff (Respondent):** NORTHROP Corp.

**Defendant (Appellant):** John HUGHES Ceramic Tile Contractor, Inc.

**Opinion By:** John E. MICHOS Examining Attorney

**Prior History:** One day in 1988 John Hughes a 20 something entrepreneur from Taylor, Texas was driving his pick-up truck and thought the stale condom market needed fresh thinking. He figured a catchy name coupled with an equally catchy slogan would catapult him to fame and fortune.

He established Stealth Condoms Inc., a family enterprise in his hometown of 12,000, designed carton packages resembling an airplane. He farmed out actual production to a company in New Jersey, producing it in the three patriotic colors; one red, one white and one blue and selling them at $5 for a box of 3.

His parody slogan on the boxes read: "They'll Never See You Coming." And when he wasn't in the office, his telephone answering machine responded: "WE ARE OUT ON A MISSION."

He then applied for a trademark registration at the United States Patent and Trademark Office, which was granted. Then, he got a phone call from the attorneys representing Northrop Grumman, the giant US defense contractor, manufacturer of the then thought to be invisible Stealth bomber.

They thought the condoms' package design was too close to the actual bomber, that it might confuse, deceive consumers. It seems Northrop and its lawyers think it's really easy to be mistaken by a $5 box of condoms and an $800 million Stealth fighter airplane at the check-out counter.

**Before this Court:** In this petition filed with the Trademark Trial and Appeal Board Northrop claims it will be damaged by the trademark for Stealth

Condoms because, a trademark infringement likely to cause consumer confusion.

**Verdict:** This court holds, there is no likelihood of confusion with an actual Stealth bomber; the two products are vastly different. The trademark application was registered, but subsequently it was cancelled or invalidated and removed from the registry. Further, John HUGHES Ceramic Tile Contractor, Inc. also ceased to exist.

## 4-Playing Ball

**Court:** United States District Court, N.D. California

**Date:** 1984 SEP 07

**Report:** No. C-84-1039-WWS

**Case number:** 591 F. Supp. 1573

**Link:** https://merillionpress.com/cases/XII-004.pdf

**Plaintiff:** Robert A. HEIMBAUGH

**Defendants:** CITY and COUNTY of San Francisco et al.

**Opinion By:** William W. SCHWARZER, District Judge

**Prior History:** On September 4, 1982, Heimbaugh, a lawyer by trade, was playing softball in an area of Golden Gate Park in San Francisco with a sign posted prohibiting softball playing. Officers of the San Francisco Police Department informed him, that he was in violation of the Park Code and that he could not play in the area. He refused to leave and stated he wished to be cited. The officers informed him of the law and the citation procedure. Following his repeated request, the police issued him a citation. Heimbaugh was then arrested following his refusal to sign the citation.

In this suit he complains that the City and County of San Francisco and its elected officials and employees, are interfering with his softball playing at Golden Gate Park. As a consequence, he alleges that he has been deprived of his rights under the First, Fourth and Fourteenth Amendments. He seeks monetary damages for a number of alleged torts suffered by him.

Defendants ask for dismissal as well as reimbursement for its attorneys' fees.

**Before this Court:**

1-Heimbaugh claims that by playing softball "they (he and his friends) are making a statement about the right to democracy in recreation as opposed to elitism." Playing softball in this context has not been shown to have been intended to convey a message. Even if it was so intended, there is no indication that persons observing him playing softball in Golden Gate Park would understand his conduct to be a message "about the right to democracy in recreation as opposed to elitism."

2-The Park Code is content neutral, it is tailored to serve a significant governmental interest in safety, and the park provided an alternative playing field, thus leaving open an "ample alternative channel" for whatever message he purports to convey by playing softball.

3- His Fourteenth Amendment claim is an equal protection claim. In essence, he contends that the City is not making its facilities available in an equal manner and that the distinction between baseball players and softball players is arbitrary and invidious. The Constitution does not, however, require that laws treat every individual exactly alike to withstand constitutional attack.

4- His assertion that his Fourth Amendment rights were violated is merely an unsupported allegation.

5-His claim for attorney fees is entirely unwarranted by existing law, it is frivolous on its face. He is schooled in the law, having recently completed law school and taken the bar examination. There is every reason to hold him to the certification he made by signing the pleadings he has filed in this action.

**Verdict:** Case is DISMISSED on all counts and Heimbaugh is ordered to pay defendants the amount of $50.00.

## 5-Looking up the Sun [*sic*]

**Court:** Court of Appeals of California, Third District

**Date:** 1976 FEB 04

**Report:** No. 13828

**Case number:** 55 Cal. App. 3d 67 (1976) 127 Cal. Rptr. 217

**Link:** https://merillionpress.com/cases/XII-005.pdf

**Plaintiff (Appellant):** Thomas MIDGLEY, a Minor, etc.

**Defendant (Respondent):** S.S. KRESGE Company

**Opinion By:** Robert K.PUGLIA, Presiding Judge

**Prior History:** Thomas Midgley was 13 years old when he purchased from Kresge a refracting telescope manufactured in Japan. Its components were in a cardboard box accompanied by a booklet of instructions on assembly, use and maintenance. The box bore the legend "Manufactured in Japan for S.S. Kresge Company...." The telescope itself bore a label "K-Mart" accompanied by the phrase "Quality Guaranteed." Kresge, owner of K-Mart Discount Stores, the retailer, was the only named defendant.

One component of the telescope is a sun filter consisting of a dark lens labeled "Sun." The instruction booklet with the piece reads: "Sun and moon glasses are deposited in the eyepieces cases; screwed into the eyepiece bottom. Be sure to use sun glass for solar observation and moon glass for moon observation. CAUTION: Please refrain from looking up the sun [*sic*] without attaching the sun glass. Also the sun should not be seen through the finder scope."

Reading the warning, Thomas knew he should view the sun only through the sun filter. He also knew before purchasing the telescope that it was dangerous to look at the sun with naked eye.

In the first two months of ownership, he used it to view the sun 15 to 20 times, always through the sun filter. In doing so, he would remove the eyepiece lens and replace it with the sun filter. Properly assembled for sun viewing, the eyepiece lens should remain in place and the sun filter be screwed into the opposite or bottom end of the cylinder. When properly assembled the system is safe for sun viewing. As assembled by Thomas, however, harmful sunlight leaked around the sun filter into his eye sustaining a solar burn on the retina of his eye, irreparably impairing his vision.

They sued for damages and a jury trial cleared Kresge of wrongdoing.

**Before this Court:** This appeal presents the perplexing question whether liability for failure to warn of dangerous properties of a product is measured by the doctrine of strict liability in its generally understood sense or, alternatively, by traditional negligence concepts imposing a duty of care, requiring warning of danger only when there is actual or constructive knowledge of the danger.

Kresge marketed a technically complex product intended for use by technically unsophisticated consumers, to be assembled and used by them in accordance with instructions prepared and supplied by the technically knowledgeable supplier. Failure to assemble or use the product in accordance with these directions may well cause physical injury and thus constitutes a potential danger. Therefore, the supplier is strictly liable for injury proximately resulting from the set of instructions for assembly and use, which does not adequately avoid the danger of injury.

**Verdict:** We have determined that the jury should have been instructed on the theory of failure to warn in the context of strict liability in tort. The omission so to instruct was detrimental to Thomas' case and requires REVERSAL.

## 6-Adultery and Alimony

**Court:** Supreme Court of South Carolina

**Date:** 1992 FEB 10

**Report:** No. 23576

**Case number:** 414 S.E. 2d 157, 307 S.C. 199

**Link:** https://merillionpress.com/cases/XII-006.pdf

**Plaintiff (Respondent):** Bobby RUTHERFORD

**Defendant (Petitioner):** Carol RUTHERFORD

**Opinion By:** Jean H. TOAL, Judge

**Prior History:** Bobby Rutherford ("Husband") brought this action for divorce on the ground of adultery. He also sought an order barring Carol Rutherford ("Wife") from seeking alimony.

She filed an answer denying adultery and counterclaimed for support and maintenance.

A trial was held in the Family Court in Richland County. At trial Wife denied the adultery took place. Alternatively, she sought to prove that even if it had, she should not be held responsible due to her mental illness. Her psychiatrist testified Wife suffered from multiple personality disorder.

Additionally, the Wife submitted evidence of the parties' verbal agreement of support. She asserts this agreement overrode the statutory bar of alimony applicable to adulterous spouses. The trial judge denied the Husband's petition for divorce on the basis of a finding due to the Wife's mental disability; she lacked the capacity to commit adultery. The trial judge found the Wife had committed the physical act of adultery; however, at the time of the physical act of adultery; the Wife was under the control of one of her alter personalities and lacked the ability to control her actions. The lower court awarded Wife separate maintenance and support and divided the parties' property.

Husband appealed both the denial of a divorce and the award of support. The Court of Appeals reversed. In the view of the Court of Appeals, in order to successfully maintain a defense to the adultery charge of lack of capacity, the wife had the burden under the facts of this case to show that a disengaged alter ego committed the adulterous acts rather than respondent as a cognitive person.

Based on its own view of the preponderance of evidence, the Court of Appeals held Wife did commit adultery, but she did not prove she could not at least control her transformation into her alter personalities. The Court of Appeals also found Wife had not proven she was not in control of the alter personality when she committed the adultery.

Finally, the Court of Appeals held in order to sustain her defense, the Wife must show by clear evidence her mental condition deprived her of the ability to control her acts.

**Before this Court:** Wife asks this Court to modify its well established interpretation of this constitutional provision and interpret "review of the findings of fact" as a mere general directive subject to limitation in scope by the legislature. Wife's urged interpretation is particularly illogical since the statute intending to narrow this Court's review of domestic suits uses the identical language as the Constitution to define the appellate scope of review in all other equity suits.

Thus, we would be required to apply two different interpretations to identical language.

The question of whether a mental disability is a defense to at-fault grounds for divorce and what degree of mental impairment is required has never been presented to this Court.

**Verdict:** REVERSED and remanded for further evidentiary hearing on the defense of mental illness as it pertains to the grounds for divorce and alimony.

## 7-Extrasensory Empathy

**Court:** United States District Court, Southern District of New York

**Date:** 1980 FEB 19

**Report:** No. 78 Civ. 2035. MDL No. 306

**Case number:** 484 F. Supp. 850

**Link:** https://merillionpress.com/cases/XII-007.pdf

**Plaintiff:** Martha BURKE

**Defendants:** PAN AMERICAN WORLD AIRWAYS, Inc., KLM Royal Dutch Airlines, and the BOEING Co.

**Opinion By:** Robert J. WARD, District Judge

**Prior History:** Martha Burke is the surviving twin sister of Margaret Fox, a passenger killed in the March 27, 1977 crash between a PAN AM Boeing 747 aircraft and a KLM 747 aircraft on the airport runway at Santa Cruz de Tenerife, Canary Islands, in Spain.

Burke sues not for the wrongful death of her sister, but rather for her own physical and emotional injuries allegedly sustained while at home in California through "extrasensory empathy" at the time of her twin's death.

Specifically, Burke alleges that shortly after she awakened on the morning of March 27, 1977 at her home in Fremont, California, she began to feel nervous and upset. She then purports to have felt, at the precise time of the Tenerife crash, a painful burning sensation inside her chest and abdomen, and sensations of being "split" and of emptiness "like a black hole" within her body.

She alleges that she knew then that her twin sister, who was travelling abroad, had somehow died. An hour later, she heard that two airplanes had collided at the Tenerife airport. Later in the day, she heard that one of the planes was her sister's and that her sister was missing and presumed dead.

**Before this Court:** This Court finds that Burke's alleged injuries were not reasonably foreseeable. She was not present at the scene of the crash, either at the moment of the accident or during its aftermath. Indeed, at all relevant times she was in California, thousands of miles from the Canary Islands.

Moreover, any injury to Burke did not result from a direct emotional impact on her from her sensory and contemporaneous observance of the accident. Although Burke claims to have known at the moment of the crash that her sister had died, she did not know the circumstances of her sister's death until she was informed of them by third parties.

Thus, she had no contemporaneous observance of the accident. What Burke alleges is not sensory, but rather extrasensory perception. As such, her injury is outside the realm of foreseeability as defined by California law.

Burke appears to contend that her injuries were foreseeable because pain sharing between twins is a documented phenomenon. This argument ignores the specific guidelines for determining foreseeability established by the California courts to protect defendants from liability for the "remote and unexpected."

**Verdict:** Accordingly, the complaint is DISMISSED.

## 8-The Returning Boomerang

**Court:** Appellate Court of Illinois, First District, Third Division

**Date:** 1967 APR 06

**Report:** Gen. No. 51,033

**Case number:** 227 N.E. 2d 80; 82 Ill. App. 2d 95

**Link:** https://merillionpress.com/cases/XII-008.pdf

**Plaintiffs (Appellants):** Joseph MARAMBA, a Minor, by Daniel MARAMBA, His Father and Next Friend and Daniel MARAMBA, Individually

**Defendants (Appellees):** Gerald C. NEUMAN, Individually and as Guardian for James NEUMAN, a Minor, and James NEUMAN and POLK Bros., Inc., an Illinois Corporation

**Opinion By:** Michael J. SULLIVAN, Presiding Justice

**Prior History:** Joseph Maramba, a child, was playing with James Neuman, age 10, in Prospect Park, Cook County, Illinois. James threw a boomerang which struck Joseph in his right eye, causing a serious impairment of vision. It was alleged that the throwing of the boomerang was negligent or, in the alternative, intentional.

The boomerang was given to the father of James' father by the defendant, Polk Bros. Inc., a short time prior to April 13, 1963. According to the complaint, at the time the father secured the boomerang from Polk Bros., it was aware that the boomerang was going to be used by the son James, who at the time was ten years old and neither experienced nor expert in the use of a boomerang. It was further alleged that, Polk Bros., knew that a boomerang was a dangerous instrumentality in the hands of a child inexperienced in its use.

Their suit was dismissed and they appeal.

**Before this Court:** The main point argued on this appeal is that every person owes to all others a duty to exercise ordinary care to guard against injury which may naturally flow as a reasonable, probable and foreseeable consequence of his act.

A child can be injured by an ice skate, a roller skate, a bicycle, a baseball or bat, a croquet mallet and many other items which are commonly used by children. Had Polk Bros. given the father of James Neuman a bicycle and James Neuman was not experienced in operating the bicycle, could it be said that Polk Bros. would be liable because James Neuman, age 10, had injured the plaintiff while operating the bicycle? We think not.

We conclude that a boomerang, which is used by children, is not a dangerous instrumentality as such, merely because after it is thrown its flight cannot be controlled, any more than a baseball, a dart or many other articles, which are classified as toys, can be held to be dangerous instrumentalities.

We further conclude that an injury occasioned by the use of the boomerang in question by an inexperienced child, even where the merchant could reasonably have foreseen that the boomerang was to be used by that ten-year-old child, does not impose liability upon him.

**Verdict:** Judgment AFFIRMED.

## 9-Steak Dinner

**Court:** United States Court of Appeals for the Seventh Circuit

**Date:** 1996 NOV 15

**Report:** Nos. 96-1730 & 96-2606

**Case number:** 100 F. 3d 519

**Link:** https://merillionpress.com/cases/XII-009.pdf

**Plaintiff (Appellant):** David M. SCHLESSINGER

**Defendants (Appellees):** George SALIMES, et al.

**Opinion By:** Frank H. EASTERBROOK, Circuit Judge

**Prior History:** David Schlessinger and two friends visited Anthony's Steakhouse in Geneva, Wisconsin, for dinner on January 8, 1994. Schlessinger ordered his steak medium-well done. Before the main course arrived, Schlessinger deemed that he was "receiving substandard service at the restaurant, so I demanded better service." Judging the meat he received "burned," he complained long and loud. George Condos, the owner, told him that the food had been properly prepared and asked him to stop disturbing the other patrons.

He was unwilling to eat the food, to leave, or to pay until his demand for a new entree had been met. Schlessinger's affidavit continues: "I feared trouble by the escalating situation and called the police [from my cellular phone] to get the situation corrected." George Salimes and another officer answered the call. Condos suggested to the officers that Schlessinger might be under the influence of drugs. Salimes told Schlessinger that, unless he paid the tab and left, he would be arrested for disorderly conduct and theft of services. The trio then paid and left.

Most people dissatisfied with a restaurant's service or cuisine would tell their friends not to go, resolve not to return themselves, and perhaps write a letter to the editor of the local newspaper or the Better Business Bureau, then let the matter drop. But having played the wise guy in calling the police, Schlessinger encored that performance by filing this suit against Condos, Salimes, and everyone else in or out of sight–including the Town of Geneva, the Town Board and its members, the Town's police department, and the Town's chief of police.

He launched his lawsuit on a variety of state-law theories, none of the claims reached first base.

This goofy lawsuit deservedly met an abrupt end in the district court. Frivolous at the outset, and likely maliciously retaliatory as well, the case has deteriorated on appeal.

**Before this Court:** On appeal, his indifference to Wisconsin's law persists. Attaching two newspaper articles to his brief, one from the Wall Street Journal, observes that high jury verdicts have led to proposals for statutory caps; it has nothing to do with the rules Wisconsin uses to compute punitive damages in defamation cases. The other, from the Washington Post, begins: "A former cafeteria manager at the Smithsonian Institution's National Museum of American History was awarded $400,000 Monday in a human rights lawsuit after a jury heard testimony that his boss addressed him as an 'old fart.'"

What this suit, dealing with a hostile working environment, has to do with accusations of crime in Wisconsin he does not endeavor to explain. No argument based on Wisconsin law has been preserved, so this appeal was doomed. Because he took his cue from the newspapers rather than from the law books, Schlessinger's lawyer (yes, he has one) neglected to notice that many jury awards are trimmed as legally unjustified.

Schlessinger's suit is absurd and likely malicious. It trivializes the constitutional rights he asks us to vindicate. If your meal is not tasty, you do not throw a tantrum, upset the other diners, and then sue the mayor of the town where the restaurant is located. We therefore direct Schlessinger and his attorney to show cause, within 14 days, why they should not be penalized for pursuing a frivolous appeal.

**Verdict:** District court decision AFFIRMED, ORDER to show cause issued.

## 10-I Hate Your Ass to Death

**Court:** United States Court of Appeals for the Fifth Circuit

**Date:** 1993 MAY 13

**Report:** No. 92-1835

**Case number:** 992 F. 2d 66

**Link:** https://merillionpress.com/cases/XII-010.pdf

**Plaintiff (Appellee):** United States of America

**Defendant (Appellant):** Marlon Keith BARTON

**Opinion By:** William L. GARWOOD, Circuit Judge

**Prior History:** Barton's story begins on April 10, 1991, approximately three months before he wrote the threatening letter, at the Dallas Central Appraisal District where he worked. On that morning, Barton acted strangely at work. Barton arrived at work an hour or so earlier than he normally did, but refused to speak to any of his co-workers. One co-worker asked him to come to her office, which he did. She asked him questions, but he remained mute and simply stared at her.

Later he returned to his desk and sat at his computer, neither working nor speaking to anyone. Soon, the personnel manager brought Barton to the hospital and attempted to have him admitted. Initially Barton manifested his consent by filling out the admitting forms, but he then tore up the forms. The hospital refused to admit him and Barton went home.

The next day, Barton surrendered to the Dallas County Jail for a probation violation of failing to regularly contact his probation officer. Barton remained in jail from April 11, 1991, to August 2, 1991.

While in jail, Barton wrote the following letter to President Bush: "Hello, Mr. Bush, I'm angered and filled with hatred that you sent my brothers over to fight a war we knew nothing about or had any reason being over there. For that I promise to kill you when I get out. I hate your ass to death." Barton signed the letter, and his return address appears on the envelope.

On July 15, 1991, a White House mail analyst received the letter and turned it over to the Secret Service. Not long after, Barton was arrested and charged with threatening to kill the President.

After his arrest, the district court ordered a mental health evaluation of Barton to determine his competency to stand trial. Initially, the Metropolitan Correctional Center at Miami found that Barton was suffering from a severe mental illness, was incompetent to stand trial, and was in need of psychiatric care. He was then sent to the Federal Medical Center in Rochester for an evaluation of his competency and criminal responsibility and treatment. Barton arrived there on January 7, 1992.

Staff psychologist Dr. Thomas Kucharsky said that Barton arrived at the center mute, bordering on catatonia, and with a passive bland affect. He diagnosed Barton as suffering from Brief Reactive Psychosis, a mental illness with symptoms "essentially the same as symptoms of schizophrenia. The major distinction being that the duration of the illness is less than six months."

Barton recovered enough to stand trial where he was convicted of the crime to send a letter in the mail threatening to kill the President. At trial, Barton raised the defence of insanity. Implicit in the jury's verdict of guilty was its finding that Barton was not shown to be criminally insane unable to tell right from wrong when he wrote the letter. His sole contention on appeal is that the evidence conclusively established his insanity defence.

**Before this Court:** Although there is substantial evidence that he was insane beginning in April of 1991, we think that Barton failed to prove by clear and convincing evidence that at the time of the offence in July 1991 he was by reason of his mental illness unable to appreciate the nature and quality or the wrongfulness of his acts.

A week after Barton went to jail, one of his co-workers called him. Over the phone he apologized for his actions and the problems he had caused. This suggests that Barton could appreciate the nature and quality and the wrongfulness of his conduct. Similarly, after his Aunt Darleen's visit, he wrote her a letter in which he indicated that he was sorry and wanted to change his life.

Barton argues that the fact that he signed his real name to the letter and gave his return address proved that he was unable to tell right from wrong because sane people who commit illegal acts would not leave such obvious evidence of their conduct.

While it is true that a person's attempt to hide his commission of a crime suggests that the person knows the action is wrongful or illegal, we cannot say that disclosure of one's participation in an illegal act necessarily demonstrates an inability to appreciate the nature and quality or the wrongfulness of the conduct. Sane people openly commit offences and confess to crimes they could not otherwise be convicted of. Barton's placing his name on the letter does not conclusively establish that he was then unable to determine right from wrong.

**Verdict:** Barton failed to prove by clear and convincing evidence that when he threatened to kill the President he was so mentally ill that he was unable to appreciate the nature and quality or the wrongfulness of his conduct. The district court's judgment of conviction is AFFIRMED.

## 11-Bill

**Court:** United States Court of Appeals for the Sixth Circuit

**Date:** 1997 APR 15

**Report:** No. 96-1025

**Case number:** 115 F. 3d 361

**Link:** https://merillionpress.com/cases/XII-011.pdf

**Plaintiff (Appellee):** United States of America

**Defendant (Appellant):** Antoine Andre MILLER

**Opinion By:** Robert B. KRUPANSKY, Circuit Judge

**Prior History:** On December 13, 1993, a handwritten envelope marked "confidential" and addressed to "President Bill Clinton, The White House, Washington, D.C. 20005," which carried the return address of Antoine Andre Miller, prisoner #202901, State Prison of Southern Michigan (located in Jackson, Michigan), was postmarked at Lansing, Michigan.

The inmate mail from the Jackson facility is routed through Lansing. The enclosed handwritten letter dated December 12, 1993, inscribed on prisoner stationary, similarly reflected authorship by Antoine Andre Miller, prisoner # 202901, Southern Michigan Prison. That missive recited:

Bill,

You fucked up!

I told you not to cross me, but you did anyway! Now, you will have to pay!

You, your wife, your daughter, Al and Tipper too!

I will have all of you killed! When? You'll never know! Where? You'll never know! Why? Only me and you know Bill.

I thought that my having the Trade Center bombed, would let you know to "never" cross me and to leave my people alone. But, I see that it didn't.

So, I had to have the shooting spree on the subway committed, but I see that you still haven't learned your lesson yet. Therefore, you, Hillary, Chelsa [sic], Al, and Tipper "Must" Die!

There ain't-no-doubt-in-my-mind that I can have you all killed at will, and you can't prove shit because I'm already locked up.

This letter don't mean shit!!

Signed:

You know who!

He was charged for mailing a threatening message to the President and the Vice President of the United States from a Michigan state penitentiary. A jury convicted him of all charges and was sentenced to imprisonment, which he appeals.

**Before this Court:** Miller claims that a rational person would not believe that the subject communication published a "true threat" to kill or injure the President or the Vice President because he was incarcerated in a penal institution at the pertinent time and because the letter's content evinced a delusional originator.

However, the author's imprisonment does not automatically transmute a facially threatening letter into an innocuous prank. The writing menacingly suggested its author's motives for inflicting injury upon the President and the Vice President, pointedly asserted that his claimed associates outside the prison would carry out the threatened assassinations, and confidently proclaimed his perceived immunity from prosecution by virtue of his incarceration alibi.

The manifest instability and irrationality of the perpetrator of these menaces did not objectively diminish the letter's credibility but instead predictably heightened apprehension by its recipients that the author could be sufficiently imbalanced to seek the realization of his proclamations.

Expert testimony proved that the letter had been transcribed in Miller's handwriting, complete with his left index fingerprint; Miller nonetheless denied that he drafted the document. Rather, he averred that prison guards framed him by forging the letter on prisoner stationary taken from Miller's prison cell, in retaliation for his civil lawsuits against them. In support of this defense, he argued that he could not have successfully posted the letter from within the institution because prison officials screened his non-legal correspondence prior to mailing and consequently would have intercepted a communication of this type.

The trial court implicitly concluded, correctly, that Miller improperly sought to garner the jurors' sympathy for himself, and inflame them against the authorities, through the introduction of distracting and immaterial collateral allegations against the prison guards.

**Verdict:** No reasonable doubt exists about Miller's guilt and his conviction is AFFIRMED.

## 12-The International Journal of Verbal Aggression

**Court:** United States Court of Appeals for the Seventh Circuit

**Date:** 1994 AUG 04

**Report:** No. 93-3372

**Case number:** 31 F. 3d 550

**Link:** https://merillionpress.com/cases/XII-012.pdf

**Plaintiff (Appellee):** United States of America

**Defendant (Appellant):** Reinhold AMAN

**Opinion By:** Kenneth F. RIPPLE, Circuit Judge

**Prior History:** In early 1989, the Dr. Aman's former wife, Shirley Aman, retained Charles Phillips to initiate divorce proceedings against him. A trial on division of assets was conducted before Waukesha, Wisconsin County Judge Marianne Becker. After the divorce decree was issued, Dr. Aman began sending these three individuals threatening letters. Based on these letters, Dr. Aman was indicted on five counts of mailing threatening communications. One reads as follows:

"Shooting Old Bitch Becker and Filthy Phillips would be too fast and too painless. Those two bastards must die a very slow and painful death, so that they can appreciate all the suffering they have inflicted on others. If there is a God or Just Fate, those two pigs – now protected by their immoral legal buddies – won't be able to get protection from all the Waukeshit storm trooper cops but will rot away like diseased sewer rats and burn forever in deepest hell, punished by a Power higher than those hypocritical, corrupt, self-important little gods at the Appeals Court and Supreme Court of Wisconsin."

At trial, he explained that, early in his academic career, he began to specialize in "maledicta," a Latin term he coined meaning bad words. Maledicta encompasses "insults, slurs, curses, threats, blasphemy, obscene words, nasty proverbs, and jokes about racism, religion and professions." He incorporated this expertise into an annual journal: Maledicta, The International Journal of Verbal Aggression. Dr. Aman testified that there were two ways for people to vent anger: physical aggression and verbal aggression. Verbal aggression, he explained, is the means used by "civilized people."

Dr. Aman was convicted of three of those counts and was sentenced to twenty seven months' imprisonment. He now appeals and challenges his conviction and sentence.

**Before this Court:** Dr. Aman claims that, although his letters were a means to vent frustration and anger, they were not "true threats." In stating that he would "destroy" the recipients, he meant that he would destroy them professionally. The postcard ("Man Kills Ex-Wife"), he testified, was mailed in order to keep Ms. Aman's guilt alive and to make her spend another $125.00 reviewing it with her attorney.

In defining a "threat" we explicitly have held that the inquiry is governed by an objective standard: "It is not what the defendant intended, but whether the recipient could reasonably have regarded the defendant's statement as a threat."

A "threat" is a serious statement expressing an intention to inflict bodily injury upon someone, which under the circumstances would cause apprehension in a reasonable person, as distinguished from idle or careless talk, exaggeration, or something said in a joking manner.

We also recognize that (1) that Dr. Aman wrote a letter addressed to a certain person containing a threat to injure the person of the addressee or of another, (2) that he knowingly caused the letter to be forwarded by the United States mail.

Dr. Aman submits that retroactive application of the newer sentencing guidelines, which includes Judge Becker within its definition, results in a harsher sentence. The increase in offense level translated into an increase in sentence as well; the applicable sentencing range increased from 18-24 months to 27-33 months. Because a sentence based on an incorrect guideline range constitutes an error we must vacate his sentence.

**Verdict:** We AFFIRM his conviction, but remand for resentencing.

## 13-The Horror of It

**Court:** Court of Special Appeals of Maryland

**Date:** 1991 OCT 02

**Report:** No. 1738, September Term, 1990.

**Case number:** 88 Md. App. 588 (1991) 596 A.2d 116

**Link:** https://merillionpress.com/cases/XII-013.pdf

**Plaintiffs (Appellants):** Susan ABRAMS, et al.

**Defendants (Appellees):** City of ROCKVILLE, et al.

**Opinion By:** Alan M. WILNER, Chief Judge

**Prior History:** During the school years 1986-1988, the City of Rockville, through its Department of Recreation and Parks, operated what it called the Student Total Enrichment Program (STEP), designed to provide a variety of after-school activities to elementary school children of working parents.

Jenifer Flannery and Steve Chriqui were employed to operate the program at the Fallsmead Elementary School.

It was customary at the Fallsmead program to show a video-tape movie to the children on Friday afternoons. On Friday, May 13, 1988, Flannery and Chriqui selected the movie Poltergeist, a ghost story; indeed, it was chosen because that day was Friday, the 13th. One of the children in the program was seven-year-old Andrea Abrams who, according to her parents, became so traumatized by the movie that she began and continued to suffer great anxiety and psychological distress, manifested by sleeplessness, nightmares, and a fear of being left alone.

On January 26, 1990, Andrea and her parents filed a four-count complaint against Flannery, Chriqui, and the City in the Circuit Court for Montgomery County. Alleging that the movie was rated PG-13 and thus was suitable only for children over 13, they charged all three defendants with negligence, causing emotional distress of various kinds. In an opinion and order filed September 20, 1990, the lower court returned a verdict in favor of all defendants and the Abrams appeal.

**Before this Court:** The Abrams alleged that the defendants acted "in reckless disregard of the well-known fact that Poltergeist is a very frightening motion picture and would have an adverse effect on some children," that "it was foreseeable that some children would be damaged by viewing it and that the damage would be in the form of emotional distress," and that "Defendant [singular] had actual knowledge of Andrea's vulnerability to scary stories."

In response to these averments, the defendants stated, that

(1) Poltergeist "was requested by many of the children in the program since it was Friday the Thirteenth and many indicated they had seen it previously at home."

(2) The movie was rated PG and "had been shown throughout the world in theatres and on network and cable television."

(3) Some parents entered the room (including Andrea's father) while the movie was being shown but made no comment about it.

(4) The children were advised that Poltergeist "is a ghost story that employs special effects to produce unreal situations," that it was stopped prior to the beginning of the special effects and the children were advised "that it is all Hollywood special effects, e.g., veins are only spaghetti; the blood is only ketchup; toys do not really come alive; none of this can happen in real life."

(5) The children were also told at that point that "if they didn't like scary movies, they should not watch any more, but should go out and join other children playing outside."

(6) The defendants could recall no particular reaction from any of the children who watched the movie.

The defendants agreed at oral argument that the purpose of the movie was to frighten; its success, both artistically and at the box office, derives from the manner in which it achieved that purpose, in part through spectacular special effects. The issue, however, is not whether it is a good movie, but whether it was a suitable movie for the defendants to show to young children without prior notice to the parents. Under the circumstances alleged, a jury, we think, could find that it was not.

The remaining question, then, is whether the nature of her injury the anxiety and psychological damage alleged will suffice in light of the requirement that mental distress is not actionable unless it results in some "physical injury." That test is met here. Inability to sleep, hysteria, and nightmares have all been regarded as sufficient physical injury.

**Verdict:** Lower court's decision AFFIRMED in part, REVERSED in part and the case REMANDED in part for further proceedings.

# CHAPTER XIII

# WORK

*"We're a different sort of thief here, Lamora. Deception and misdirection are our tools. We don't believe in hard work when a false face and a good line of bullshit can do so much more." Scott Lynch is an American fantasy author*

Embarking on the final chapter the grievances and complaints here encompass a variety of cases happening in the workplace, businesses and some occupations not quite obvious. The inescapable inference from most of them is the party being sued.

That is, governments, large corporations, in other words, deep pockets. Sleeping on the job, promiscuous absenteeism from work while caring for a favorite pet, or going postal, somehow, seldom happens in the private sector, especially small businesses where half the people work.

## 1-The Size of Graveling

**Court:** United States Court of Appeals for the Seventh Circuit

**Date:** 1993 OCT 29

**Report:** 92-4148

**Case number:** 8 F. 3d 584

**Link:** https://merillionpress.com/cases/XIII-001.pdf

**Plaintiff (Appellant):** Robert E. TAYLOR

**Defendant (Appellee):** ILLINOIS Central Railroad Company

**Opinion By:** Jesse E. ESCHBACH, Senior Circuit Judge

**Prior History:** On March 19, 1988, Taylor was working as a conductor on a train originating in Bluford, Illinois, bound for Mattoon, Illinois. En route, the crew made a stop at a rail yard in Effingham, Illinois to remove and add some rail cars. The engineer, D.C. Brubaker, was moving the train away from an automobile intersection at a speed of approximately 7-10 miles per hour when Taylor attempted to board the engine car.

Rather than board the train near the intersection, where the ground underneath the tracks was primarily asphalt pavement, Taylor walked approximately 120 feet south of the intersection where the ground underneath the tracks consisted of "mainline" ballast. Mainline ballast is primarily limestone or other rocks, between one and three inches in diameter. While attempting to board the moving train, Taylor stepped up with his right foot but slipped with his left foot.

He felt a "pop" in his left leg, and was taken to the hospital where doctors treated him for a broken leg.

He sued Illinois Central for negligence, alleging in part that the ballast Illinois Central used under the tracks was too large and therefore unstable, causing him to fall. A jury found Illinois Central was not negligent in providing a reasonably safe workplace and the district court dismissed his claim. He appeals that decision.

**Before this Court:** This issue boils down to whether a pile of large rocks is harder to stand on than a pile of smaller rocks. Taylor alleged in part that Illinois Central was negligent in not using "yard" ballast, a smaller ballast consisting primarily of rocks one-half to one inch in diameter, in lieu of mainline ballast at the location of his fall, arguing that yard ballast would have provided safer and more stable footing than the larger mainline ballast. In an effort to demonstrate the importance of ballast caliber, Taylor sought to introduce the testimony of an expert witness regarding unsafe ballast conditions. The district court excluded the expert's testimony because ballast caliber and its relation to stable footing was within the ordinary juror's lay understanding.

The expert's testimony about other alternatives would have been superfluous to the evidence already present which demonstrated that larger rocks provided less stable footing that smaller rocks and alleged that Illinois Central was negligent in failing to provide a reasonably safe workplace. Because the expert testimony was both unnecessary for lay jurors and cumulative, the district court correctly excluded the expert's testimony.

Proof of a safer alternative is not necessarily proof of negligence – Illinois Central could have provided a reasonably safe workplace notwithstanding the fact that safer workplace alternatives exist. Taylor was the sole cause of his own misfortune as the jury properly concluded.

**Verdict:** We find no reason to disturb the district court's decision and we AFFIRM.

## 2-Getting an Earful

**Court:** United States Court of Appeals for the Seventh Circuit

**Date:** 1994 FEB 18

**Report:** No. 93-2246

**Case number:** 17 F. 3d 199

**Link:** https://merillionpress.com/cases/XIII-002.pdf

**Plaintiff (Appellant):** Willie GREEN, III

**Defendants (Appellees):** WHITECO Industries, Inc. and Joel J. NYGRA

**Opinion By:** Harlington WOOD, Jr., Circuit Judge

**Prior History:** Green is a drummer in the band "The Neville Brothers." On the night of July 7, 1988, the band was performing at the Holiday Star Theater in Merrillville, Indiana. Whiteco owned and operated the theater. Whiteco had contracted with the Neville Brothers to perform at the theater. The contract provided in part that Whiteco would provide a "professional quality sound system ... and engineer/operator." Whiteco provided a sound system, which it had leased from another party and hired Joel Nygra to operate the sound system for that concert.

Green alleged in his complaint that during the concert he signaled to the stagehand that he needed to hear more saxophone from his speaker, which was three feet from his head. He next alleged that the stagehand relayed this message to Nygra. Finally he alleged that after the stagehand gave this message to Nygra, the volume of the speaker shot upward causing a sound blast and knocking him from his stool.

He also claimed that this sound blast permanently damaged his ear and caused hearing loss. Count I of the complaint alleged that the sound blast resulted from the negligence of Whiteco and Nygra. Count II alleged that the sound system was in a defective condition unreasonably dangerous and Whiteco should be liable for strict products liability.

The magistrate dismissed all his claims and Green appeals.

**Before this Court:** The lower court ruled that Whiteco could not be liable for products liability under Indiana law because it did not fit the definition of a "seller." It also held that Whiteco could not be held vicariously liable for any negligent acts of Nygra because, based on the undisputed facts, Nygra was an independent contractor.

Next Whiteco argued that it was entitled to judgment because there was absolutely no evidence that it breached any duty to provide a safe sound system or sound system monitor. In fact the only evidence, the court found, showed that the sound system operated properly the entire evening.

Even drawing all reasonable inferences in Green's favor, he has failed to identify any evidence suggesting that Whiteco was "engaged in business as a manufacturer, a wholesaler, a retailer, a lessor or a distributor."

Consequently no reasonable jury would be able to conclude that Whiteco was a "seller" as that term is used in the Indiana statute. He has failed to make a sufficient showing to establish this essential element of his case, on which he would have the burden of proof at trial; therefore, summary judgment in favor of Whiteco is not only proper but mandated.

**Verdict:** For the above reasons, the orders of the magistrate judge granting summary judgment in favor of Whiteco are AFFIRMED.

## 3-Work Boots

**Court:** United States Court of Appeals for the Seventh Circuit

**Date:** 1994 JUN 14

**Report:** No. 93-2300

**Case number:** 26 F. 3d 761

**Link:** https://merillionpress.com/cases/XIII-003.pdf

**Plaintiff (Appellee):** Michael HIATT

**Defendant (Appellant):** ROCKWELL INTERNATIONAL Corporation

**Opinion By:** Daniel A. MANION, Circuit Judge

**Prior History:** Michael Hiatt began working at Rockwell's Centralia, Illinois plant on January 25, 1984. He held a succession of production positions during his employment and was covered under union agreements. He was terminated by the company in October of 1989. He sued his former employer for retaliatory discharge. He claimed that Rockwell discharged him for pursuing his rights under the Illinois Workers' Compensation Act.

During the course of his employment Hiatt sustained two injuries to his left knee and developed carpal tunnel syndrome. His first knee injury occurred sometime in 1984 for which he sought and received workers' compensation benefits. He then filed a subsequent claim under workers' compensation for his carpal tunnel syndrome.

Rockwell contested this claim, but eventually settled with Hiatt after he was fired. The third claim for workers' compensation arose in October, 1987, when Hiatt re-injured his left knee. The company did not contest this claim at first, but later denied it when Hiatt failed to provide the appropriate medical documentation. The company offered to cover this third injury under its sickness and accident program. Hiatt refused, stating that he was entitled to workers' compensation for this injury. The record indicates that Hiatt took two and a half months medical leave for his first knee injury and took almost a year off for the second knee injury.

The facts surrounding Hiatt's termination revolve around a provision in one of the collective bargaining agreements between the company and the union. Each contract year employees at the Centralia plant are entitled to a certain level of reimbursement from Rockwell for one pair of safety shoes. To obtain reimbursement, employees must show proof of purchase by either submitting a receipt or bringing in the shoe box. The events surrounding the October reimbursement gave rise to Hiatt's termination. He submitted falsified documents as proof of purchase.

The jury returned a verdict in favour of Hiatt, awarding him $36,188.00 in compensatory damages and $413,812.00 in punitive damages. Rockwell appeals the decision.

**Before this Court:** Our task is to determine whether there is any evidence in the record from which a jury could find the necessary fraud, actual malice, deliberate violence or oppression, wilfulness, or gross negligence to support the award in this case.

The evidence shows that Hiatt violated a plant rule and was fired, but only after a series of formal meetings convened for that purpose. These meetings, required by an agreement between the union and the company, ensured that Hiatt received adequate notice and an opportunity to defend any claim brought against him.

This also gave the company time to re-think its decision and investigate any allegations made. The record shows that this is exactly what occurred in this case. Hiatt's union representatives were active in his defence and he was provided with the opportunity to explain his actions. Hiatt has pointed to no evidence, and we have found none, that would demonstrate that the employees of Rockwell responsible for his discharge knew or acted in such a way as to show a wanton disregard for Hiatt's rights.

Rockwell urges that the evidence in this case demonstrates a valid reason for Hiatt's discharge (the falsified shoe receipt–which, we note, Hiatt does not contest) and that the evidence presented at trial did not support Hiatt's allegation that this reason was a mere pretext.

**Verdict:** From our review of the record, it is clear that the facts of this case do not justify the imposition of punitive damages. We therefore REVERSE the award.

## 4-Eye Was Put Out

**Court:** United States Court of Appeals for the Seventh Circuit

**Date:** 1994 JUN 10

**Report:** 93-3499

**Case number:** 26 F. 3d 52

**Link:** https://merillionpress.com/cases/XIII-004.pdf

**Plaintiff (Appellant):** William D. REARDON

**Defendant (Appellee):** PEORIA & PEKIN UNION RAILWAY Company

**Opinion By:** Frank H. EASTERBROOK, Circuit Judge

**Prior History:** Reardon, a locomotive engineer, whose eye was put out by a pellet fired from a BB gun as the train rolled slowly near a public housing project, sued his employer, contending that the railroad had not taken precautions such as posting guards to patrol the area, installing bullet-proof glass, or providing goggles.

The district court dismissed his suit, concluding that it could not have foreseen an attack at the place where the shooting occurred. Although the record revealed that stones had been thrown at trains occasionally, such infrequent occurrences (less than one a year at the site in question) did not require the railroad to foresee and take precautions against random shootings, the court concluded.

Hazards from projectiles are not confined to one stretch of track. Data compiled by the American Association of Railroads and proffered by the engineer show that shooting at trains is depressingly common. Hazards that accompany the train should be dealt with by precautions that accompany the train – not by guards at the Taft Homes in Peoria, Illinois, but by capital expenditures such as bulletproof glass. The locomotive involved in this case had, this equipment. Even the best safety precautions are of little value if employees defeat them, and this crew left the windows open.

Attempting to recover from the recognition that the railroad had taken the very precaution the complaint said it was supposed to take, Reardon offers two justifications for leaving the window open: heat and fumes. It was a warm day, and the crew would have been uncomfortable in the cab, which was not air conditioned. Moreover, he implies, closing the window would have made the cab unsafe, given the exhaust fumes inside.

**Before this Court:** In this appeal no evidence at all suggests that the train would have been *unsafe* with the windows closed. Regrettable though the injury is this record shows that the railroad provided the means of its prevention.

Reardon testified that the cab was "warm and humid" and did not mention fumes. Only eight months later, as part of a last-ditch effort to stave off dismissal of his case, did Reardon file an affidavit stating that "heat and fumes" led the crew to leave the window open. This statement was contradicted by both his co-workers with him in the cab at the time.

The idea that these were exhaust fumes, rather than the ordinary smell of diesel oil and other volatile substances around an engine, appears to be the invention of his lawyer.

**Verdict:** The Federal Employers Liability Act does not make the railroad an insurer against injuries, and it does not require the railroad to provide precautions that are impossible to defeat. The lower court's decision is AFFIRMED.

## 5-Failure to Steal "Test Letters"

**Court:** United States Court of Appeals for the Seventh Circuit

**Date:** 1994 NOV 08

**Report:** No. 93-3247

**Case number:** 40 F. 3d 164

**Link:** https://merillionpress.com/cases/XIII-005.pdf

**Plaintiff (Appellee):** United States of America

**Defendant (Appellant):** Erica HILL

**Opinion By:** John L. COFFEY, Circuit Judge

**Prior History:** In February 1991, Anita Henry filed a federal individual income tax return for the year 1990. One month later, the Internal Revenue Service ("IRS") notified Henry that she would receive a tax refund of $712.87 within six weeks. On May 10, 1991, the IRS in Kansas City mailed a United States treasury check in the amount of $712.87 to Henry at 1170 West Erie Street, Chicago, Illinois 60622.

In the ordinary course of the mail, this check would have first arrived at the Main Post Office in downtown Chicago. At the Main Post Office, the check would have been segregated by zip code for delivery through the Wicker Park Post Office. At the Wicker Park Post Office, the check would have been further separated by street address for delivery on carrier route 8.

During the month of July 1991, Henry received a letter from the IRS notifying her that the check had been cashed at the Manufacturer's Bank in Chicago with an enclosed copy of the negotiated check that allegedly contained Henry's endorsement but where in fact it was in someone else's. Henry stated that she had never been in Manufacturer's Bank nor had she ever authorized anyone to cash the check.

A jury convicted Erica Hill, a former postal employee, of stealing and cashing a United States treasury check from the mail. The district court sentenced Hill to three years' probation on condition that she participates in work release for the first thirty days of probation, and ordered her to make restitution in the amount of the check. On appeal, Hill challenges the sufficiency of the evidence offered in support of her conviction as well as the exclusion of evidence that she failed to steal "test letters" from the mail.

**Before this Court**: In September 1991, Henry took a copy of the check to the Manufacturer's Bank. It was quickly established if postal employees were in uniform or had previously done business at the bank no identification was required before a bank officer would authorize the cashing of a check. Codes on the back of Henry's check indicated the date, teller window no. 7, the 41st transaction of the day, and that the person who cashed the check did not have an account at the bank. In addition, when bank officials displayed the videotape to supervisors at the Wicker Park Postal Office, they identified Hill.

At that time, Hill was still working for the Wicker Park Postal Office and was responsible for stamping "Return to Sender" on undeliverable mail. On October 8, 1991, postal inspectors placed three "test letters" that were undeliverable in Hill's mail tray containing food stamp coupons, a credit card, and a greeting card. Postal inspectors observed Hill properly handle the "test letters," mark them "Return to Sender," and forward them for further processing.

Given Hill's awareness in September 1991 that she was a suspect in the May 1991 theft of Henry's check, her failure to steal the three "test letters" in October 1991 was only tangentially relevant to whether she intended to embezzle the check five months earlier.

Contrary to Hill's argument, the jury was convinced, as are we that the evidence established the check came into Hill's possession on May 13, 1991, in the ordinary course of her postal employment. The evidence also established that Hill was the person who possessed and cashed the check on May 13, 1991. Viewing all the evidence a rational jury could have found Hill guilty of postal embezzlement beyond a reasonable doubt.

**Verdict:** The district court's decision is AFFIRMED.

# 6-Back Breaking Paint Job

**Court:** United States Court of Appeals for the Seventh Circuit

**Date:** 1996 MAR 20

**Report:** No. 95-2079

**Case number:** 79 F. 3d 64

**Link:** https://merillionpress.com/cases/XIII-006.pdf

**Plaintiff (Appellee):** United States of America

**Defendant (Appellant):** Larry Richard BUSH

**Opinion By:** Terence T. EVANS, Circuit Judge

**Prior History:** Larry Bush was a painter. He wasn't the sort of painter who did oil on canvas – Bush worked with a roller. In this case he tried to roll his employer and its insurance company. And he almost got away with it. But greed and a spurned spouse did him in. Bush worked for the River City Painting and Sandblasting Company which was doing a job for a water treatment plant in Bloomington, Illinois, under a subcontract with the River City Construction Company.

Over the weekend of October 1, 1988, Bush ruptured a disc in his back at home while trying to fix the engine on his pickup truck. Although he was in considerable pain, he dragged himself to work on Monday, telling a co-worker, named Hopkins, that he did not expect to do much work that day. He had a plan to make his employer pay for his injury.

Bush and Hopkins were assigned to paint a 12-foot-deep concrete pit. Bush selected an old worn rope, loosely tied it to a heavy, cast-iron paint pot, climbed into the pit, and directed Hopkins to lower the pot to him. Bush falsely claimed that he injured his back doing this operation.

Soon after, he underwent an operation to repair his back. After the operation he applied for worker's compensation benefits by filling out insurance forms for the Liberty Mutual Insurance Company, his employer's insurer.

Sandra joined her husband in filling out the forms, which falsely claimed that Bush ruptured his back at work. After the claim for benefits was filed, an insurance adjuster contacted Bush and Hopkins to confirm the details of the accident. Both said that the phony accident actually happened.

Bush received disability checks from Liberty Mutual totaling $16,426.56. Liberty Mutual then stopped paying because Bush refused to attend occupational therapy sessions. He also received medical benefits totaling $11,944.04 and eventually settled a claim for permanent partial disability for $37,805. Thus, the phony scheme netted Bush a sweet sum, $66,175.60.

He should have quit while he was ahead.

Then, Bush got greedy and sued the treatment plant and River City for the same phony injury. He demanded $282,000. Bush produced the rope which, he said, broke as the paint pot was lowered to him. But the jury didn't believe him when Sandra, now divorced from him, told the lawyers for the defendants the claim was a fake and she went along with the scam only because Bush had been abusive to her.

In September 1994, Bush was the beneficiary of a four-count indictment in federal court and was convicted on all counts. He was sentenced to 48 months imprisonment on each count, to be served concurrently, followed by 3 years of supervised release. He now appeals, asserting that the district court erred by enhancing his sentencing range for more than minimal planning, and for his role as organizer of the criminal activity.

**Before this Court:** The district court enhanced Bush's sentence two levels for more than minimal planning, finding that the staging of the accident and Bush's subsequent collusion with his wife and Hopkins on a common version of the events constituted "more planning than is typical for commission of the offense in a simple form. Bush asserts that this was error because the offense was a "simple crime of opportunity." The appeal on this point is meritless.

The district judge also added a two-level enhancement because he concluded that Bush organized the scheme to defraud, directed Hopkins to lie to the insurance adjuster, and Sandra to complete the fraudulent workers compensation claim form. On appeal, Bush contends that the control which he exercised over his wife and Hopkins was too attenuated and incidental to qualify for the enhancement.

Bush here misses the boat–control is simply one factor for the court to consider. He clearly was the organizer of the criminal activity: he devised the scheme, recruited the assistance of his wife and Hopkins, formulated the story to tell the insurance adjuster, and coordinated the efforts of both his wife and Hopkins.

**Verdict:** For these reasons, Bush's challenge to his sentence is DENIED, and the judgment of the district court is AFFIRMED.

## 7-An Expensive Cop

**Court:** United States Court of Appeals for the Seventh Circuit

**Date:** 1996 JUN 12

**Report:** No. 95-2776

**Case number:** 86 F. 3d 107

**Link:** https://merillionpress.com/cases/XIII-007.pdf

**Plaintiff (Appellant):** Donald M. STEWART

**Defendants (Appellees):** County of BROWN and Sheriff Michael DONART

**Opinion By:** Diane P. WOOD, Circuit Judge

**Prior History:** Stewart started working in the Brown County Sheriff's Department in 1978 as a patrol deputy. Over the years, he received many commendations for his performance. On the other hand, his work history showed that he tended to be excitable. Unfortunately, he also began to suffer from stress, induced both by high pressure situations on the job and by the fact that he was also running a full-time business on the side, which meant he got very little sleep.

On the job he continued to have problems with his temper. He participated in an altercation with citizens of the Greenleaf section of the county and subsequently was charged with using excessive force, violating departmental rules. In the investigation of the incident, Stewart referred to the residents of Greenleaf as "the kind of sewer trash that had been puked up in the south end of Brown County," and made a number of other equally derogatory remarks.

Starting in May 1988, he had a complete physical and was diagnosed with depression. For the next 5 years he bounced from one psychiatric treatment to another, sick leave and very little actual work. Sheriff Donart decided he had enough and started proceedings to discharge him. In a letter dated April 22, 1993, he informed Stewart that he would be reassigned to a courthouse security position effective April 26, 1993.

In his new position, Stewart sat in the courthouse security room watching video screens that monitored courthouse activity.

This new position unleashed another series of ailments ranging from the ergonomics of the security room, suffered from spinal symptoms (i.e., neck and back pains) and headaches, the lighting in the courthouse security room to be changed to soft lighting, and that he be provided with a more comfortable chair.

The county did everything he asked for, it also modified his work schedule, which according to his description in his deposition appears to have been exceptionally light:

From 9:00 a.m. until 10:00 a.m., I am in the monitoring room. From 10:00 a.m. until twelve noon, I am free to roam about the courthouse. From noon until 1:00, I come back into the monitoring room. From 1:00 until 1:45, I leave the courthouse to take my lunch. From 1:45 until 3:00 p.m., I go over to the Y, and I do a variety of exercises. From 3:00 until 4:00, I come back and wander around the courthouse, and, from 4:00 until 5:00 p.m., I man the monitoring room. At 5:00 p.m., I go home.

Notwithstanding all these efforts, Stewart continued to be dissatisfied. He filed a charge of disability discrimination with the Equal Employment Opportunity Commission (EEOC) on March 4, 1994, obtained a right to sue letter on May 31, 1994, and filed this case on August 1, 1994.

Stewart presented two claims to the district court. The mental disability claim and the failure to accommodate physical disabilities claim.

The district court dismissed his first claim as time barred. And dismissed the second, for Stewart failed to demonstrate, that he met any of the criteria for "disability" recognized in the statutes. This is his appeal.

**Before this Court:** With respect to Stewart's accommodation claims, we confess that it is difficult for us to imagine how much more Brown County could have done with the security room and the conditions of his employment to make life more comfortable, short of giving Stewart a blank check and full authority to order a complete rehab of the building. The fundamental problem with Stewart's theory is his erroneous assumption that "accommodation" means the same thing as "a perfect cure for the problem."

We have little to add to the district court's analysis of this case.

**Verdict:** We therefore AFFIRM its decision.

## 8-An Outing's Consequences

**Court:** City Court, City of New York, Trial Term, New York County

**Date:** 1948 MAY 26

**Report:** No Number in Original

**Case number:** 194 Misc. 942; 83 N.Y.S. 2d 297

**Link:** https://merillionpress.com/cases/XIII-008.pdf

**Plaintiff (Respondent):** Eino KOISTINEN

**Defendant (Appellant):** AMERICAN EXPORT LINES Inc.

**Opinion By:** Frank A. CARLIN, Justice

**Prior History:** Koistinen, a seaman, rated as a fireman and water tender, on the S. S. John N. Robins, was injured while on shore leave in the port of Split, Yugoslavia, (now Croatia) on February 3rd, 1946.

He went ashore about noon; in the exercise of a seaman's wonted privilege he resorted to a tavern where he drank one glass of wine like to our familiar port. Thereafter in the course of a walk about town he visited another liquid dispensary, where he quaffed two glasses of a similar vintage. There he met a woman whose blandishments, prevailing over his better sense, lured him to her room for purposes not particularly platonic.

While there 'consideration like an angel came and whipped the offending Adam out of him.' The woman scorned was unappeased by his contrition and vociferously remonstrated, unless her unregarded charms were requited by an accretion of 'dinner' (phonetically put). The court erroneously interpreted the word as showing that the woman had a carnivorous frenzy which could only be soothed by the succulent sirloin provided at the plaintiff's expense; but it was explained to denote a pecuniary not a gastronomic dun.

She then essayed to relieve his pockets of their monetary content but without the success of the Lady that's known as Lou in Service's Spell of the Yukon where the man from the creeks, unlike plaintiff, was not on his toes to repel the peculation. Completely thwarted, the woman locked plaintiff in her room whereupon he proceeded to kick the door. While he clamoured for exit, not thus persuasive, he went to the window, which was about six to eight feet above the ground.

And while there contemplating departure he was quickened to resolution by the sudden appearance of a man who formidably loomed at the lintels. Thus, tossed between the horns of a most dire dilemma to wit, the man in the doorway and the window, the plaintiff eyeing the one with the duller point, elected the latter means of egress. Undoubtedly at the time, labouring under the supposition that he was about to be as roughly used, as the other man in a badger game. Parenthetically it may be observed that it is a matter of speculation for contemporary commentators as well as for discussion by the delegates to the U.N., how the refinements of that pastime came to penetrate the ferruginous arras of Yugoslavia, especially as the diversion is reputed to be of strictly capitalistic American origin.

So the plaintiff thus confronted leaped from the window and sustained injuries which hospitalized him in Yugoslavia and the United States. During the extensive period of his incapacitation his wages and hospital bills were paid by his employer.

**Before this Court:** The only question confronting the court is his claim for maintenance over a period of thirty-six days. The defendant resists the claim contending, that it is founded in immorality. It further defends against the claim on the ground that during all the times involved in this action the United States and not the defendant was the owner of the ship and, therefore, was exclusively liable in the event plaintiff had a claim.

This court finds that the drinking of three glasses of wine did not render plaintiff intoxicated; nor did his jump from the window denote inebriation; to hold otherwise would argue strongly against his ability to choose the means of escape and would indict him for an error of judgment which is not the law against one who chooses in an emergency one means of safety when another might have been more conducive to that end.

Peculiarly the plaintiff chose the only means of escape even though it resulted in his injuries; had he elected to go out the door with the threatening man, there barring the way, his injuries reasonably might have been more dire and serious than those sustained by his jump from the window; at least he's still alive.

It may be argued that plaintiff's immoral indiscretion first put him in the woman's room but it did not impel him to jump from the window; that was occasioned by the barred door with the man there at menacingly looming.

**Verdict:** The plaintiff in the court's opinion is entitled to recover. JUDGMENT for plaintiff against defendant for $187.20 for thirty-six days of maintenance at $ 5.20 a day ($2,000 and $55.0 respectively today).

## 9-Eye Bank Fraud

**Court:** United States Court of Appeals for the Sixth Circuit

**Date:** 1995 JUL 12

**Report:** No. 94-1451

**Case number:** 58 F. 3d 1111

**Link:** https://merillionpress.com/cases/XIII-009.pdf

**Plaintiffs (Appellants):** Diane M. WHALEY, William E. JONES, et al.

**Defendants (Appellees):** County of TUSCOLA, Armando HERRERA et al.

**Opinion By:** Bailey BROWN, Circuit Judge

**Prior History:** Diane M. Whaley and the others in this suit are the next of kin of deceased persons whose bodies were the object of autopsies by Dr. Ronald Hines at the Saginaw Community Hospital. Dr. Hines is a pathologist who was employed on a contract basis by the Saginaw and Tuscola County Medical Examiners to perform autopsies.

Dr. Hines's assistant, was the now-deceased Armando Herrera who, coincidently, owned and operated the Central Michigan Eye Bank and Tissue Center and was a certified "enucleator" – having the ability to remove eyes and corneas without causing damage to them. Herrera, as Hines's assistant, apparently had a business agreement with Saginaw and Tuscola Counties, in which he would pay all the counties' expenses in performing the autopsies whenever corneas were removed and half those expenses when they were not.

Herrera would sew up the body after Dr. Hines finished the autopsy. Allegedly, he would also remove the corneas and sometimes the eyeballs at this time and sell them out of his Eye Bank. In all of these cases, this was supposedly done without the next of kin's permission: According to the district court's opinion, in some cases the next of kin were never asked, in other cases the next of kin specifically refused to give their consent. The plaintiffs allege that this was authorized by both Tuscola and Saginaw Counties.

Once the operation was discovered, Whaley and the others sued in state and federal court claiming both state and federal law violations. After hearing arguments, the district court dismissed their claim and they appeal.

**Before this Court:** The interesting question raised in this consolidated appeal is what relief the Constitution might provide when a state actor steals the eyes of a dead man. Specifically, we must decide whether Michigan law provides the next of kin with a constitutionally protected property interest in a deceased relative's body, including the eyes.

There is no issue in this case of the possessory right of a spouse or other appropriate member of the family to the body of a deceased person for the purpose of preparation, mourning and burial. The law is not primarily concerned with the extent of physical injury to the bodily remains but with whether there were any improper actions and whether such actions caused emotional or physical suffering to the living kin. We believe the district court mistakenly focused on the label attached to the right rather than its substance.

**Verdict:** We disagree, REVERSE the district court's decision, and REMAND for further proceedings.

## 10-JUST DID IT

**Court:** United States Court of Appeals for the Seventh Circuit

**Date:** 1993 SEP 28

**Report:** No. 92-3303

**Case number:** 6 F. 3d 1225

**Link:** https://merillionpress.com/cases/XIII-010.pdf

**Plaintiff (Appellee):** NIKE, Inc., an Oregon corporation

**Defendants (Appellants):** "JUST DID IT" Enterprises, and Michael STANARD

**Opinion By:** Daniel A. MANION, Circuit Judge

**Prior History:** Humor, like beauty, is in the eyes of the beholder. When artist Michael Stanard designed and sold T-shirts and sweatshirts with a "swoosh" design identical to Nike, Inc.'s, but with the word Mike instead, Nike saw no humor and sued for trademark infringement.

NIKE, the swoosh design, and the slogan JUST DO IT have gained widespread public acceptance and recognition.

Stanard is an award-winning commercial artist whose works include, among others, the trademark "Louisville Slugger," printed on its baseball bats. As a summer project, he and his daughter decided to market his first name, Mike, as a takeoff on the NIKE logos. They named the enterprise JUST DID IT.

Stanard marketed T-shirts and sweatshirts ($19.95 to $39.95) to the general public with the given or first name of Michael, focusing on the northern suburbs of Chicago. He also mailed brochures to college athletes and celebrities named Michael. Approximately two-thirds of those purchasing his shirts were named "Mike." Stanard asserts that the other one-third probably bought a T-shirt for a friend, relative or loved one named "Mike." Although JUST DID IT Enterprises mailed over 1,400 brochures, the project lost money.

Only one letter separates MIKE from NIKE. Stanard sees this whole matter as a "joke on Nike's image which has become a social phenomenon," a "trick upon the perception of the viewer," and his own "personal pun." The district court disagreed and he appeals.

**Before this Court:** The requirement of trademark law is that a likely confusion of source, sponsorship or affiliation must be proven, which is not the same thing as a "right" not to be made fun of. When businesses seek the national spotlight, part of the territory includes accepting a certain amount of ridicule. The First Amendment, which protects individuals from laws infringing free expression, allows such ridicule in the form of parody. But the parody has to be a takeoff, not a rip-off and have a legal hurdle to overcome. Federal law prohibits copies or imitations that confuse consumers.

The primary consideration in this case is parody and if successful, the customer would not be confused, but amused. A parody must convey two simultaneous – and contradictory – messages: that it is the original, but also that it is not the original and is instead a parody.

Stanard has forthrightly proclaimed his knowledge of Nike's marks and his attempt to create a parody of them. Some observers may not think his creation is funny. That does not much matter. What matters is whether the "Mike" shirts confused the consuming public into thinking that they were a Nike product. Based on the facts of record, this court cannot conclude that confusion reigns. Stanard does not sell his shirts off the rack at stores. His was a mail-order business.

To purchase a shirt, the customer had to make a check payable to JUST DID IT Enterprises. Not so with Nike. Certainly Nike would not have us compare the similarity of MIKE and NIKE on actual shirts, because the customer never sees the actual MIKE shirt until after purchasing it. Thus, in order for a customer to be confused in this case, he must see MIKE as similar to NIKE, and continue to be confused while making a check out to JUST DID IT Enterprises.

On the record as it now stands we conclude that a jury could infer that Stanard intended to amuse, not confuse, and that MIKE was intended as a parody, not an imitation designed to be passed off to purchasers as a Nike product.

**Verdict:** The district court dismissed Stanard's defense. We REVERSE and remand.

## 11-Deadly Distraction

**Court:** Supreme Court of Oklahoma

**Date:** 1996 APR 02

**Report:** No. 84374

**Case number:** 922 P. 2d 592

**Link:** https://merillionpress.com/cases/XIII-011.pdf

**Plaintiffs (Petitioners):** DARCO Transportation and State Insurance Fund

**Defendants (Respondents):** Elmer O. DULEN and the Workers' Compensation Court

**Opinion By:** Marian P. OPALA, Justice

**Prior History:** Dulen was injured when a tractor-trailer rig, which he was driving, entered a railroad crossing and was struck by an oncoming train.

Dulen and Polly Freeman (Freeman), his co-driver, were hired by Darco to transport goods cross-country. On the night of September 7, 1993 Dulen stopped his rig behind another truck (also a Darco rig) when the signal arms at a railroad crossing lowered. The arms malfunctioned and came up before the train had reached the intersection. The first Darco truck proceeded across the tracks and Dulen followed. While the first truck avoided being hit, his rig was rammed by the train.

Freeman died as a result of the accident and Dulen was severely hurt. At the scene of the collision a female traffic investigator (with the local police department) noticed that Freeman, who was clad only in a T-shirt, sustained physical injuries primarily to the right side of her body. She observed that Dulen's pants were unbuttoned, unzipped and resting mid-hip when he was readied for transportation to the hospital. Her report also reflects that the passenger door on Dulen's rig was intact but the driver-side windshield and door were knocked out.

Apart from the investigating officer's report and testimony, there was other evidence about Dulen and Freeman's attire on the night of the accident.

It shows that on occasion male truck drivers, when on long hauls, do unbutton their pants for comfort's sake.

After Dulen was admitted to the hospital, the investigator approached him there for information to complete a supplemental accident report. The officer questioned the claimant – then in apparent shock and suffering from lacerations and fractures of the face, jaw and body – about how the accident had happened. She noted in her report that Dulen said, "I was fucking her and now, oh, my God, I have killed her."

In later testimony Dulen explained that – by his earlier statement at the hospital – he meant that he had been living in an intimate relationship with Freeman for five months before the accident and felt responsible for her death because she was driving with him.

The trial judge found the claimant's injuries (1) occurred in the course of and arose out of his employment and (2) resulted directly from the railroad-crossing arms' malfunction.

The answers to two questions are dispositive of whether Dulen's (employee or claimant) injuries are compensable under Oklahoma's workers' compensation regime. The pertinent queries are: (1) Had the claimant abandoned his employment when he was injured? and (2) Is the risk of being struck by a train at a railroad crossing purely personal or does it have a causal connection with, so as to arise out of, Dulen's employment with Darco Transportation.

**Before this Court:** There is competent evidence to support the trial tribunal's decision that Dulen's injuries were caused by the railroad-crossing equipment's malfunction.

Two insuperable hurdles absolutely militate against overturning the trial tribunal's findings and exonerating the employer as a matter of law. Assuming Dulen and Freeman, at the critical temporal point, were engaged in sexual intercourse,

(1) there is undisputed proof that, when the collision occurred, Dulen remained at the steering wheel and hence cannot be deemed to have then "abandoned" his assigned work station and

(2) there is competent evidence to support the trial judge's finding which ascribes the accident's cause, not to copulation-related inattention, but to defective railroad-crossing warning equipment.

**Verdict:** The opinion of the Court of Appeals is VACATED and the order of the Three-Judge Panel SUSTAINED (With four dissents).

## 12-Old Fart

**Court:** District of Columbia, Court of Appeals, Washington DC

**Date:** 1998 APR 30

**Report:** No. 95-CV-441

**Case number:** Non citable

**Link:** https://merillionpress.com/cases/XIII-012.pdf

**Plaintiff (Appellant):** DAKA Inc.

**Defendant (Appellee):** James W. BREINER

**Opinion By:** John A. TERRY, Associate Judge

**Prior History:** At all times pertinent to this case, DAKA (an acronym for Dining and Kitchen Administration) was a contract food service provider for the Smithsonian Institution at its Museum of Natural History.

In April 1990, Sakell, a senior manager at DAKA, hired James Breiner, who was then fifty-four years old, as building director of one of the Museum's buildings. As soon as he started in his job, Sakell started to address him as an "old man" or "old fart." At the regular weekly meetings, Sakell would address Breiner in front of the other managers as the "senior citizen," the "older guy," or the "old fogey." Although Sakell laughed at these remarks, no one else did.

As time went on, Sakell's insults became more frequent and more caustic. Eventually, the persistent insults about his age "started to bother," "irritate," and "really hurt" Breiner. He felt inadequate and wondered whether his job skills had eroded to the point that he was getting too old to do his job properly.

Eighteen months into his job, his superiors began to have doubts about his managerial ability. He had his performance evaluation in October 1991 and received a raise and a $5000 bonus in October – and a month later he was fired. Breiner filed suit against DAKA alleging age discrimination and wrongful termination.

After a five-day trial, the jury found that Breiner had not established a *prima facie* case of wrongful termination, but it returned a verdict in his favor on his age-related hostile environment claim, awarding him $10,000 in compensatory damages and $390,000 in punitive damages.

DACA appeals.

**Before this Court:** It is evident from the submissions that Breiner sought to discourage this behavior by making it well known, especially to Sakell, that he found these insults inappropriate.

On three separate occasions he approached Sakell and told him his comments were "against the law" or "illegal." But Sakell was undeterred by these complaints and, if anything, became more abusive toward Breiner. Not only did he insult Breiner in front of, and directly to, Breiner's subordinates, but he also condoned or encouraged other DAKA employees when they made similar remarks.

In this case, although the issue is a fairly close one, we are satisfied that there was sufficient evidence of malice or evil motive to support the jury's award of punitive damages. Because there was no formal grievance procedure the defendant was aggravated by egregious conduct and a state of mind that justifies punitive damages.

Given our limited and highly deferential scope of review and the trial court's broad discretion, we have no basis for holding that the compensatory damages award was excessive. "We are satisfied that . . . the award reasonably reflected injuries which Breiner actually suffered despite their intangibility."

As the trial court noted, the $390,000 punitive damages award represents a mere 2.9 percent of DAKA's income from the Smithsonian during the time of Breiner's employment. Because it is so small in relation to DAKA's total income, we conclude that it does not "exceed the boundaries of punishment and lead to bankruptcy."

**Verdict:** The judgment of the trial court is in all respects AFFIRMED.

## 13-Chesty Love

**Court:** United States Tax Court, Washington, DC

**Date:** 1994 MAY 04

**Report:** No. 11036-92S

**Case number:** 1994 U.S. T.C. Summary Opinion 1994-79

**Link:** https://merillionpress.com/cases/XIII-013.pdf

**Plaintiffs (Petitioners):** Reginald R. HESS and Cynthia S. HESS

**Defendant (Respondent):** COMMISSIONER of Internal Revenue

**Opinion By:** Joan Seitz PATE, Special Trial Judge

**Prior History:** Cynthia S. Hess resident in Fort Wayne, Indiana worked as a self-employed professional entertainer and exotic dancer since 1986. She obtained contracts to perform at various night clubs through a theatrical booking agency.

In 1986 and 1987, she used the stage name "Tonda Marie." At that time, she grossed from $ 416 to $750 per week. In the summer of 1986, she underwent her first breast implant operation which augmented the size of her breasts a small amount.

At the urging of her agent, in 1988, she underwent multiple medical procedures to replace and to substantially enlarge her implants, and which finally expanded her bust size to an abnormally large size (56FF).

The implants were so large that they each weighed approximately 10 pounds. During 1988, she was reintroduced into the market under the stage name of "Chesty Love." At that time her fees almost doubled.

In December of 1988, because of the added weight and imbalance created by the implants, she slipped and fell on ice, rupturing one of her implants. Afterward, she contracted a severe bacterial infection and the implants had to be removed and she could not work at all during 1989.

In 1991, she received custom made implants in an even larger size (56N). Due to the enormous size of her breasts, she was featured on several television and radio talk shows, was chosen to have the "largest freakiest breasts." During a 20-weekperiod, she realized gross income in excess of $70,000.

In addition to medical problems, she and her husband were subjected to considerable humiliation: she was ridiculed by people on the street, her husband suffered off-color comments and insults, and she was ostracized by most of her family. When her career is over, she plans to have the implants permanently removed.

She views the implants as a necessary "stage prop" that has demonstrably increased her earnings. She contends that she is entitled to depreciate her implants (on her income tax return) because they are assets used in her trade and she derives no personal benefit from them. On Schedule C of her 1988 income tax return she included as part of her deductible business expenses $2,088 as depreciation on the implants.

Commissioner of the IRS maintains that the cost of the implants and resultant medical care are personal expenditures and are deductible only as medical expenses. As a result Mrs. Hess' ended up owing money to the IRS.

**Before this Court:** The sole issue for our decision is whether Cynthia S. Hess may depreciate the cost of implants in connection with her business. She has shown that her implant surgery was "incurred solely in the furtherance of the business engaged in" and "incurred in producing revenues to the business". The sole reason she enlarged her breasts to such a horrendous size was to increase her success (and concomitantly her income). In this endeavor she has succeeded, inasmuch as her fees have increased substantially since the surgery.

These costs were not "incurred for the convenience, comfort, or economy of the individual in pursuing [her] business." The implants under consideration here are not those usual breast implants that women seek to enhance their personal appearance.

**Verdict:** We HOLD that the cost of petitioner's implant surgery is depreciable.

## 14-Failure to Say Please

**Court:** United States Court of Appeals for the Fifth Circuit

**Date:** 1989 SEP 20

**Report:** No. 88-2794 Summary Calendar

**Case number:** 883 F.2d 429

**Link:** https://merillionpress.com/cases/XIII-014.pdf

**Plaintiff (Appellant):** Charles B. BUREN

**Defendant (Appellee):** UNITED STATES POSTAL SERVICE

**Opinion By:** William L. GARWOOD, Circuit Judge

**Prior History:** Buren's ongoing odyssey through the federal courts may be traced to March 21, 1981, the date he was hired by the Postal Service. Buren proved to be less than a model employee. In 1983, he was fired because, to use his own words, he "evidently beat up a lady's three dogs, threw the mail in the lady's face and called the lady and her daughter a bitch." For reasons not altogether clear, Buren was reinstated in 1984. However, all was not well. On October 13, 1984, he was involved in an altercation with a supervisor, during which he held the supervisor in a bear hug and "placed a pen to the supervisor's throat." As a result of this incident, the Postal Service fired him for the second time.

Buren immediately turned to the Equal Employment Opportunity Commission (EEOC), where he filed at least 217 charges detailing his grievances against the Postal Service, including such noteworthy complaints as the failure of an area manager to say "please" when requesting Buren to return a box of flag pins (intended for children) that Buren had taken. Turning to Buren's more serious complaints, the EEOC rejected his claim that he had been discharged on a discriminatory or retaliatory basis, finding instead that he had been legitimately fired because of his assault on his supervisor. The EEOC also reprimanded Buren for "blatantly overburdening the administrative system" with his frivolous complaints.

After his failures with the EEOC, Buren then turned to the courts. On February 8, 1985, Buren filed a *pro se* complaint in the Southern District of Texas. After the district court held four separate conferences seeking to determine the nature of his claims, it found that Buren had at least fifteen other employment discrimination federal court suits pending against the Postal Service. Upon this discovery, the court consolidated all of these cases. Nevertheless, only six days later he filed another *pro se* complaint against the Postal Service, listing nine new claims, and after this suit was consolidated with the others he sought to amend his complaint to add another 142 claims!

Unfortunately, Buren's sojourn through the courts has continued. On May 9, 1988, he filed yet another complaint. This complaint, like the multitude preceding it, alleged discriminatory and retaliatory discharge by the Postal Service. The district court dismissed this suit on May 24, 1988, and admonished him that it would set a criminal contempt hearing if he persisted in filing further frivolous actions. He then filed a motion to amend the above order, which was denied on June 14, 1988. This appeal followed.

**Before this Court:** We agree with the district court that Buren's complaint was frivolous. Furthermore, it is clear to us that this complaint is simply one more example of an ongoing pattern of vexatious, multiplicious, and frivolous litigation that has now extended for more than four years. In our first opinion regarding Buren, we observed that "plaintiff should be thankful that the district court merely dismissed his complaint rather than impose monetary sanctions." He should heed our advice. Enough is enough. The law allows us to "award just damages and single or double costs to the appellee" if we deem an appeal to be frivolous, and Buren's litigation gives new meaning to the term "frivolous."

**Verdict:** We AFFIRM the dismissal of Buren's complaint and award the Postal Service double costs in addition to damages of $500.

## 15-Working Overtime

**Court:** Appellate Court of Connecticut, Hartford, CT

**Date:** 2003 AUG 12

**Report:** No. 22888

**Case number:** Not citable

**Link:** https://merillionpress.com/cases/XIII-015.pdf

**Plaintiff (Appellant):** Anne FRANK

**Defendant (Appellee):** Department of Parks and Recreation of the TOWN of GREENWICH

**Opinion By:** C. Ian MCLACHLAN, Judge

**Prior History:** In 1983, Frank began employment with the defendant as an account clerk. In 1987, her direct supervisor began having an affair with Joseph Siciliano, who held the positions of superintendent and acting director of marine facilities and operations for the department.

Throughout the course of the affair, her supervisor and Siciliano would leave their respective offices during business hours and be unavailable. As a result, she had to perform her job responsibilities and those of her frequently absent supervisor. That, in turn, caused her to work numerous hours of overtime without pay.

To compensate Frank for that overtime, her supervisor asked her to keep track of her hours and told her that she could use them as compensatory time. Accordingly, she kept her own records of her hours and routinely presented them in a request to take time off from work, which the supervisor consistently approved. At one point during the affair, she had accumulated 1500 hours of compensatory time.

In 1998, almost eleven years after it had started, the affair ended when the supervisor left for other employment. In September, 1998, Siciliano became the director of the department and Frank's direct supervisor. In 2000, Siciliano forbade her from taking additional compensatory time. She then had 800 hours of compensatory time remaining, which were worth approximately $28,700.

In her complaint, the Frank alleged that when she protested the denial of her earned compensatory time, Siciliano retaliated by removing many of her responsibilities, and she was not allowed to work overtime hours while other employees were allowed. She further alleged that on November 26, 2000, she submitted a grievance to her union and that the union did not process the grievance for two months. When the union responded to her grievance, it concluded that she had no grounds for a grievance.

Frank commenced this action on August 22, 2001. The lower court dismissed her case because she had failed to exhaust her remedies as established by the grievance procedures in the collective bargaining agreement. This appeal followed.

**Before this Court:** In the present case, the collective bargaining agreement describes the procedure to be followed when an employee accrues overtime. It provides that "by mutual agreement of the employee and the employee's supervisor, in lieu of cash payment for overtime, an employee may be granted compensatory time at the applicable rate. Compensatory time must be used within sixty (60) calendar days of the date on which it was earned and may be accumulated to a maximum of thirty-five (35) hours."

Put succinctly, the remedy provided in the collective bargaining agreement was inadequate because the supervisor had no authority to grant Frank more than thirty-five hours even though she had accumulated 800 hours of overtime over the course of almost eleven years. Furthermore, the supervisor was without authority to order compensation for the hours, which were not used within sixty days after they were accrued.

Given the limitations placed on the supervisor's authority, we conclude that it would have been futile for Frank to follow the procedures established in the collective bargaining agreement. We conclude, therefore, that the court improperly dismissed the case for lack of subject matter jurisdiction.

**Verdict:** The judgment is REVERSED and the case is remanded for further proceedings in accordance with law.

## 16-Traffic Ticket Romance

**Court:** United States District Court For the Northern District of Illinois, Eastern Division

**Date:** 2012 MAR 08

**Report:** Non in original

**Case number:** 1:11-CV-09296

**Link:** https://merillionpress.com/cases/XIII-016.pdf

**Plaintiff:** Evangelina PAREDES

**Defendants:** Christopher COLLINS, Joseph A. KRETCH, and Village of Stickney, Illinois

**Opinion By:** Gary FEINEMAN, District Judge

**Prior History:** On Saturday October 22, 2011, Paredes was driving in Stickney, Illinois on her way to work when she was stopped and pulled over purportedly for speeding by Village of Stickney Police Officer Christopher Collins. After being pulled over, Collins took her driver's license and registration and returned to his vehicle. She was issued a citation for speeding.

On the morning of Monday October 24, 2011, Paredes left her home and went to her car where she found an envelope affixed to the windshield of her car. The envelope was stamped and addressed to Paredes. The return address on the envelope was "Chris Collins, 4025 Euclid Ave., Stickney, IL 60402." The sender had not mailed the envelope, instead had placed it on the windshield of her vehicle. Inside the envelope was a handwritten letter asking her on a date:

"Hello,

It's Chris I'm that ugly bald Stickney cop who gave you that ticket on Saturday. I know this may seem crazy and you're probably right, but truth is I have not stopped thinking about you since. I don't expect a girl as attractive as you to be single, or even go for a guy like me but I'm taking a shot anyways. Because the truth is I'll probably never see you again unless I do, and I could never forgive myself. Listen if I never hear from you I understand, but hey I did cost you $132 least I can do is buy you dinner. Little about me real quick I just turned 27, did 4 years in the Army, and been a cop for just over 3 years. Hope to hear from you one way or another. Thanks!!!"

The letter caused Paredes to suffer great fear and anxiety. She could not believe that a police officer would use his access to her personal information to find her home and stalk her. She instantly felt unsafe in her own home and feared for her safety and the safety of her children. Collins used his authority and position as a police officer not to protect the public, but to attempt to manipulate her into going out on a date with him.

The policeman's use of this private information was highly offensive and has caused her to suffer severe emotional distress, as a result of these actions. WHEREFORE, Plaintiff prays for entry of a judgment in her favor and against Defendants awarding:

A. Compensatory damages;

B. Punitive damages;

C. Reasonable attorneys' fees and costs incurred in filing this action; and

D. Such other and further relief as this Court deems appropriate and just.

**Before this Court:** Paredes failed to appear at a hearing scheduled for February 27, 2012.

**Verdict:** Plaintiff having filed a voluntary dismissal with prejudice, this case is CLOSED.

## 17-Unsafe Caricature Mask

**Court:** Supreme Court of Nevada

**Date:** 1995 APR 27

**Report:** No. 25207

**Case number:** 893 P. 2d 367

**Link:** https://merillionpress.com/cases/XIII-017.pdf

**Plaintiff (Appellant):** Thomas PRICE

**Defendant (Respondent):** BLAINE KERN ARTISTA Inc.

**Opinion By:** PER CURIAM

**Prior History:** Thomas Price filed this action against Blaine Kern Artista, Inc. ("BKA"), a Louisiana corporation that manufactures oversized masks in the form of caricatures resembling various celebrities and characters ("caricature mask"). The caricature mask covers the entire head of the wearer.

Price alleged in his complaint that the caricature mask of George Bush which he wore during employment as an entertainer at Harrah's Club in Reno was defective due to the absence of a safety harness to support his head and neck under the heavy weight. He also alleged that his injury occurred when a Harrah's patron pushed him from behind, causing the weight of the caricature mask to strain and injure his neck as he fell to the ground.

The district court found that his injuries resulted from the patron's push that precipitated Price's fall constituted an unforeseeable superseding cause absolving BKA of liability. The district court dismissed his complaint and he appeals.

**Before this Court:** The focal point of this appeal is whether the unknown assailant's push that caused Price to fall to the ground is an intervening, superseding cause of Price's injuries, insulating BKA from liability.

Under the circumstances of this case, the trier of fact could reasonably find that BKA should have foreseen the possibility or probability of some sort of violent reaction, such as pushing, by intoxicated or politically volatile persons, ignited by the sight of an oversized caricature of a prominent political figure.

Indeed, while the precise force that caused Price's fall is uncertain, shortly before the fall, an irate and perhaps somewhat confused patron of Harrah's took issue with the bedecked Price over Bush's policy on abortion rights.

We note that Price's injuries were not the immediate result of the assailant's push. Rather, the shifting of the weight of the caricature mask was allegedly the immediate cause of his injuries, and the risk of such an occurrence and the resulting strain on Price's head and neck may be found to be within the realm of risks that should have been considered and addressed by BKA in the design of its product.

In the final analysis, the initial cause of Price's fall appears to be of little consequence, considering the reasonable prospect that among the quantity of users of BKA's products, some of them will sooner or later fall for any number of a variety of reasons.

Assuming, as we must on appeal, that the caricature mask of George Bush was defective, we are unable to conclude that the defect was not a substantial factor in producing Price's injuries, despite the role of the third party. Stated in the negative, a jury may reasonably find that a push or shove of the nature and magnitude occurring here would not have caused the type of injuries sustained by Price if he had been wearing a non-defective caricature mask.

**Verdict:** Accordingly, we REVERSE the district court's entry of summary judgment and remand for trial.

# 18-Facebook and Icing on the Cake

**Court:** The Human Rights Review Tribunal, Napier, New Zealand

**Date:** 2015 MAR 02

**Report: No.** HRRT 027/2013

**Case number:** [2015] NZHRRT 6

**Link:** https://merillionpress.com/cases/XIII-018.pdf

**Plaintiff:** Karen May HAMMOND

**Defendant:** CREDIT UNION BAYWIDE

**Opinion By:** PER CURIAM

**Prior History:** On 31 March 2012 Karen Hammond uploaded to her Facebook page a picture of a cake made by her for a private dinner party held on the evening of 31 March 2012 for a close friend of hers, Jantha Gooding.

Both Hammond and Gooding had recently resigned from Credit Union Baywide trading as NZCU Baywide (NZCU Baywide). The party was attended by ten close personal friends, five of whom were current employees of the firm.

What would otherwise have been an unexceptional set of circumstances was transformed by two factors. First, the top of the cake had been iced with the words "NZCU FUCK YOU" while the side of the cake bore the "CUNT" word. The privacy setting on Hammond's Facebook page meant only those accepted by her as "friends" had access to the photograph.

Second, on NZCU Baywide gaining access to the Facebook page a screenshot of the cake was taken. That screenshot was then distributed to multiple employment agencies in the Hawke's Bay area by email which, along with contemporaneous phone calls from NZCU Baywide, warned against employing Hammond. At the same time an internal email was sent by the Chief Executive Officer of company to staff disclosing information about the circumstances in which Hammond had earlier resigned her employment. The company also placed severe pressure on her new employer to terminate Hammond in her new job.

Hammond contends NZCU Baywide breached Information Privacy Principles 1 to 4 and 11. For its part the company denies breaching the first two but admits breaching Principle 11. That admission relates to the disclosures to the employment agencies and to the internal email sent by the CEO. NZCU Baywide denies, however, there was any consequential interference with Hammond's privacy.

**Before this Tribunal:** After 4 days of hearings and testimony we see few, if any mitigating circumstances for NZCU Baywide's conduct. There was a gross over-reaction to news that Hammond had made a cake for a private party held for Gooding and had iced that cake with words some might find offensive but which in context commented on the circumstances in which Gooding had been "let go" by the firm.

Members of the executive team were unable to access Hammond's Facebook page so a new and very junior employee was inappropriately and unreasonably pressured to provide access. The screenshot obtained was almost immediately disseminated to four HR agencies in the Hawke's Bay area with the intent that Hammond either be unable to obtain employment, or that finding another job difficult. Her existing employer was simultaneously pressured to terminate her or face a financially crippling embargo on referrals prepared by Hammond at a time when its owner was known to be seriously ill.

Belatedly it was acknowledged at the Tribunal hearing the entire episode was badly handled by NZCU Baywide but that acknowledgement was not made with any enthusiasm and the apology given was lacking in sincerity. Had management's personal animosity towards Hammond been reined in and had more mature counsel prevailed, NZCU Baywide could have avoided the enormous harm inflicted on Hammond and eventually, upon itself.

On the facts we see nothing that could possibly justify the withholding from Ms. Hammond of a formal declaration that NZCU Baywide interfered with her privacy and such declaration is accordingly made.

**Verdict:** The total sum of $168,070.86 (US $115,000) is awarded to Ms. Hammond (comprised of; loss of earnings, legal fees, career regression and humiliation). An ORDER is made, that NZCU Baywide is to send a retraction of all correspondence related to the case; emails sent to agencies and personnel and any screenshots of the cake sent by her (and any copy) be deleted from their records.

# ACKNOWLEGMENTS

Apart from the judges named in each case and the list of authors in the Bibliography section can't really think of anybody other than librarians. What fool should be thankful for causing and facilitating 14-hour workdays, getting deep vein thrombosis in front of computer screens while tackling the heroic work of 1,100 dashes?

Be as it may, the following people share some of the blame in no particular order:

Michel, Michael, Carlito, Rudi, Noemi, Tahir, Robert, Alex and her husband and others.

Thank you all.

# GLOSSARY

**Affirm:** The Supreme Court affirmed the lower court's decision. To assert that one will give true testimony equivalent to that which would be given while under oath.

**Allegata and Probata:** The allegations made by a party to a suit, and the proof adduced in their support. It is a general rule of evidence that the allegata and probata must correspond; that is, the proof must at least be sufficiently extensive to cover all the allegations of the party.

**Answer:** A formal written statement made by the defendant setting forth the grounds for a defense to a lawsuit filed by the plaintiff.

**Appellant:** One who appeals a court decision.

**Appellee**: One against whom an appeal is taken.

**Certiorari:** A writ seeking review of a lower court decision by a higher court.

**Complaint**: A cause or reason for complaining, a grievance or resentment.

**Cross-action**: An action brought by the defendant against the plaintiff or against another defendant.

**Demurrer:** A pleading that admits an opponent's point but denies that it is a relevant or valid argument.

**Genuine issue of material fact:** Is a legal term often used as the basis for a motion for summary judgment.

**Et al.**: An abbreviated form of *"et alia,"* Latin for "and others."

**Guardian ad litem:** A person appointed by the court during litigation to protect the interests of a party who is incompetent.

**Habeas Corpus:** Latin for "you shall have the body" is the name of a legal action or writ by means of which detainees can seek relief from unlawful imprisonment.

**In forma pauperis (IFP):** Latin legal term meaning in the character or manner of a pauper. A phrase that indicates the permission given by a court to an indigent to initiate a legal action without having to pay for court fees or costs due to his or her lack of financial resources.

**In re:** In the matter of. Used in case captions to designate cases that lack parties, such as one concerning the probate of a will.

**Intervener:** A person who becomes involved in a case either for his own or for the public interest.

**Joinder:** The union in one lawsuit of multiple parties who have the same rights or against whom rights are claimed as co-plaintiffs or co-defendants.

**Mandamus:** A writ issued by a court requiring a public official or entity to perform a duty associated with that office or entity.

**Motion:** A written or oral application made to a court or judge to obtain a ruling or order directing that some act be done in favor of the applicant. The applicant is known as the moving party, or the Movant.

**Motion for nonsuit:** No case to answer.

**Non-pecuniary Damages:** Damages which are not readily quantified or valued in money, such as proposed compensation for pain and suffering.

**Non-suit:** A non-suit (British English) or nonsuit (American English) is a legal procedure.

In the United States, a *voluntary nonsuit* is a motion taken by the plaintiff to release one or more of the defendants from liability.

**Per Curiam**: A Latin term meaning by the court. A phrase used to distinguish an opinion of the whole court from an opinion written by any one judge.

**Petitioner:** A formal written application seeking a court's intervention and action on a matter.

**Plaintiff:** The party who initiates a lawsuit (also known as an action) before a court.

**Pleading:** A formal written statement of a party's claims or defenses to another party's claims in a civil action.

**Pro se**: In propria persona. Latin legal term meaning for "himself, for herself, for themselves."

**Proximate causation:** Proximate means immediate, nearest, next in order, and in its legal sense, closest in causal connection.

**Remand:** To send back. A higher court may remand a case to a lower court so that the lower court will take a certain action ordered by the higher court. A prisoner who is remanded into custody is sent back to prison subsequent to a preliminary hearing before a tribunal or magistrate until the hearing is resumed, or the trial is commenced.

**Resident:** A euphemism for inmate; a "law clerk" is an inmate, who assists other inmates with their legal problems, i.e.: a "jailhouse lawyer."

**Res ipsa loquitur:** Latin term for "the thing speaks for itself."

**Respondent:** The party, who is required to answer a petition for a court order or writ requiring the respondent to take some action, halts an activity or obeys a court's direction.

**Rule 11:** Triggers sanctions by the courts.

**Statute of Limitations:** A type of federal or state law that restricts the time within which legal proceedings may be brought.

**Summary judgement**: A judgment rendered by the court prior to a verdict because no material issue of fact exists and one party or the other is entitled to a judgment as a matter of law.

**Tribunal:** A general term for a court, or the seat of a judge.

**Tortfeasor:** A wrongdoer; an individual who commits a wrongful act that injures another and for which the law provides a legal right to seek relief; a defendant in a civil tort action.

**Vacate:** To make void or annul (an erroneous lower court decision): vacate a death sentence.

**With prejudice:** Cannot be filed again.

**Writ:** A written order issued by a court, commanding the party to whom it is addressed to perform or cease performing a specified act.

# SELECTED BIBLIOGRAPHY

Les Tribunaux comiques, ©1881 by Jules Moinaux, published by Chevalier-Marescq, 438 pages

The Judicial Humorist ©1952 by W.L. Prosser, published by Little, Brown & Co., 284 pages

The Myth of Mental Illness ©1961 by Thomas S. Szasz, published by Harper Perennial, 368 pages

Bardot M.P.? ©1965 by A.P. Herbert, published by Methuen, 185 pages

The Trouble with Lawyers ©1968 by Murray Teigh Bloom, published by Simon & Schuster, 351 pages

Uncommon Law ©1969 by A.P. Herbert, re-published by Methuen, 516 pages

Woe Unto You Lawyers ©1980 by Fred Rodell, re-published by Berkley Books, 180 pages

Prisoner's Self-Help Litigation Manual ©1983 by Daniel E. Manville, published by Oceana, 680 pages

Frivolous Lawsuits & Frivolous Defenses ©1987 by W. Friedman, published by Quorom, 160 pages

Disorderly Conduct ©1987 by Rodney R. Jones, Gerald F. Uelman and Charles M. Sevilla, published by W. W. Norton, 171 pages

Terrible Truth about Lawyers ©1987 by M. McCormack, published by Beech Tree Books, 260 pages

Naked Promises ©1989 by Jeffrey Miller, published by Random House Canada, 192 pages

Supreme Folly ©1990 by Rodney R. Jones and Gerald F. Uelman, published by W.W. Norton, 205 pages

Corpus Juris Humorous ©1990 by J.B. McClay and W. L. Matthews, published by MAC-MAT 685 pages

The Litigation Explosion ©1991 by Walter K. Olson, published by Dutton, 416 pages

World's Wackiest Lawsuits ©1992 by K.R. Hobbie, published by Sterling Publishing Co., 128 pages

Lawyers and Other Reptiles ©1992 by Jess M. Brallier, published by McGraw-Hill, 128 pages

The Death of Common Sense ©1994 by Philip K. Howard, published by Random House, 216 pages

The Excuse Factory ©1997 by Walter K. Olson, published by The Free Press, 384 pages

Whores of the Court ©1997 by Margaret A. Hagen, published by Regan Books, 330 pages

Jurismania: The Madness of American Law ©1998 by Paul Campos, published by Oxford University Press, 208 pages

Presumed Ignorant ©1998 by Leland Gregory, published by Dell/DTP, 216 pages

Moral Judgment ©1998 by James Q. Wilson published by Basic Books, 125 pages

The Rule of Lawyers ©2003 by Walter K. Olson, published by Truman Talley Books, 352 pages

The True Stella Awards ©2005 by Randy Cassingham, published by Dutton, 352 pages

Our Corrupt Legal System ©2009 by Evan Whitton, published by Book Pal, 326 pages

Law and Disorder ©2014 by Charles M. Sevilla, published by W.W. Norton, 256 pages

The Trouble with Lawyers ©2015 by D.L. Rhode, published by Oxford University Press, 245 pages

The Myth of the Litigious Society ©2016 by David M. Engel, published by University of Chicago Press, 248 pages

# AUTHOR'S BIOGRAPHY

Leslie M. Carwell – a resident of Montréal – is the author of this collection.

He boasts very modest experience in journalism in the automotive field and some of his articles have appeared in English, French and German language publications in Canada, Germany, and Switzerland. However, marginal talents – then, as now – have to make decisions between eating, or not. The decision turned out to be manageable.

He developed his searing judicial insight two decades ago when he was thrown in jail for a traffic accident in the Middle-East and subsequently had to face a blind judge for the "crime" in a Sharia Court.

He has attended law school for 2 years, but it wasn't to his liking and while debating the pros and cons of a legal education came to the conclusion, that the legal profession was not only overcrowded but also faces a bleak future. Dropping out was also manageable.

This collection started as a hobby with newspaper clippings decades ago and with the spread of computers and the Internet age, morphed into a database with several thousand records today. Not quite hypnotized by the profession he remains a distant observer with no agendas or affiliations of any kind.

Anymore résumé embellishment would reek of multiple-personality disorder, or if not, a lawyer drafting a legal document paid by the number of words.

This, in a nutshell, is his legal career.

CPSIA information can be obtained
at www.ICGtesting.com
Printed in the USA
LVHW051259280420
654553LV00012B/259